RAISING CHILDREN
in Love, Justice and Truth

MOST PARENTS find it difficult to cope with all the demands made on them. Many can't communicate with their children. More and more families suffer from the negative influences of the world or struggle to survive separation and divorce. In most households the irritations and tensions of family life are accepted as perfectly normal.

For parents who are spiritually aware, any lack of harmony in the home is disturbing. It is distressing to witness the God-given gift of a baby child growing up in a world of conflict and confusion.

Many mothers and fathers express a keen desire to put things right, for the child's sake and for their own. When parents meet Barry Long, a spiritual master with a very practical approach to life, they are able to ask his advice and receive his guidance. This book is his response to their need and their questions.

BARRY LONG offers a wide-ranging view of the human condition and shows how parents today can give their children the best possible preparation for adult life.

This spiritual perspective on the family will be revealing to every reader. The book is based on dialogues with mothers and fathers from different countries and deals with many incidents in the life of the child, from toddler to teenager.

The central theme is the importance of getting a right basis for the parent-child relationship. Love alone is not enough. This book uniquely demonstrates what it means to bring the spiritual dimensions of truth and justice to family life.

RAISING CHILDREN
in Love, Justice and Truth

Conversations with Parents

BARRY LONG

BARRY LONG BOOKS

First published 1998

BARRY LONG BOOKS
BCM Box 876, London WC1N 3XX, England
Box 5277, Gold Coast MC, Qld 4217, Australia
17470 Sonoma Highway, Sonoma, CA 95476, USA

Cataloguing in Publication Data:
A catalogue record for this book is available from The British Library.
Library of Congress Catalog Card Number: 97-92756

ISBN 1 899324 13 5

Compiled and edited: Clive Tempest
Cover design: Rene Graphics, Brisbane
Cover Photo: International Photographic Library
Photos of Barry Long and child: Tibor Hegedis

Printed in England on acid-free paper by Biddles Ltd

CONTENTS

3

BALANCE IN THE WORLD

Bringing innocence to experience

FOREWORD

B arry Long has had two children of his own, a boy and a girl, and three stepsons, and has lived a family life in three marriages. His own childhood was spent in New South Wales in the Depression years of the 1930's. None of his playmates in the Sydney schoolyard could have had an inkling of what Barry would become. The aunts and uncles he visited out on the farms in school holidays would surely not have believed that from the hard school of life he would one day graduate as a man whom many people from many different backgrounds now see as their spiritual father.

After leaving school at 15 he became a journalist and by his mid-twenties was married and thriving in the cut and thrust of a successful career. By all the outward signs his life was pretty good, but inwardly something had changed. People who knew him found that he was really only interested in talking about one thing — the truth. His spiritual awakening was already well advanced when at the age of 38 he separated from his wife and two children. He went first to India, then to England. He sought to live without compromise and by 1969 his self-realisation was profound. Continuing to live as an ordinary man in the world, he remarried. His wife, Julie, brought with her two stepsons, one a teenager. The marriage lasted for sixteen years until in 1982 Julie died of cancer.

He was teaching meditation classes in London and beginning to attract the attention of spiritual seekers when in 1985 he married his third wife, Kathy and acquired another stepson, Simon, who, as you will see, has made his own mark on this book. The following year they moved to Australia and made a home on Tamborine Mountain, Queensland. After four years he again separated and divorced.

Throughout the 1980's he was giving talks and seminars in England and Australia, introducing people to the stillness at the centre of their being and at the same time helping them to face the responsibility of a life lived in the truth. During the early 1990's he went around the world, giving seminars on 'The Truth of Life and Love' and teaching his 'Course in Being' in many countries.

Barry Long's teaching has attracted many thousands of people and at each public meeting or seminar he is open to questions which range across the whole experience of man and woman. The fundamental concerns and anxieties of the individuals in the audience are more or less the same, no matter what their walk of life or where they live. There are always parents in the audience who are concerned for their children and want to get their family life right. They want to do their best for their children and ask Barry Long for guidance. This book is based mainly on those questions. It includes conversations with mothers and fathers at seminars in Europe, Australia and America; and teachings given to a number of families with whom Barry Long has stayed in touch for several years. Some individuals appear by name. The names given in the book are fictional, except in the case of Barry Long's own family.

The conversations cover the life of the child from cradle to adolescence and hundreds of situations that commonly occur in every home. The questions will be familiar to every reader, for they touch on the common core of family life. Recordings of the conversations and questions have been collected, transcribed, substantially edited and arranged to make a coherent book. Barry Long has personally revised and approved the text and its purpose is to provide you with an authentic and complete record of his teaching on the parenting and education of children.

The material has been arranged in three parts, broadly dealing with life in the family, how to introduce children to the wider world and how to help them become responsible for themselves. These themes relate to every age group, as do the essential principles of Barry Long's teaching, and so the book does not follow a strictly chronological progress from infancy to adolescence. Whether you are the parent of toddlers or teenagers, or have no children of your own, this is a book to be read right the way through.

What Barry Long proposes throughout is that justice, honesty, clarity and harmony can actually become the basis of the parent-child relationship, ridding the family of the friction, confusion and mutual resentment that has become the norm. To so radically change the drift of history must necessarily engage the whole life. This is not a book of quick-fix remedies. It can certainly be consulted for guidance on specific issues and for that purpose there is an index. The book is primarily for you, the parent, because teaching the child is your responsibility. Nevertheless, much of it can be read to the children or passed on directly to them.

Thanks are due to the many parents and children who have made their contribution to this book. Their candour, honesty, dedication and love has allowed Barry Long to demonstrate that spirituality means nothing unless grounded in the practical business of leading a responsible life, including life around the family table.

Clive Tempest

1

HARMONY IN THE HOME

Raising children in love, justice and truth

The True Parent – The Embrace of Love
Tears and Tantrums – Piggy Out – Life with Simon
Rules of the House – Straight Talk
Fear and the Dark – Love Comes First

As usual I had invited questions from the audience. A man stood up: 'I'm having trouble closing the gap with my seven-year old daughter,' he said. 'I really want to talk to her about life but I don't seem able to. What can I do?'

'That's because you haven't communicated with her in the past,' I said. 'You've got to start communicating now. What's she interested in?'

'Gymnastics.'

'And what do you know about gymnastics?'

'Nothing. I'm not interested in it myself.'

'Typical,' I said, 'putting yourself first. If you love your daughter, and you want to communicate with her, you'll have to find out about what she loves. Then you'll have something to talk about. It's not a matter of whether you're interested in it. You can only communicate through what she loves.

'All it needs to close the gap (at any age) is sufficient love — love that goes beyond your own selfish interests. For you are guru, Dad, to your children. And to be guru is to give of your love, your self, your life.'

THE TRUE PARENT

Travelling around the world and teaching the people as I do, I have found that there is a great need in mothers and fathers for practical guidance in raising their children. Parents frequently ask: 'How can I cope with the difficulty of raising a child in this world?' I address their questions and endeavour to help them all I can. This book is mainly an account of my response to these questions and it also includes reports of my own experience as a father and guardian, as guru or wise father to the people and as an ordinary man in the world.

We are going to be looking at how parents and children can be straightforward and true in their dealings with each other, from the very beginning. Bringing up a child rightly is such a total activity that it concerns every aspect of living together. Therefore I address the whole of life in this book. All self-discovery is a return to the beginning and whether you are a parent or not, you were once a child; so I endeavour to show you how and why unhappiness arises in every child and in every family. I make suggestions about what can be done to keep unhappiness out of the home and how to raise children in justice, love and truth so that as adults they can cope with the demands of the world and face life as it is.

The truth is always simple — simple enough to be demonstrated to a seven year old child — so I frequently give illustrations of the truth in the form of conversations or dialogues with a child. But primarily I am addressing you, the adult. The truth begins with you. Unless you are endeavouring to be straight and true, or to be more love, how can you raise your child in love and truth?

The first family is the family of the earth, the human family. The purpose of our lives is for each of us to contribute something of lasting value to it. As parents we have a special opportunity to do this. But if we look at the human family around us, including ourselves, we will notice that yesterday's parents didn't make a very good job of it.

Most adults have deep personal doubts, fears and insecurities arising from their own childhood. Very few know what life's about. Ignorance abounds. Moodiness and worry are accepted as natural. Emotional manipulation of each other is the normal practice and the selfish right to be resentful, angry and unpleasant is exercised regularly, even with loved ones. No one can be joyous for long. The sorrows and hurts of the past soon rise up again; anxiety, self-doubt, guilt or depression quickly follow. Yet most of this emotional pain and suffering is unnecessary. It is self-made, the habit of it originating and persisting from the childhood years, mainly through lack of right parental guidance and instruction.

Love is not enough in raising children. There must be justice and there must be truth.

How do we know the truth? So much of what we know comes from what we've read or heard or been taught by someone who read it or heard it somewhere else and then invested it with their own values, beliefs and notions. So how do we tell what is really right or good or true? Everybody thinks they know. Everybody thinks they can create a better world. But the only thing man and woman create from thinking is trouble. That's why the world is in such an awful mess.

Most people in fact go by their feelings. But as soon as we develop a feeling for what is right, we have to have a feeling for what is wrong. These are the two aspects of feeling — feeling good and feeling bad — and by the way of things there cannot be one without the other. While people follow their feelings and believe in 'good and bad' all that results is confusion and unhappiness.

If feelings are not the truth, what is? What should I believe in? What am I to do? First I must empty myself of all beliefs and notions. I can't empty my memory of what I remember but I can detach myself from believing in anything that any spiritual teacher or any priest has ever said to me that is not the truth for me now. I can be rid of every belief ever professed by anyone who sought to tell me the truth, along with every notional 'truth' put into me by scientists or newspapers or television. For as I clear myself of all this thinking, believing and feeling, I start to discover the truth that is always within me. How simple it is! How simple life is! And how self-evident is what's right, or not so right.

The beauty, wonder and truth of life is already created. All I have to do is get back to the natural simplicity of the truth of life, the creation of God. Then I am true to my being as the centre of it all, I am true to everyone and everything in existence and I am a responsible parent of the human family. Inasmuch as you are that, what I say in this book will affirm what is the truth for you and you'll be able to say 'Yes, I see the truth in what he says.' Then having realised what you already know, you will have more power to live the truth and help your children live it.

I said this book is about raising children in love, truth and justice. What do I mean by 'justice'? Parents who would raise their children to be as free as possible of unhappiness must start by first taking responsibility for their own destructive emotions. What they ask of the child they must do themselves. That's justice.

You have to begin at the very beginning, preferably the very moment the child is born. Some men and women were practising my teaching when they first came together and before their children were born. These children are being raised in love and truth to the best of their parents' ability. But most of the people who ask me questions come to me when their children are already at least five or six years old, or are teenagers. It is much more difficult to apply this teaching as a way of life when you have imbibed the ignorance of our society or have not been rightly informed about the spiritual life in a practical way. But if you are willing to make a start, this book will guide you, and you will teach the children.

You are a parent, or one day will be. Or you are a childless adult who cannot escape the consequences of having been born into your family. The question I ask you is: What do you want of life? Do you know what you want? In this world very few people really know what it is they want.

'We want to get married and have children. And we want everything to be all right and the children will grow up happily and get married and have children of their own. And our grand-children will visit us and we will be one big happy family.'

But life seldom works out as you wanted. Nobody's life comes delivered as a ready-made package. In truth there are only two options for what you can want. You can want to be true to life; or you can want anything and everything but the truth, which will make you often confused and unhappy.

Practically everyone starts off wanting anything but the truth. The result is lots of confusion and unhappiness. Look at the people in your neighbourhood. Look at your Mum and Dad. They all got more or less what they wanted and then passed their wanting on to us. They taught us to want the same things. So off we went, wanting and getting the same things with the same result. Look at your own life. It might be all right for now but confusion and discontent are not far away unless you've based your life on wanting one thing first — the truth.

'I want the truth of life. I want life as it is. I want to be true to life.'

For a parent this means being true to the life I am responsible for. The first life I'm responsible for is my life. And that responsibility translates into emptying myself of attachment to anger, wanting, resentment, jealousy and suffering. The next life I'm responsible for as a parent is the life of my children. Inasmuch as I have taken responsibility for my own life by detaching from my unhappy emotions, I will be able to address my children with the truth. Then, through them and my life, I make a lasting contribution to the good of the human family.

THE EMBRACE OF LOVE

I t is a great shock to the new-born baby body to emerge from the enclosing warmth of the womb. Until this moment there has been no need to breathe or open the mouth for food, no need for any awareness of space or time. Suddenly the environment is strange and hostile. There's the feeling of suffocation, the need to breathe; the difference between warmth and coldness; and a sense of distance or isolation, the separation of myself from the fluid world that was embracing me. In the trauma and shock of that moment my very first need is to be embraced by the warmth of another body. It is the warmth my body will desire for the rest of my life, until I slip back into the psychic womb of death to be embraced by what awaits me there.

When the baby first comes into the world it is vital for the child to feel the physical embrace and warmth of the mother. If in the first moments that is not possible, then midwives, nurses and doctors carry a great responsibility. It is most important to wrap the arms around the little body and hold it close. The baby needs this firm reassurance in the moments of transferring from one dimension to another.

'It's all right. I love you. It's all right. I am here with you. I love you.'

Don't think the infant cannot hear you. The baby hears the love in the voice, and that is determined by the love in the speaker. It rises from the sweetness of life that the speaker has realised as his or her inner wellbeing; and that is what communicates to the new-born.

'Hello, here you are. You've arrived in this world. It's a strange world, because we're so isolated here; we're individuals and separated from each other. And it's cold here, though we try to keep you warm. But I want you to know that these are my warm arms around you and I love you. You've come from a lovely warm place where you didn't have to breathe and you didn't have to cry, you didn't have to do anything there; but there are lots of things to do here, I know, and it's a very strange existence, although there is love here. So everything's all right. I am going to look after you as best I can and prepare you for living in this strange world. You can feel the warmth of my arms and my voice carries my love and my assurance that I will look after you.'

Talk to the new-born just like that, as though every word is understood, because the being of the child receives the words. Even a flower receives your 'Hello!' when there's meaning in it because there is a correspondence between all living things. We are psychic creatures and the energy of the voice carries psychic meaning as long as we actually live what we are saying and are being true to what we are saying.

'I love you. You can feel my arms around you. It's very important in this world to feel the warmth of another's love. And these arms are going to be around you as long as I can be with you. These are the arms of love. My arms of love are around you. Isn't it nice to be lying in my arms like this? It is good to feel them around you. And it is good for me to hold you. It's very beautiful for me to have you lying in these arms of love.'

As you go on speaking quietly in this way you are giving the baby your loving attention. This is then stored in the battery of the baby's experience as the knowledge 'I am loved.' A baby spoken to like this will make fewer demands for attention. There will be less insecurity when the parents are out of the room, less demand for attention when the toddler suddenly misses mother's physical presence around the house. There will be less reaching out — trying to relate by touching and holding on — because there is already frequent physical contact with the mother and father. When your children are four or five years old, they will know that cuddling is a most natural thing and that any time of the day Mummy or Daddy can come over and pick them up and say 'Hello, little one, hello, hello' and give them a cuddle. When the physical contact they need is already there, children do not need to demand it.

I have spoken to thousands of people at my seminars in different countries around the world and it is amazing how many people tell me that they were never cuddled. Their mothers or fathers couldn't reach out to embrace them.

So many people are still trying to find love. So many have told me how difficult it is for them to truly embrace their partners and they attribute this to the fact that their own mothers and fathers did not want to embrace them, or could not.

So many people have said to me, 'What is love? I don't know that I've ever loved or been loved. I don't think I even know what love is.' But it's only the thinker speaking. There's no love in the mind, so of course the thinker doesn't know what love is.

So many people avoid the simple actions of love. 'What should I do to find love?' they ask. Their love is so covered over with trying to find love and thinking about it — instead of being like the innocent baby, back at the beginning, simply knowing 'I need love because everything needs the warmth of love.'

The simple beginning of love is in the warm and firm embrace of those first moments of life. But the embrace of love is just as important as the child grows. As a parent reading this book you must take responsibility for your love, for the child who needs your loving, firm embrace. In the morning when it's time to go to school, don't be too busy to embrace your young sons and daughters before they leave for the day. And when they return, welcome them home with a cuddle. This should be the loving action of both parents, not just the mother. Each gives a different psychic vibration that enters the child's body of experience. It is just as important for the father to hug his children, for his way of playing and being with them is different and they love his masculine embrace; indeed often they are waiting for it. Take the little one's hand and play or be together. It's no good saying you are too busy or too tired. Make time for it. If you're going to put your work before your love, why have a child? You must love what is in your care. You must be responsible for your love, your child.

I often use the word 'must' for emphasis — but I do not tell you what to do if it is not the truth for you. When it is the truth for you, it is the truth. All you have to do is apply it. That's not easy in a world where there are so many forces that also think they have the truth; but inasmuch as you are responsible for your love and do your best to live the truth, you will find your way through the labyrinth of forces that necessarily oppose every one of us in this existence.

Man: May I say something?

Go ahead.

Man: You said the child needs the embrace of both father and mother. But many children these days are brought up by only one parent . . .

14

If the father or mother leaves — or dies — must the child suffer? We cannot assume so. If the child has the love of only one parent, then obviously that parent has to be more love.

Since the truth is always seen in the fact, single parenthood is evidently the right situation for that family, so one parent's love must be sufficient. If there is sufficient love you can fly on one wing.

Man: My son lives with his mother, miles away, and I can't get to see them very often. But I love him and I think he knows that.

A mother: It's important to hug a child, of course. But do some need more cuddles than others? I notice my little boy wants to push me away sometimes.

Every child has to be encouraged to live the physical life. Your boy might have a certain predisposition not to be cuddled — everybody is born with predispositions — but it is important to overcome a negative tendency such as rejecting your embrace.

Man: What would cause a predisposition like that?

It can be brought about before a child is born — by an unhappiness in the womb . . . Speaking to the mother, if this was so in your case you will know it . . . If a mother during pregnancy is unhappy in love, she may reject the sensation of being embraced. That could give her child the predisposition to reject physical contact with love.

Parents help their children overcome this conditioning by cuddling them as babies; and, as they grow up, giving them the warmth of their embrace. In this way they'll always know the sensation of physical love. One day it will be very important for them to be able to embrace the one they love. Right from the beginning the child needs the security and warmth of your love as physical experience.

We have to teach our children what love is. Otherwise they pick up the world's notion of love; the same ignorance and confusion that we ourselves acquired from the world.

— 'Nanny sends her love to you.'

— 'For your birthday, with lots of love from Uncle Jack.'

The greeting on the card, the token love of everyday talk, makes love as unreal as the love in a doll or pet rabbit.

The man who privately says 'I don't really know what love is' turns to his child and says 'I love you.' Such is the ignorance of a world where men and women do not live what they say and the common condition is utter confusion about love.

We have to make love more substantive than mere words. To show children what love is we must encourage them to feel the love in their own bodies; because real knowledge is the experience of our own body. I suggest you sit down with the child at an early age and have a cuddle together. Don't just give a hug. There must be depth to the experience. There must be the warmth of love.

'Mummy and Daddy love you. Can you feel the warmth of our love? Do you feel the firmness in my embrace?'

First embrace the child firmly and then give a half-hearted sort of hug. 'Now, do you feel the difference? There's no firmness, no meaning in it, is there? Whereas, if I hug you with love, you can feel the love in it.

'Now I'll take my arms away. Do you feel what happens?

'Come and let me cuddle you again. Do you feel the warmth again?'

In this way you begin to demonstrate the real warmth of love in the embrace. There are two aspects to it. The first is the temperature, the warmth of the physical body, which is superficial. The second and deeper warmth is psychic. My body warmth is given me by life. Psychic warmth is given me by my consciousness. As I consciously bring love into me I bring warmth into my psyche. When I communicate my love psychically it is a far more potent and lasting warmth.

You can recognise this in your own adult love-life. We are all children of the earth who yearn for the warmth of the love of man or woman. We are always looking to be and to receive this invisible, immeasurable quality of psychic warmth.

We have to demonstrate to the children what love is; and also we have to show them where it is. When the time is right, sit down together, Mum, Dad and child. Pick your time, to suit the child's attention span.

'Let's sit down and have a game. This is a game of discovery. We're going to show you where love is. Now, do you love Mummy?'

'Yes,' the child says.

'Where do you feel your love of Mummy?'

The child is likely to indicate the tummy region.

'You feel you love Mummy there?'

'Yes.'

'And Daddy? Same place?'

'Yes, yes.'

The purpose is to transfer the notion of love into a bodily sensation. Then the child will grow up with the substantive experience of love: 'Ah yes! I feel love. That's where my love is.'

There are many opportunities to teach this: 'Do you see the little bird over there? Isn't it lovely to hear it sing? Do you love it? Can you feel the love of it in you?'

If you can introduce a child to the substantive feeling of love in the youngest years, then later on, when the body starts to zing with sexual energy, the feeling of love will be unmistakable.

Man: Supposing the child doesn't get it first time? He might not point to his tummy. He might point to his head!

Then I would say: 'Do you really feel it there? I don't think so. The head doesn't have much feeling really. I feel it down here, across the top of my tummy. It's got a sort of a warmth in it.'

Go on directing the child's attention to the sensation. 'Do you feel anything in your tummy? You know how when you have your breakfast in the morning, you can feel the warmth of the cornflakes down in your tummy? The warmth is a form of love. That's because the body grows on love and food is a form of love for the body. We have something called digestion, which is a process that goes on down in our tummies. The digestion turns food into energy, which makes it possible for us to walk around and see the world. It's like putting fuel onto a sort of fire down in our stomachs. So love is like that. It has warmth in it.

'Now, do you see the lovely leaves on the trees? Just have a look at them. Can you see the changing colours in the autumn leaves with the western sun catching them in all their glory? Isn't that lovely? That's the same feeling of love. Can you feel it?. . . Yes? You can still feel it, can't you — the beauty of what you've seen?

'So, you see, you don't have to think about love. We can't think about it. We feel it. And it's a good sensation, isn't it?'

The more you speak to small children like that the more you communicate that love is a sensation — not the notional love that most people tend to carry around in their heads. The more experience they have of the physical sensation of love in their own bodies, the more prepared they are for sexual love later in life. As they grow up they will increasingly enter the mental world and gradually lose touch with sensation — until the sexual drive brings them back into their bodies in adolescence. Being in the body as much as possible in the earlier years will help them later when they pass through the inevitable pain of sexual confusion and disappointment.

*

We come out of the land of love. Gradually we take on this divided, personal existence. And in defending ourselves from it, we take on self.

New mother: The beautiful, sweet little baby in my arms is becoming her own person. She's so beautiful. I'm besotted with her. I've never known so much love. The moment she was born I was suddenly in heaven. I didn't know I had such capacity for love. I just love her so much that sometimes I feel I don't know quite what to do with it . . . Then I see I'm getting fearful of what is sure to happen, that the love will be lost. Already she's starting to get a bit more independent and a little bit wilful. She's starting to crawl, and I already feel that she's being torn away . . .

It's so unnatural to be divided. In your baby you see one who is still so near to the land of love, who is not divided. That's the extraordinary experience of having the new-born in your arms. But you know that she must leave the land of love, as we all do. And you have to face that.

New mother: I know what I have to do. I have to just be there for her, as she needs me, and let her go as she needs to go.

Young mother: I have a four year-old. He's become quite independent, already a strong character. Can you tell me what I can do to help him grow into a loving man?

The most important thing is to let him know that you love him. Do not be afraid to show him love physically. Remember that the boy needs to know the love of his Mum and Dad physically. So hold him in your arms. Play games with him. Roll on the floor with him. If he is not to be afraid of physical love later in life, he needs that physical contact with the warmth of your love.

Mother: What about older children? My son will be twelve soon and he's starting to go out into the world. I want him to be able to go and get his experience of love, though love sometimes hurts. I'm aware of how much I still want to protect him from hurt, from the 'coldness' of love and the fact of aloneness.

Of course. A mother who loves her child as an extension of her own being, her own self, is naturally moved to protect him from any sort of hurt. You are a mature woman who knows the reality of love. You know that love in its pristine reality is indeed cold. It is without sentimentality. It is not cosy or comfortable. You know 'the fact of aloneness' — that finally I am alone — because that is the final truth for everyone. And, as a mother, you also know that your son cannot receive the coldness of love before he's received its warmth.

This 'coldness' of love is not the emotional chill of feeling unloved and it's not the loneliness of feeling rejected. There are no feelings in love's reality. Love's coldness is an impersonal quality that acts utterly without consideration for feelings. Wherever there is a sentimental attachment to love as a feeling, or dependence on love as shared warmth, the reality of love is cold.

Children who are raised to depend on emotionality, in families where love is shown mostly through sentiment, become so attached to personal love that they suffer terribly when by the evolutionary process love shows itself in its true impersonal colours.

You prepare your son for the reality of love in two ways: by freely giving him the warmth of the love you feel for him, and by giving him the truth of your honesty and straightness. As you hug him he receives the warmth of your embrace. Be interested in what he's doing; he receives the warmth of your love in the communication. As he grows up, speak to him openly and honestly about love, life and truth. Put him straight about man and woman, from the truth of your own experience.

You have to get the balance between the coldness and the warmth. You have to weave the two into your family life. You'll find that you are able to do this as long as you endeavour to live the truth as best you can, and always put love first. Then you will find the courage and the presence to bring your son to a right maturity, not forcing him to mature too fast and not allowing his development in love to be retarded.

Man: That balance seems very important, because the warmth mustn't be suffocating. What happened to me was, I think, a case of too much mother love. She loved me so much — she really mollycoddled me — and I think it led to a reaction and a denial; because I went round for years saying there's no such thing as love.

Yes, this is the common reaction when the mother's love is overly sentimental and cloying. The child becomes withdrawn and shuns displays of affection. A boy like that in later life is likely to be closed to love. And that is why it is so important to give our children the balance of love and truth, as best we can through our own living example.

✳

Love must be accompanied by truth and justice. Mother and father have to get the love of each other straight before there can be right love of the child. If the parents are not honest and do not get their love-life right then it's very likely the children will carry that dishonesty and lack of love into their own relationships.

Mother and father are kind and nice to each other during Sunday dinner and by bedtime they're tearing each other's hair out. Because we live a life of double standards, as adults we're inured to this dishonesty. But as children we think it's for real. It is not easy for children to be cunning and dishonest but gradually they are taught by adult example. What happens when parents argue and fight? The children take it on and it becomes a life-long burden.

Woman: That's so true. I sometimes feel I'm terrified of love or being loved. Any sweetness or intimacy and I just pull back, quite unconsciously, without really wanting to. I'm sure this is because my mother and father were always fighting. They loved each other but were very emotional and always arguing.

And that little girl was appalled at what went on. She wept and ran away and came back and cried 'Mummy, Daddy, stop it. Please don't do it, please.' She shrank inside to see what was happening. The contraction went into her subconscious. Something like that doesn't just go away.

How many have cried? How many have tried to stop the arguing? Well, it happened to me. The boy in this body cried and cried, 'Stop it. Please, please stop it.'

The little one takes on the pain of the conflict: 'I am responsible for their unhappiness,' or, 'I am responsible for bringing them together again and keeping the peace' — a terrible strain inside the child; the burden of wrong responsibility and guilt. The emotion stays in the body and as soon as someone comes to be kind and caress the child there's a withdrawal. The child doesn't believe it.

Man: I can identify with that too, because that's how it was for me, as a boy, and I carried on the same sort of emotion myself, in my first marriage. A reluctance to face emotional situations. A fear to love, or lack of trust. And I probably passed the same thing on to my own children. I think of what it says in the Bible: 'The sins of the fathers shall fall upon the sons and daughters, generation upon generation.'

The old saying is true; except that the word 'sin' carries the punitive curse of the Christian religion and is outdated. For 'sins' of the fathers substitute their unhappiness and ignorance. The solution is then simple. Get rid of the unhappiness in this generation. Get rid of the ignorance in you.

Man: Easier said than done. But I'm working on it, with my new partner. She's really making the difference, although I still get frustrated at times.

You'll get rid of the frustration as you get your love-life right. That means you have to be honest with each other. And you have to make love rightly. You have to dismantle your habitual sexuality and learn how to make love fresh and new. [That's the subject of my Making Love tapes.] For if you do not get your love-life right then it's very likely that your dishonesty in love will pass into the children.

Man: It's probably too late for them. They'll have to find their own way now. But still I hope in some way I'm undoing the damage, because the more loving I am the more love there is and then there's a kind of healing. I see this in the woman I'm with. Love really is a salvation, isn't it?

Yes, and a man of love who can love the pain out of a woman is indeed her saviour, for she can't save herself. But to save her, man must truly love her. In doing that he redeems himself. But I am talking of real love here. Selfless love.

23

Self is always unhappy. Woman is already unhappy enough. If you love with your self you only put more self, more unhappiness, into her. Man must love woman with such love that all her past relationships are loved out of her — her mother and father, all her previous lovers, all her fears and false notions, pains and contractions. Man must love the child out of her, the one who is still weeping inside. That's what real love is.

*

Of all the stresses acting on the love of man and woman, the most enduring is the presence of a child or children in the house. But, despite their need for love and attention, the children must never be allowed to get in the way of the parents' love for each other. Right from the beginning the mother and father must remember that their love for each other comes first. Of course, this is not easy, and the arrival of a new baby puts a tremendous strain on the household.

New mother: It is the hardest time of my life! I am always tired. I do my best not to identify with the tiredness, but the baby's constant need for attention means that making love is usually out of the question. It's hard enough to find time to just be together.

Father: Before the baby came we had been taking it for granted that we could be together whenever we wanted. Now I have to let her be with him . . . she has to let her attention go to him.

Are you prepared, in your great love of the child, to show him that the two of you need time to be together? You have to communicate that as soon as possible.

'For our love to continue, to be the love that we all are, your

Mummy and Daddy have to have time to be together — but we will never exclude you from our love.'

It is most important to impart to the children that as parents we must have time to love each other, otherwise they will want to interfere and come between us; and then they will become demanding, wanting attention when we should be having our time alone.

'I have to leave you for a while so that Mummy and I can be on our own. We are going to go into our room to love each other. A mother and father have to make love in order to love their child. If we don't love each other, there will not be enough love for you. But because we love each other, you will be all right on your own, because you know we love you.'

Once the message has been received, the boy as he grows will be able to go and play contentedly on his own, in his own way, without demanding attention.

Woman: I've been in a relationship for a few years now with a much younger man and I've had a child with him, my first. In the last couple of years the relationship has become very complacent, perhaps because I was overwhelmed by the baby. We're still very much in love with each other, but the passion isn't there any more. I know that in the course of a relationship the initial passion does fade, but with a child in the house it seems to be inevitable.

You can't afford to let love slip. You must not get too tired to make love and he mustn't make excuses. 'I'll be late home from the office again tonight. I've got to work harder now there's three of us, you understand . . .' (He should be working really hard to get the love back again.)

You can't expect to keep your love alive if he goes down to the club or off to the football without you. Although one of you might suddenly rediscover your passion every week or ten days, in between you will both be busy with your separate lives. And that's not living love; it's living death.

Do you want a complacent relationship? May I ask, when did your partner start to become disinterested?

Woman: Well, it was around the time the baby was born.

You have to be the vigilant woman watching for signs that the baby is coming between you and your partner. If he loves you he will be doing his best to act out of love, but as much as he tries to conceal his disinterest, making love will start to become an effort. The relationship loses its sparkle and a deadness comes between you. You have to give him as much attention as the child — because at heart he's really only a boy who needs your love.

When all a woman's love and attention goes into her baby she starts living through the child and then, later on, there is nothing to talk about except the children, and finally no reason to stay together except 'for the children'. That's living death between man and woman.

'What are we doing with our lives? We've drifted further and further apart. We've got a nice home, plenty of money, two cars and we've got the children. But what about us?'

Why has the passion and the desire gone? — because you are so busy with the child and your partner has become disinterested in love. There's only one thing to do. Go and have an intelligent conversation with him. Be honest with each other about what you want. And bring your bodies back together again.

It is very difficult for any couple to keep love fresh and new, but tragically children often bring the end of love. Man and woman are made to be together, with nothing between them. When the baby arrives there's suddenly a third party. The man knows the baby is getting more attention than him, but he loves the child too and feels he has to put up with the situation.

Although they try to go on loving one another in the same way as before, it's just not the same.

Woman: Are you saying there would have been more love if I'd not had the baby? I can't believe that. I feel there's a lot more love in my life now because, in some kind of way, the child is my love made into a baby-body.

I hear what you say, but the first question I would ask you or any woman is: Why do you want a child? If you love the man, why do you want to have his child? The answer, as far as I am concerned, is that wanting a child is giving in to the instinctive need to perpetuate the species. That's all very well and serves the need. But I still say children come between the love of man and woman. I am not saying you shouldn't have a child. I am just saying how it is. Children separate us as man and woman because they introduce another element into our existence together. They are the introduction of more existence, more separation. That's why it is vital for man and woman to keep their love alive, and ensure that their union remains undivided.

You have to put the love of your partner before your child. The two of you come first.

TEARS AND TANTRUMS

If children are allowed to demand attention they will learn to demand things from the world; and then they will get frustrated and unhappy because neither life nor love ever gives us what we demand. You have to take the demand out of children; the demand for this, the demand for that, the demand for attention. Allow the demanding to go on and you'll make a cross for yourself and a cross for the child.

Children must have our attention, of course, and we must join in their interests. That is our love. We must endeavour to provide everything they require — without fulfilling their demands. They must be taught not to demand, because love does not demand.

One of the hardest things to give your children is your time, especially as they get older and you get immersed in your own life. A mother may give all her time to her new-born baby but gradually she withdraws into jobs around the house. These days both parents may go out to work and when they get home they have to make time for each other as well as the children. It is rarely easy to abandon the other calls on your limited time so it gets harder and harder to be with the children. But because you are withdrawn from them, and they want to be with you, they will start demanding your attention.

So how do you handle this? How do you teach them that it is not right to demand?

— As much as possible, address the demand as soon as it arises.

— Find out what the child wants.

— When speaking with children, always give them your full attention.

— Continually inform them of the situation.

— Whenever they are unnecessarily demanding make it clear that there's really no need for the demand.

'You're trying to get attention. What do you want? I can't just give you attention for attention's sake. What is it you want? If you don't want anything except my attention, I have to explain something to you. You are no more special than anyone else here. You must take your place in this house. But if you want something, just tell me what it is and I'll do what I can to get it for you . . .'

Generally what the child wants can be given as long as it does not disturb the situation. If there is a disturbance it means there is a demand to be special: 'You are trying to make yourself special. Can you see that? Either everybody is special or no one is special. In this house nobody is special, so none of us can demand special attention.'

'When you want something that you need, all you have to do is ask me for it. If it's a real want and I can provide it, I will. But you have to know I might not be able to give you what you want because it always depends on the situation. Now, tell me: What do you want?

'Okay, you want to go for a walk. All right, I am not so busy that I can't go for a walk with you. So yes, let's go for a walk.'

Or: 'No, we cannot go for a walk because I have work to

do.' (You have to give the reason.) 'I have to work to earn the money so that we have electricity for the lights and food to eat and so that we can all live in this house. Your Mum and I are doing our work so that you can sleep comfortably in bed tonight. Right now our work has to come first, and what you want has to take second place. The work has to come first because what the house wants is what we all want.'

One of the most important things in instructing children is to communicate that they take their place in the context of the whole situation: 'You take your place in the context of everything that goes on in this house. This house is the situation that we're all in. It's a total situation, not made for any particular person. Each of us who lives here is welcome to make a contribution. But no one can demand special attention for themselves. We all have needs which arise from time to time and when one of us has a need for something we address it and satisfy the need as much as possible. We endeavour to address it in the moment. We look at the whole situation. If possible we fulfil the need. And then everything can settle back into the context of the whole.'

The demand in the child must not be tolerated. It is best to start right from the beginning. It is possible to inform the baby, even while suckling at the breast: 'We cannot demand love in this existence. As you suckle my breast there is no demand. Your body needs the food. You look for it and it's there. If it's not there, then you cry for it because you want something you need, some nourishment. And my breast or your food is there for you. There's an interaction between what your body needs and what is supplied. And that's love.'

The child grows and the moment comes when you say: 'You cannot demand what you do not need. To demand what you do not need is selfishness in you, and you will never be satisfied. So in this house never demand what you do not need. If you need a glass of water, or warm clothes, or if you need anything, we can attend to it. I am always here to fulfil your needs, as much as possible, because you have my love. You will not miss out but you must remember that in this house we will not tolerate demand.'

Children will not make unnecessary demands if they know where the limits of acceptable behaviour are: 'If you want a cuddle, come and say so. But there are limits to what I can do and if I say I cannot do something, you must accept that.'

Keep reminding the child of the rules: 'If you want something, you come to me and ask for it. But when your mother and I are talking, or when there's something else going on, you must play with your toys and be quiet. Or you can sit with us and be still. If you have to come and interrupt us in what we are doing, we will stop and listen to you. But then you must know what you want so that you can tell us what it is.'

Take the time to sit down with the child and explain what life is, so that you put the house rules in the wider context of the world: 'Sit down. I have to speak to you. You're being demanding. You cannot demand anything — from me, from your mother or from life — because if you demand things from life sooner or later you are going to encounter someone who will not give you what you want. Then you will be unhappy. Or someone will demand things from you which you don't want to give up and then there will be a conflict and everyone concerned will be unhappy. We don't want to be unhappy, do we? So that's why I endeavour to teach you not to be demanding.'

*

Mother: What I want is a bit of peace and quiet. I have to give my baby constant attention. It's so demanding and I get very tired. She's fourteen months now and still not sleeping

long enough to give me a good night's sleep. It's wearing me
down. I get angry with her — waking me up and crying in the
night.

That's what you take on when you have a baby; and we all
know it's not easy. I know what it's like to be woken in the
night. I've been through it. But let's tackle first thing first. Which
means addressing you, the mother.

You have to use the opportunity to sink more into your
body, into your stillness or your love. You do this at any time
of the day, but especially when the baby has woken you and
you're lying there trying to get some sleep. Where there's any
feeling of irritation in your body you have to get around it with
your attention and steady it down with your intelligence. You
have to physically relax the tension.

Is there any striving in you for perfection? Or desire for the
situation to change? Anything like that will drive you out of
your body, away from your being now. As soon as you're out
of your body you will start to feel uncomfortable, irritated, or
even get a feeling of failure. Any effort to get back into your
body will simply perpetuate the irritation. You can't try to get
back into your body or try to make things right — it's the
trying that's 'trying'. So you have to just give up and sink into
the body.

Any agitation in a mother will affect her child. So it is up to
you, in the first instance, to steady yourself and quieten down
any irritation you might have. But any association the baby has
with other people or other children may also be subconsciously
winding up the restlessness in her.

Are there any signs that the baby's pattern of sleeping and
waking is not right? Sometimes these short cycles of sleep
continue for quite a while. Is she just waking because she's
hungry? Or is she fitful and crying too much?

Mother: She's my first, so I don't really know if it's right.

She does cry a lot. But it's been like this from the start.

Something is causing her to wake so frequently. You may be able to discover the cause of her restlessness, although of course there are unseen factors that make a young child wake up.

Father: This is a confusing issue for us, and probably for everyone who's in this situation. Our instinctive feeling is not to just let her cry but go over and comfort her. Then we wonder if we are not just reinforcing her pattern of behaviour. Of course it's hard on us to have to keep getting up and attending to her. Other people say you should just let them cry themselves to sleep.

There is a time for leaving a child to cry. But there are many times when the child should not be left to cry. First thing first: Why is the child disturbed? I'm not saying you can always find out. But it must be the first question. Is she hungry? Is she uncomfortable? Is she sick? What is it? You look at all the obvious things. Then you search through your life (your whole life together) to see if there is anything you know of that could be disturbing the child. Observe her during the day to see if any agitation arises; and if so, what is the cause of it? Does it give you a clue as to the agitation that's going on at night?

As you say, by attending to a crying baby all the time you can set up a habit pattern. Yet your instinctive feeling is not to leave her to cry. I suggest that when the baby cries you go and speak to her and see if you can pacify her.

'It's all right. There's no need to cry. Mummy and Daddy are with you. You're not going to cry any more. Now, be still, be easy.'

Speak to her subconscious. Speak about ease and peace and tell her she is not alone. Tell her all is well and that you are with her.

'It's all right. Even while you're asleep we are with you. We are always with you. We are deep inside you where you love us and where we love you. And in that place, in sleep, we meet, and we are all together. So sleep now little one. Be still. It's all right. We are close at hand. Just sleep.'

In addressing the baby's subconscious like this, you are suggesting peace and stillness to her, informing her that there is no virtue in agitation. Your words will counteract the suggestion that the whole world will soon be putting into her: 'Everyone is agitated and unhappy. You have every right to cry and be moody.' But you can't speak to her of peace if you're agitated yourself. If you're irritated because the baby has woken you, at least one of you, mother or father, will have to give up the irritation before you go to her. At night, under these circumstances, it's not easy, but you have to do it. You have to sink into your body and give up, knowing what you are doing and why. If one of you is calmer than the other, then that's the one who should go and speak to the baby. You will have to be prepared to go on doing this for several successive nights or perhaps weeks. Speak to her with love, and remember: you are speaking to the subconscious, a most powerful place, putting in the suggestion of union and love.

When she stops crying: 'That's good. Now go to sleep or be still and I will come in again later (or in the morning) and be with you.'

There is a time for going in to be with the baby and a time for leaving her alone to cry. You will know when those times are. You will find the balance between the two. You have to go by what you register in yourself as right at any one time. That's what this life's about, isn't it? There's nothing for sure. All we can do is stay open to what is right in this moment and then do the best we can.

You will have to steel yourselves for the times when you must let her cry. Again you have to go and speak to her subconscious: 'Now, listen, you are not alone. I can hear you crying but I cannot stay with you at this time. I am going into the other room now and I will return later when it is right.'

If she still doesn't stop, return in say fifteen minutes and repeat the exercise again: 'There is no need for you to cry any more. Everything is all right. You are loved.'

Sometimes you may have to be very firm with her: 'I cannot come to you again until you stop crying. As soon as you stop crying I will come in and see that you are all right and tuck you in again. But now it is best that you just lie there. I won't be able to come in while you keep crying like this, because there's nothing to cry about. Everything is all right.' Then go out. But you will have to overcome your agitation and anxiety as you listen from the other room.

Mother: That is so difficult for me — even when she's not crying. I do get very concerned about her. I am always wondering if she is all right; if there's anything wrong . . .

The child picks up the mother's agitation along with her love. Be still. Give up a little more. And ask your partner to help you: 'Whenever you see that I am getting too concerned about the baby, will you tell me, please, and I will endeavour to pull back from my agitation and give it up.'

*

Mother: This is also a question about crying, but in my boy's case it isn't so much during the night as the day, and not so much crying as outright wailing! I feel this as a real onslaught on the peace of my home. I admit I'm perhaps over-sensitive about this because I didn't have the baby until I was 33 (he's two and a half now) and up to then I'd always been able to arrange my life pretty much as I wanted it. Until the baby came along I suppose I thought my partner and I had more or less got our act together, so to speak. We are loving and supportive and I thought that with so much love, centering, relaxation and genuine love-making (from which our baby sprang) we would have a totally happy, contented child.

Actually, he is a joy to be with — generally. But there are times when he is fractious all day and seems to be completely possessed; and then I just can't stop him wailing. He's inconsolable. It is very disturbing to me to let him 'cry it out'. It pains me to see him in pain. Aside from the obvious things, the crying seems to have no apparent cause. It is not that he is unloved. We can't understand why he is so unhappy and just don't know what to do about it.

I suggest that while he's crying you kneel down beside him, keeping yourself as psychically detached as possible from the disturbing fact of the crying, and then speak to him like this: 'Be steady. Be still. I love you. You are loved. There is no need for you to be disturbed or to cry like this. Mummy is with you. I am not going to pick you up or try to comfort you with things you don't need. You must wait. I will come to you and cuddle you and give you your dinner when the time is right. Now settle down and know that you are in a house of love and it is always a house of love even when you are unhappy. I love you and I am with you even when I am in the next room.'

Remember that there is an energetic or psychic transmission between you and your child and you can speak to him as straight as you would speak to your partner. When he is in a good mood sit down with him and tell him that there is no need for him to cry. Tell him that you will always see that he is physically comfortable, but you will not come to him just because he cries for no good reason.

When he is older and can communicate verbally with you he will have to tell you what he is crying about, what his problem is. No child should be allowed to cry without knowing why, and yet that is how every child gets away with emotion; and as an adult, is able to get away with being moody and unhappy without taking responsibility for the immediate cause.

Father: When a toddler is bawling, most of it is a demand for love and attention. I can understand that, but I still find it difficult to deal with our boy when the wailing goes on and on. If I get into a confrontation with him it only makes matters worse. So I try to create some sort of distraction, which works for a while . . .

But only for a while. The secret is to realise that young children become emotional mainly because of their need to demand. Every demand expresses itself very quickly as emotion. You cannot confront the emotion; in that situation you can't win. What you have to do is confront the demand.

'Stop screaming. There's no need for it. If you want something you do not have to cry to get it. You should ask for it. It is my pleasure to give you whatever I can.'

The child starts screaming . . . (I am talking now about young children or toddlers who can talk to you.) As his father I would go over and say 'What are you screaming for? Why are you behaving like that? Why are you crying?'

'Don't know . . .yaaaah . . . baaah . . . don't know.'

'Then you are absolutely irresponsible. You have to know why you're crying. You have to be sharper, more intelligent. Come on, tell me why you are crying. Or else stop it. Which is it to be?'

This is how you start to teach responsibility, in the very first instance: 'You are responsible. If you cry you are responsible for what you're crying about. Tell me what the matter is and I'll try to fix it. That's what I'm here for. But if you can't tell me what the matter is, stop crying.'

Even when children are very young you have to speak truth like that. You train children in the truth by informing them about life and speaking straight. Later, when the child is old enough, you will be able to inculcate real responsibility: 'Look, son, this is my life and your life is yours. You have to be responsible for your life as I am responsible for mine. Be responsible for what you want. Know what you want, take action to get it and if you don't succeed or get into trouble getting it, don't turn round and complain.'

I say that nobody cries without a reason. Is that the truth?

It seems nobody in the world knows this truth, so children are usually allowed to get away with screaming and bawling. You'll see them in their prams when the mothers are shopping: 'Waaaaaaaah.' Toddlers walk around quite content and then suddenly they're screaming — for no reason. The parents tell them to shut up, pick them up, carry them around, put them down: 'Waaaaaaaah!' What this spectacle means is that unhappiness is creeping into those children, as it creeps into every body in this existence, to possess them. It needs to express itself with enough force to get a sense of its own existence. The children cry out automatically so that the unhappiness can get the feedback. When it gets possession of a child's brain like that it can use the body whenever it wants. The child will then cry for no apparent reason and the parent in ignorance accepts it.

A child raised in truth and justice is told: 'If you cry, you must always tell me why, because I will do everything I can to help you, whatever the problem is.' Then, with your instruction, the child will be vigilant, looking for the reason.

When he has stopped crying and has looked for the reason, he might say: 'There's no reason. I just feel it in me.' And then it can be simply explained: 'Well then, the reason must be that unhappiness was trying to enter you. Well done for being straight with me. Now let's get rid of it. Come here and I'll give you a cuddle . . . '

39

Mother: Are there some children more prone to this behaviour than others? It's hard to understand why our little boy gets these wailing fits when we love him so much . . .

You have to remember that every body is born with pre-dispositions. No one is the same. Your son has come into the world to live through his predispositions, just as you are doing. His wailing is part of what he brought with him to this world. And as you know in your own experience this world is a very hostile and unhappy place. Our whole society is raised on negativity and fed on shared unhappiness. The entire globe is orientated towards greed, cruelty and sex. Scientific materialism seeps everywhere. You can close your front door and create as peaceful and harmonious a home as you possibly can, but the corruption flows through everything; down the street, under your door and into your home.

There is a psychic reality inside every body and it is that which governs our lives. Every child is psychically exposed at birth to the negativity of the world and infected by our ignorance of love. As long as I have anger, jealousy, guilt, fear, resentment, or any negative emotion inside of me, then my child will be possessed in some way or other by unhappiness. Even in the womb the intelligence is being conditioned by lack of love and the world in which we live.

As we all live in the past it is a world of past. That's what everybody talks about; even talk of the future is an extension of the past. Who ever talks about the present? So every new-born child is soon buried in the past, in ignorance, and the parents go on speaking of the past or the future and very rarely of what life is about now. Though the baby has not yet learned the language of the words we speak, he is an open consciousness, ready to receive whatever psychic influence he is exposed to — ignorance and the past, or love and the present.

You have to know that all children must carry some of our past, some of our ignorance, just as we had to carry some of the ignorance of our forefathers and by living it, endeavour to enlighten it. Everyone has the opportunity to enlighten the human consciousness a little more, for that's what everyone's life is; the enlightenment of the terrible condition of man and woman on this earth. Because each of us has our share of that burden to carry, from time to time we get depressed. We are likely to get drawn into more of the ignorance and then get even more depressed. But then again there are beautiful days of wonder, or love or rightness, and life is good — for a while. The good and the not-so-good — that's living.

Taking on the burden of our forefathers means taking responsibility for what we have done to this planet, to our love; for what man has done to woman, or woman to man, and for all the cruelties we have inflicted on each other. That is being a responsible parent of the human family. But even so, in preparing our children for what they have got to deal with, we can only do our best.

The voice that has love in it counteracts the waves of ignorance floating through the house. But despite our parents' love and their best advice, we each have to go and live our lives. All you can do as parents is love your child, even with his burden, and prepare him for life in a just and knowledgeable way so that he can take responsibility for his unhappiness whenever the time comes.

*

Mother: I think it's very frustrating for children when they aren't old enough to communicate everything they want to say. My daughter is two and a half now and for the last six months she's been going through a phase of having tantrums and I am finding her quite difficult to handle. She screams and gets red-faced and is totally confused about what she wants. Whatever I do for her, she wants the opposite. The only thing it seems I can do is leave her alone until her rage burns itself out. I feel it comes from the frustration of not being old enough to express what she wants. But I have noticed that she is definitely worse when I am emotional myself, especially when I'm emotional because of my husband.

Yes. I understand. Generally speaking all children go through this frustration and rage and they struggle and scream or beat the floor. It's part of the frustration that comes from being born. But then there are other influences, as you say. When you and your husband are in disagreement or conflict, it goes into the child. That's how it is. You can't help that. The child is like an absorbent tissue. She is absorbing the emotions of you and your partner.

All children absorb the psychic vibrations of those around them, and the hidden element that people don't usually know about is the sexual frustration, particularly of the male partner. All men are sexually frustrated, as a rule. The father's psychic energy of frustration goes into his children, boys and girls; and daughters especially are very open to it because they come from the opposite sexual polarity.

All you can do, as much as possible, is for you and your husband to get rid of the emotion in you both. But we can't live ideals; we have to be down-to-earth. Your child has to go through this stage and absorb the emotion. She will get through it. It's a bit like an infection. Once it's started you can try all the medications, but the infection has just got to work through you and there's nothing much you can do about it.

When she is older your daughter will be able to communicate the frustration she feels by speaking about it to you and then you'll be able to help her deal with it more consciously. You will be able to demonstrate the difference between the love or the good inside of her and the frustration that comes over her: 'Can you feel the love in you? Can you feel any warmth? Your body enjoys that, doesn't it? It doesn't at all enjoy the agitation and frustration, does it? So when you feel the frustration coming over you, call Mummy and we can get rid of it by talking about it and being together.'

The cause of the frustration is deep inside her, a pain like the pain you and I had in us from childhood. Eventually, when she is old enough and has suffered enough and wants to find the truth or God or life inside her, she will have to go right back through the frustration of her whole life and rid herself of the pain energetically. That's the spiritual way. She will also need the love of a man who loves her. His love will help to take the pain out of her: that's what man's love is for. It's a long unavoidable process for everyone who loves God or life enough. But in the end life is just.

Mother: And if we do not allow her to make demands, and we don't give in to them, that will help to prevent her unhappiness from building up?

Yes, it will limit her future suffering. The world is not going to tolerate her demands, is it? Go out into the world and make demands, and you soon get trodden on, don't you? Demands and expectations make everybody unhappy.

We must teach the children not to have expectations: 'Listen to me, my son or daughter. You can ask me for something but you must never expect to receive it. Why? Because I might not give it to you. Then you'll be unhappy and it would have been better not to have expected it.

'Do not think that I "should" give anything to you. Life doesn't have any "shoulds". When we start thinking that something should be one way or another, we are soon shown that life isn't like that. But if you are contributing to the house in a harmonious and loving way, it's possible that everything you need will be provided.'

Why wouldn't everything a child needs be provided by the parents? They are like gods, you see.

'My son or daughter, it is my pleasure for you to enjoy your life. I shall never leave thee nor forsake thee and all that I have is thine — but only what I have. If you make demands on me you will make me selfish and emotional. I will not give you my emotion, which is my self, because I can give you only what I know to be right. My love and guidance you can have endlessly.'

Isn't that so? It is your pleasure that your children enjoy their life, isn't it? So you give them all the things that are right and are within your power to give. That's what the heavenly father's pleasure is — that we might enjoy our lives. And then all is provided for us.

PIGGY OUT

In the early days of my realisation of truth I used to write verse that spontaneously suggested itself to me and described what I was seeing about my self. It became quite a long saga, as you can imagine. One part is a battle between Life and a cunning opponent — the bit of self which always opposes the good of life.

> No ordinary foe is he,
> he'll even come disguised as me . . .
> Aha, the simpering inner beast,
> considerate, smiling, gentle, kind.
> That's mine host, the contented mind.
> But spill one drop from its twisted cup
> And watch the filthy mess erupt.
> The pacifist he turns to war.
> What for? There is no war.
> 'Yes, there is, my friend, you see,
> every war begins in me.
> I am your Guardian of Strife . . .'

I called this creature 'The Pigmy', because in the battle for transcendence I had gone back through my self and reduced it to a desperate nucleus:

> Look at you, once so fat and sleek,
> You're sickened, starved and shame-faced weak.
> — 'No, Life, that is not so,
> Rough it's been, but I'll not go.
> I'm thin from slipping through the door.
> But I get in!'

Unhappiness is always trying to get in. It is so intransigent and deeply embodied that to keep it out is a continuing battle.

We have seen in the last chapter how a core of unhappiness exists even in the very young. The self starts to form around that nucleus and quickly grows, inhabiting the innocent body and gradually possessing it. From time to time it seems to take over completely, suddenly eradicating the child's sweet nature in a sulky mood or storm of screaming. All parents know the ugliness of the child possessed. Now we will have a closer look at what can been done to deal with that unhappy self and, in the words of one particular family, 'keep Piggy out'.

*

Nobody in truth wants their child to be unhappy. You raise children in the truth with your love and honesty and by informing them about life. This way they can be responsible for their unhappiness and make themselves free of it, with as little pain as possible. Then their lives have purpose.

The reason so many people get bored sick with their lives is that they've got no purpose. They may have many goals, but purpose doesn't have a goal. Ambition has goals. Future plans and schemes have goals. Purpose is always known now. The whole of my teaching has purpose — to get rid of your unhappiness now. And a real family has the same

46

purpose — to free the home of unhappiness, as much as possible, every moment.

'Know this, above everything else, my son and daughter, we do not want unhappiness in this house. We don't want it sticking to the walls.

'The walls of our house are built in the psyche. In existence they are made of thick bricks, as solid as our bodies; but behind the bodies and the bricks is the psyche, where you feel love or where you feel hungry or sad. Every sensation is in the psyche. Our bodies are not just physical. Inside is psychic energy. But the walls of the house absorb or reflect that energy, just as when you shout at a wall you get an echo bouncing back at you, so you get a psychic echo. In an unhappy house the sadness, screams of pain and hurt come back at you. We don't want that in our home. Our purpose is to keep it clean.'

That's good housekeeping for a real family.

'But, children, you may not be able to tell others this. People in the world might not want to hear it. All the same you will know the truth of it, because your mother and I are both living the truth as we see it, as best as we can. And we're endeavouring to keep unhappiness out of ourselves, the house and this family.'

It is most important in parenting to be open and honest with the children about what you're endeavouring to do with your life. Honesty is the way.

'If I am angry or unhappy and you come over to me and say, "Dad, are you angry about something?" then I have to be honest. If I am angry I have to be responsible for it and give it up. You can say "What are you angry about Dad?" And I'll have to see that whatever it is that's made me unhappy, my anger is not right because it's polluting the family. So I will endeavour to give it up. Or I will take some action to rectify the situation that was making me angry. Now what goes for me also goes for you, because this is a real family and we are all in it together. Okay?'

Make an announcement like that and you're likely to encounter some resistance, because some auntie or uncle or friendly neighbour is going to say you're being unrealistic: 'All children get moody. It's part of their nature. You can't treat them like adults. They are too young to understand . . . ' etc. And then of course you will have to remain true to your purpose.

Mother: It's not just other people who make it difficult. Most of the time it's me, my self, that just loves getting away with it, and letting the kids get away with it too. It's just so hard to stop it. But I also know when I am being emotional that my consciousness is there behind it all, waiting for me to stop being dishonest.

I'm confused about whether a child has this same duality, whether the consciousness can separate from the self in one so young. Do parents have to take the responsibility of acting as the consciousness for the emotional child — in the same way that you as guru appeared outside my own body?

We have two boys. The older one, who is two, has recently become ill, withdrawn, irritable and has lost his joy in life. All the people around us are sharing their concern and trying to coax him out of it — trying to distract him or get him excited. When his moods come on we confront the unhappiness: 'You are being pathetic. The unhappiness isn't you. It is trying to rise up through you, gain entry and spread amongst us. Can't you drop it?' But he is very unwilling to co-operate.

We wonder if we are asking the impossible? Does a child really have any power of his own against this invasion? We have started to tire of always confronting him. It feels like he's building up resentment towards us for challenging him. How can we get underneath this, so that we feel more together again?

The important thing is to tell him you love him before you endeavour to instruct him. When he's battling with himself he must not feel unloved, or deserted. His consciousness is there behind the emotion, as it is in you, but it is very distant and needs the support of love as much as possible.

Try speaking to him more of love — in the good times and not just when he is being moody. Talk to him when he is open and receptive: 'We love you and we always do. When you are moody and unhappy and we try to tell you to give it up, we are still loving you as our precious little boy. We just want to help you to be your joyous being — like you are now. As you are now is what you really are. Isn't it good? So we just want to help you to be stronger so that when the unhappiness is there you will be able to keep it out or get rid of it.'

Then, when he is moody, and if possible before he starts screaming, speak to him firmly: 'Now you know we love you. And you love Mummy and Daddy. We are all together. We are a family. But we can't have this unhappiness spoiling the day, can we?'

You may feel that he is not hearing you, but keep going (in your own words and your own way, of course).

'You are spoiling our day and we don't want that, do we? So come on. Put your arms around me and give me a cuddle. You're my boy and I love you. But I certainly don't love this unhappiness. And neither do you.'

It is the demonstration of your love that the boy needs. Does he perceive that perhaps you give more love to your other child than to him? See if you can find this out (without putting the suggestion into him).

He certainly does not need more excitement or to be coaxed out of his mood with any kind of distraction. But if there is something he enjoys doing, some particular thing which in its way is creative, can you join him in that, encourage it or take more interest in it? Try to give him a sense of your participation in his interests.

Do not try to directly challenge or confront the emotion. You must be firm when you are, but it can be tempered with love.

When a child is obdurately emotional — temporarily possessed — every parent feels helpless, not knowing what to do next. It is best then to let it be. Take some firm action, such as telling the child you will not speak to him until he is quieter. But do not let that go on too long. Stand no nonsense. Be firm, but caring. As soon as possible communicate your love again: 'Are you better now?'

Love and firmness work wonders, even though you may feel much self-doubt during these very trying times.

*

The scowling darkness that at times can enter and possess a child's body is in its extreme form horrific and diabolical. The potential for violence and fury it engenders is illustrated in the following conversation with another mother who had been driven to exasperation by a whining child.

Mother: I'd like to ask you about something that's quite difficult for me to talk about. I have a five year-old boy. He's normally quite happy but every so often he gets very moody, what I call 'whiny', and pulls faces at me. After a while of him whingeing and whining and being nasty I just react inside myself and get very angry. I can feel myself getting angrier and angrier. This happened again recently in quite a bad way and I was very shocked by how full of anger I was — a very deep rage and hatred. I was very disturbed by this violence in me. I felt I almost might have killed him, although I didn't actually hit him. Can you please tell me what was going on? Where does such violence come from?

There are many parents in that condition who actually do hit their children, can't stop themselves, and of course it isn't just the parents that get enraged with children and do them harm. Such violence to young children is shocking to us all, especially as it usually seems so out of character. It is apparently as inexplicable as the sudden violence and ugliness that possesses the child. So it's a good question. Where does such sudden violence come from? Well, I can show you where the whine comes from and why, when it happens, you get so terribly reactive inside.

Something enters the child's body and twists the features of the face. The eyes slip sidelong glances. The head hangs down. The shoulders hunch. Fingers and toes fidget. And then this thing gets into the voice with a high drawling whine and it speaks.

'Here I am. Here again. Look in the mirror. See? I'm in you. I'm here again.

'You know me. You've met me before. I am the complainer. I am the whiner. I am the whine in the child. I am in all bodies . . . You know me, don't you? You've seen me many times. I do the complaining in every body. You've felt me in your self. I'm always whining.

'Got something to complain about to day? Let's hear it. Come on, who can we blame today. Come on, let's have a go at someone. Go on, go on . . . lash out!

'I pursue everyone. I am frightening. I howl. Call me the accuser, the blamer, the complaining, whining, howling one. Frightening I am, in this matter, within you and without. I'll drive you to distraction. I'll push you to destruction. As you well know. For you know me well.'

That's how it speaks. What is it? It's the devil in this matter, and all matter. It does indeed pursue everyone. It is not personal. That's why its whine in the child disturbs mothers and fathers and drives them to distraction, almost to destruction — because it mirrors that same psychic place inside us all.

Our task is to outpace and outdistance this devilish thing with the creativity which is our birthright as men and women in this matter, this existence, this body. By grace or by rightness and by love we rise above the devil in all the various ways that I teach.

I tell you this about the devil for your own self-knowledge as parents; it is not for your children to hear.

*

The terrible intensity of emotion that sometimes possesses a child has to be faced with love and persistent detachment. The parents must refuse to identify with the emotion. Here is a mother's account of emotional possession in a six year-old, faced in a right way.

Mother: There is much excitement at Benny's school. The children are to give a concert and Ben has been rehearsing. After school yesterday he went to a friend's house to watch TV and when he got home he was wriggly, hard to reach, demanding and speedy, talking in a higher pitched voice. I didn't want to add to all the input he'd already had so I said he couldn't have a good-night story; he could stay up longer and play a game with us instead.

The emotional reaction that followed was quite a spectacle. Howling, wailing, shouting, slumping of shoulders, stamping of feet! He changed expression, posture and the sound of his voice from moment to moment, like going up and down the keys of a piano with great speed and intensity. It was a storm broken loose.

Wailing mournfully: 'You managed to make me cry again. You always do, every day . . .'

Stamping his foot: 'I'm going to have a story. I am! Now go fetch it!'

Complaining: 'It's not fair. I never get what I want!'

Words came out of him that are absolutely foreign to us; things I never hear any of us say. We were quite stunned.

I was still and detached, watching Ben carefully. I sat on the sofa with Dave [the father] and we said very little until he calmed down.

In the end he collapsed into an armchair and sobbed hard, which I felt was what he needed to release all the excitement and emotion. Then all was well. He was sweet, easy and tired. He told us about his day, and the rehearsals, and mentioned a few things that had upset him. Again there were tears; but then a sweet smile, a cuddle and he slept.

It was good — good that neither Dave nor I were dragged into the unhappiness; and good that we had allowed Benny to clear himself of the world in him.

Dave commented afterwards on how odd it had felt to be so still and unemotional, almost cold, in the face of so much emotion. I felt that too, and it felt good.

*

As parents in the truth you naturally teach your children what you hear me teaching you, although of course you have to adapt it to a child's level of experience.

Mother: Even if I manage to stay clear of my own emotion and I teach my daughter not to be demanding and do everything you say, it's really a hopeless task because it seems she has to have the experience of unhappiness. No matter what we do, our children have to develop a self. So they have to be unhappy.

As her mother you will help her and guide her all you can, because that is your job as a parent. And if this teaching is true for you, then you will be endeavouring to live it. It is for the evolution of our race that there are people living the particular way that I teach, knowing that it is right for them and their children. By right parenting you will contribute to the possibility of keeping unhappiness out of a child as it develops. That's what our job is, as parents.

Meanwhile every body is subject to its predispositions and everyone has to live his or her own life. But those predispositions don't necessarily have to take the child on a course of conflict. It could be a course of greater harmony, if only we can impart to the children the benefit of our experience and educate them rightly in justice and truth.

My father and my mother (every one of our fathers and mothers) always said, 'Look son, don't go and do that . . . I tell you it'll end in disaster . . .' I couldn't listen because I had to know what disaster is. But all the same, you can change the course of your child's karma to some degree.

*

There is no finer thing you can do for your children than to teach them from the earliest age how to stay in their bodies. Most children and adults spend most of their time outside their bodies.

There's a psychic space around every physical body and it's occupied by our thought processes. Most people are so often preoccupied with their thoughts, or are excited and mentally agitated, that they spend most of their time in this psychic space of thinking, dreaming and worrying. They might be walking down the street or digging up the road but if they are talking to themselves in their heads they are not in their bodies. Very few people at any one time are actually in their physical bodies — in contact with the physical sensation of wellbeing and therefore with love and what I call 'the good'.

The more you help children to find the wellbeing inside their bodies, the less they will escape into their heads. The more you remind them to stay with the good the more they will be able to counteract their moods and rid themselves of unhappiness whenever it possesses them, as inevitably it will. So it is vitally important to get your children back into their bodies as often as possible.

Keep on speaking to the child, right from infancy: 'I can feel the good. Do you feel the good? See if you can feel it. I feel it here in my tummy. Do you feel good in your tummy?

'No? . . . Okay, well this is how you do it. You look and see whether you love me. Do you love Daddy? Do you love Mummy?

'Yes? So, where do you feel that you love Daddy or Mummy? Point to where you feel it . . . Now, that's good, isn't it? That's the good.'

The more you talk to your children like that the more you engender in them the knowledge of what it is to be in the body. And the more experience they have of the good in their bodies, the more able they are to get rid of unhappiness whenever the time comes.

Getting children back into their bodies when they are light and joyous, or when they are just starting to get excited, is good preparation for doing it when they are emotional. But of course it is more difficult when they are already disturbed. In that situation try getting the child to sit down and be with the physical feeling of the upset or frustration.

'You feel unhappy, don't you? Well, look and see where you feel unhappy. Can you feel the unhappiness in your body?'

'Yes.'

If possible get straight answers. No nods. A 'yes' spoken out loud makes the communication straight and means the attention has registered what's happening. It is then possible for the child to start taking responsibility for the unhappiness.

'Okay. Where's the feeling? What's it like? Discomfort? A pain?'

As you go on asking the questions, the child's intelligence has the chance to separate out the feeling of unhappiness from the rest of the body-sensation. So you draw attention to this: 'And can you also feel the good? Can you feel the good underneath or around the discomfort?'

The sensation of the good is always there. The feelings of unhappiness or emotional pain come and go. The demonstration of this in the experience of our own bodies is one of the most important lessons we can be given — as children or adults.

After a while, it may be possible to ask: 'What's the problem? What caused it?' And that can lead to an honest dialogue.

In the best situation everyone in the household is able to feel the good most of the time, and when unhappiness does enter the house, they deal with it swiftly and honestly. If the parents put the emphasis of family life on the good, the children will help them keep it up.

There you are, Mum and Dad, starting to have an argument, and the youngest child comes up to you and says: 'Why aren't you feeling the good, you two?' You laugh; and laughing, you feel good.

*

There was a family that came to me when I returned to live in Australia in 1986 after being away in England for twenty years. They helped me get my Australian meetings started and were most giving of their service. They really loved the truth and lived it as best they could. And when they had their first child I told them that they would have to teach him where God is.

'Somehow you're going to have to give the child an idea of what we talk about in the truth. You're going to have to show him at the earliest possible age where God or life is.'

A couple of years passed and they reminded me of the conversation: 'But how do you actually do it?' they asked. 'How do you tell a small child about God, life and truth?' So I started to show them the basic practice that underlies everything that this book has been about so far.

To give you a summary of how to introduce love, truth and God into the family, here is what I suggested to them. (Always adapt it to your own circumstances, of course. And don't forget to pick a time when the child is receptive and not too restless.)

'We're going to do something very, very interesting. We're going to have a game, a fine sort of new game . . .'

'Ah!' he says. It's always good to put the truth in a context which will engage the child's interest.

'What we're going to do is this . . . We're going to find out where God is. How about that! So, the first thing is, you sit there and I'll sit here opposite you. Got your cushion? Yes? Right. Let's start.

'Now, do you love Mummy?'

And the child says: 'Yes. Yes, I love Mummy.'

'Do you love Daddy?'

'Yes. Yes, I love Daddy.'

'And when you say you love me, where do you feel your love?'

The child points somewhere in the body, usually the belly.

'That's right! Now is that a nice feeling?'

(Take some time to go into the sensation in the body, helping the child to recognise the warmth of it.)

'Is it a good feeling? Is it good to feel your love? Yes!

'Now you've heard people talk about God? Well, love is God. Love is always inside of you and God is always inside of you. So where's God? Point to where God is . . .'

Again the child points at his own belly.

'Right! Now you're pointing at your own body. But love or God is not a person. It's just a lovely sensation, isn't it? Is it good?'

'Oh yes!' he says.

'That's the sensation to stay with. It's with you all the time. It's always there and never disappears.'

It was a couple of months before I saw the parents again. They had been practising the exercise with some success, they said. But now the boy was beginning to get emotional, moodiness was setting in, and they wanted to know how to address it. So I suggested another game for when he was emotional and his face was showing signs of distortion — although at the time he might not think it much of a game. They should persuade the boy to go with them into the bathroom or bedroom and have a look in the mirror.

'See what I see? How you twist your lovely face and your eyes go red and you go all tight?

'Can you see your self? Do you know what it means?

'It means you've lost touch with your love inside. So now we've got to get back in touch with it. What Mummy and Daddy are going to do is endeavour to get you back where the love is. So let's try that now.

'Come on, you've left your body. You've gone outside it, away from your love. Come on, get back into your body. Get back to where the love is.'

The mother and father went off to try this on the little boy. When I saw them a couple of months later they again gave me their report. They had recently been to one of my public meetings, an occasion when I'd read my verses about the Pigmy, the ones quoted at the beginning of this chapter. This had given them an idea and they were making good use of it.

'We played the mirror game and eventually got our little boy to stop being demanding. And now we can usually get him to quieten down. Every time he gets overtaken by his emotion we immediately say: Come on . . . Piggy out. And God in!'

Apparently this worked very well. As soon as the child showed any sign of selfishness Mum or Dad would say: 'Now then . . . Piggy's in. Come on, come on . . . We don't want Piggy here. Come on . . . God in. Piggy out!'

They have now raised three children like this, and the 'Piggy Routine' has become a part of family life; so much so that the parents themselves cannot excuse themselves. If one of the children see Mum or Dad with 'Piggy in' they are very quick to point it out.

If Dad gets emotional, why shouldn't it be pointed out? And because Dad is living the truth he will say: 'Yeah, okay. I feel rotten and shitty and I don't care . . . No, I do care. Okay, all right, Piggy out.'

LIFE WITH SIMON

We had a deal. We agreed that none of us wanted our house to be unhappy. We often sat down together and discussed it. Even though at first Simon was only three we treated him in this like an equal partner; and he thought it was great. The three of us agreed there was only one thing that made a home unhappy and that was the emotions of the people in it.

Simon knew what emotion was and he knew it was not love. He understood the difference. His parents had been practising my teaching since before he was born and having discovered emotion in themselves, they consistently revealed the truth of it to him in his own experience. So when they decided to split up, although Simon was still a toddler, he was well prepared. Twelve months later I married his mother, Kathy, and we moved to Queensland. We set up home on Tamborine Mountain and lived there together for four years until my marriage to Kathy came to an end.

Emotion is any demand put on another individual. For instance we were able to show Simon that he was being emotional when he was grumpy and he was being emotional when he couldn't or wouldn't tell us why he was grumpy. He had to be able to say why he was grumpy or what he wanted; otherwise he was being dishonest and didn't know what he was doing — he wasn't responsible for himself.

The deal was, if ever he noticed Kathy or me being grumpy he could point it out and ask us why — why were we making the house unhappy? It was not acceptable to say that Simon's moodiness was just because he was tired. If he was tired the solution was for him to go and have a sleep. Nor was it acceptable for me to say I was grumpy because I'd had a hard day. There was always a practical solution to unhappiness, as we all discovered.

A hard day wasn't a reason to be grumpy and short tempered. I must give up my holding on to the past. The cure for a hard day was to sit down and enjoy my home and family. If I couldn't do that, why was I living there? A home free from unhappy, moody, gloomy, emotional, world-wearied people is a good home. If I enjoyed being emotional and unhappy it wasn't the home for me — or any of us.

If Simon heard us having a tiff he'd ask us 'Why are you arguing?' We'd have to tell him and that would make us responsible for finding a practical solution, or surrendering any emotional position we had adopted.

A deal was a deal. The same justice must apply to all. Then it's fair, a fair game. Children learn in fair games.

*

He woke up crying. He'd been in bed for a couple of hours. We'd been out all day with him and had a late lunch. On the way home he'd fallen asleep in the car and I had carried him to bed. I went in to him.

'What's wrong Simon?'

Sitting up and still crying, he wailed, 'I didn't have any dinner!'

'Are you hungry?'

He stopped crying for a moment: 'No.'

'Well, it doesn't matter that you didn't have any dinner does it? We had a late lunch.'

He looked at that and started to cry and wail again: 'But I didn't have any dinner.'

'I know you didn't have any dinner. We had a late lunch. You didn't need any dinner. You only eat because you're hungry. And you say you're not hungry now. So it doesn't matter that you didn't have any dinner, does it? Would you like me to get you something to eat now?'

Silence. 'No thank you.' He lay down and turned over. I kissed him, tucked him in and he went peacefully to sleep.

The habit of an idea is so strong in us; stronger often than our contentment. How often what we think we want makes us unhappy, when it is not what we want at all. It's just the habit of wanting what we've got used to having, but no longer need.

*

He was about to pour himself a glass of fruit juice. Very steadily he brought the large bottle of juice towards the glass on the table. I said, 'You're going to spill it, Simon.'

'No I'm not.'

'Okay, go ahead and let's see.' He did. Over went the glass. Juice ran across the table and dripped down to the floor.

'There you go,' I said. 'You spilled it.'

'I know that!' He was quite furious.

What he didn't know was that I had seen he was going to rest the side of the bottle on the lip of the empty glass and of course the weight would tip it over. He was very angry with himself.

'Don't be angry. We've all done it. I'll show you why it happened.'

I showed him and of course he saw it immediately. He won't spill the juice that way again.

＊

He had been naughty and I was reprimanding him. He was standing in front of me but his eyes kept darting to another part of the room.

'Do you see how you're glancing over there while I'm talking to you? Do you? There — you just did it again.'

He nodded. And immediately looked over to the other side of the room and then back to me again.

'That's not being straight, Simon. I'm talking straight to you and that means I'm looking straight at you. I can't talk straight to you if I'm looking out of the corner of my eye at something else. So you won't see my eyes darting here, there and everywhere. You can't listen straight if you don't look straight at me.

'Simon! You're looking over there again.'

'Barry, I can't help it.'

'I know that. But we're just getting it straight aren't we? You're looking over there because you don't want to listen to what I've got to say. You don't want to be told that you've been naughty and you don't want to be corrected. Do you want to stand over there, where you're looking?'

'No.'

'Well then, don't look over there. When we have finished talking you can go and be over there, or do what you like.'

Kathy was very straight with him, even before they came to live with me. She answered his questions factually, never talked down to him and expected him to address her in the same way. They delighted in each other's company and in the straightness of their communication. He was a joyous boy and because of his mother's love and straight treatment of him he didn't hold on to his moods for long.

*

'Did you turn off your light, Simon?'

He'd just come out of his room to join his mother and me in the lounge.

'Oh no, I forgot.' He turned to go back, stopped and addressed me: 'Barry, why do I always have to turn the lights off?'

'If you don't need a light you turn it off. If you need a light you turn it on and use it for as long as you need it. But when you finish with it, you turn it off.'

'Other kids leave lights on all over the place.'

'But you're not another kid. You're my boy, Simon. I'm teaching you to be responsible and to know what you're doing. By turning off your light you're learning to use only what you need. This will help you when you grow up and have a place of your own. When you've got your own place you can have your friends round whenever you want. You'd like that wouldn't you?'

'You bet!'

'It's fine to have lights on all over the house when you want them. Like when you're having a party. But you've got to remember that lights cost money. People are often surprised at how much their electricity bills come to. I want you to be in charge when you use lights and not just leave them on forget-fully or unconsciously. Then you won't be shocked at what you have to pay.'

He got the point: 'And then I'll have more money!'

'Right! We're bringing you up to be able to fend for yourself. We want you to live the best life you can. You're learning to control things. And one of the first things you can learn to control are the lights.'

*

About seven in the morning, Simon was up and playing in his bedroom opposite. I walked into his room.

'I'm going to close our door,' I said. 'Will you stay out of our room until I call you?'

'Why?'

'I'm going to love your Mum.'

'What are you going to do?'

'I'm going to cuddle her in bed.'

'Can I come?'

'No, but you can come in after and we'll both cuddle you. We'll all cuddle together.'

'Why can't I come now?'

'Well, when a man cuddles the woman he lives with in bed it's a private thing. I married her so that no one else would be in bed with us while I loved her. That's the main reason people get married, to be able to cuddle in private.'

'All right. But don't forget to call me.'

*

He came into the kitchen bleary-eyed for his breakfast and asked, 'Barry, is today tomorrow?'

'What?' I said.

'Is today tomorrow?'

I got the point. 'No, tomorrow never comes. Today is just today. But I do know why you asked the question, and it's a good question. We talk about tomorrow, but when it comes it's always today.'

Simon was just six at this time. For a child of that age there are beginning to be tomorrows. Our sense of time changes as we become more aware of past and future. The excited anticipation of birthdays, Christmas and other events sets the scene. Eventually we grow up to be so absent from now that time is measured only in memories. Watch the changes in your children and keep them in the present while you can.

On another occasion he asked: 'What's second childhood?' He'd evidently been listening to me comment on my own age.

'It's a term used to describe people when they get old and forgetful,' I said.

He was pensive for a moment: 'But what do they forget?'

'They forget everything.'

'But why?'

'Because that's how life is. You come into existence, into the world, brimful of energy in your first childhood, like you are now. You live in the moment. You forget things. It's hard enough to get you to remember to bring your reading book home from school isn't it?'

He grinned, 'Suppose so.'

'Nothing wrong with that,' I said, 'that's first childhood. And it's much the same for people in their second childhood. After you've grown up and gone through the world as an adult you start to run down a bit — like a battery runs down. You've seen the old people. They can't move as fast; neither can their minds. And in some old people one of the first things that fails is the memory. They start to act child-like — like you.'

'But I can remember lots of things!'

'Yes . . . Not as much as I can, though. An adult can remember a lot more than you because he's had a lot more birthdays. So that memory is very full. When the old people start to lose their memory they become like children again.

That's called the second childhood.

'I'll tell you a story about it. You remember Judith, my cousin?'

'Hmm . . . I think so.'

'Well, her Dad's eighty and his memory has gone. One day she took him to the hospital to visit his wife who he's lived with for sixty years. She had broken her hip and was in hospital to have it fixed. When it was time to go, Judith said, "Dad, aren't you going to kiss Mum goodbye?" And he said, "Oh yes," and slowly went over and kissed the woman in the next bed.'

Simon roared with laughter, and then said quite seriously, 'Barry, that didn't really happen?'

'Yes, it did. Quite often older people are found wandering in the streets because they can't remember where they live or who they are. I'll tell you another story. When you were a little boy, four or five years old, you wandered away and got lost in the supermarket. You started to cry because we weren't around. You couldn't remember what to do. All you could remember was that you'd be all right if you could find us, because we'd remember what to do. That's what it's like in your first childhood and in your second. We only need a memory when we have things to think about. We don't need a memory to run around and play, or to just sit in the sun all day.'

*

We were driving to Sydney and pulled up for petrol. Simon and I went into the toilets. We stood beside each other in the customary fashion. Simon, not having a fly on his trousers, started to pull them down and as he did so I yelled, 'Simon, stop!'

He stopped, looked up and said, 'What's wrong?'

'Look down round your feet, where you're standing. It's wet with urine. If you pull your pants right down to your ankles they'll get soaked in other people's pee. Do you see what I mean?'

'Yes, I do,' he said, cautiously lowering his pants to just above his knees. He went on with what he came in for.

'Don't do that!' I yelled again. He stopped, startled. 'You're splashing both of us! Point to the side, away from us, not straight at the urinal. It splashes back. Look you're making us both wet.'

He did what I asked and smiled. 'Oh good, Barry. Yes, that works.'

I always tried to show him what worked. I never told him just to do something without explaining why it was practical or right. Children learn to be practical when parents take the trouble and the time to do this in the early years.

A man came out of one of the cubicles, brushed past me and jibed, 'God, am I glad I didn't have a Dad like you!'

THE RULES OF THE HOUSE

E very child is looking for security. Every child wants the security of the mother's presence and the father's authority. Where the parents are without enough authority, the children are insecure.

The more the parents rid themselves of insecurity, the more equilibrium there will be in the household. The parents are the child's security — as love, honesty and wisdom. But to introduce those qualities to the children the parents must have the authority to deal with them justly.

Children do not find security in being given freedom. No child can be free. Security for children necessarily means that their behaviour must be limited. But the limits have to be imposed with honesty and justice.

This book is about raising children in love, truth and justice. Justice is essential. When a parent tells a child what to do, the parent must play by the same rules. If it's good enough for me to ask of you, then you have to be able to ask it of me. That's fair. That's justice.

Teaching our children justice is very rare. Yet it is essential that they acquire a sense of justice to set against the double standards of the world. It has to be done by parental demonstration; and done from the earliest age. Children who know their parents' justice when they are young will need less demonstration of it when they are older.

Justice means that everyone in the household has to be informed from the beginning what the rules are. The rules are determined both by life itself and by the authority in the house.

So I might call everyone together and say, for instance: 'This is a house in which we all contribute to the love which is the harmony of the home, so that we can all live together without unhappiness. I am contributing my love right now by telling you the truth of life, which is that everyone has to make their contribution and take their share of responsibility. I also contribute my money, which as a child you can't do.

'We all have to pay our way. You live with us because you are not old enough yet to live on your own. As you don't earn your own money, there is only one means for you to pay your way — with love. How do you pay in love? — by not getting emotional without a reason. If you are emotional you have to be able to tell me what you're emotional about. If it's because you want something that I say you can't have, I'll tell you why you can't have it. If you don't accept what I say then you are not loving.

'Any time that I'm not contributing, or your mother's not, then you are free to point it out, as long as it is a right response. In the same way we will point out when you are not contributing.'

Remember to inform children of the whole situation. Sometimes they don't realise or they forget that you have to work very hard to keep the house going.

'You can go swimming this afternoon, but I have to work. Provided you do what you're told, you have the freedom to do as you please after lunch. But I have to go back to work, even though I would like to go to the beach with you.'

Children have to be informed that life is not easy and sometimes we have to make our contribution when it doesn't suit us. But always make it clear that you're prepared to go and do what you have to, without making a problem of it, because you love them and it's your pleasure to make your contribution to the home.

Justice means being true to the situation and not to what you like or don't like. The situation of the parent is: I have a little one in front of me, for whom I am responsible. What is best for the situation is what is best for the child, not what I would or would not like for myself.

What I ask of you as parents and individuals is to give up your personal considerations. Give up the 'person' as much as possible. By listening for the truth in what I say you are becoming more impersonal. Every time you see the truth in your own experience you glimpse the vastness of impersonal justice.

If you demonstrate this lack of self-consideration when you discipline or punish your child, it will be evident that you are being just. The punishment should always be explained so that the justice of it is clear and the child knows that you are not acting out of your likes and dislikes but according to what you see as right.

Father: In my case, a major 'dislike' is the very thought of having to inflict any sort of punishment on our son. He's eight now and quite wilful. I realise my own parents let me get away with too much, really. Then, when they did have to pull on the reins, they came down on me really hard, which made everyone miserable. I was quite rebellious. Every time they insisted on me doing something, I'd refuse or demand to know why. Now, I hear my own son moaning: 'Why have I got to, Dad? Why?'

Well, as I say, the parent must endeavour to communicate the rules of the house and why they are necessary.

'The house is a physical equivalent of my psyche just as it is for everyone who lives in it with me. It's up to all of us who live here to make it a pleasant place and we all have to contribute to that. Now you haven't had enough experience of life yet to know how to keep the house free of unhappiness. So I have to guide you. I have to lay down certain rules in this house. I will give you all the freedom I can but there are certain things that are not allowed here, just as in the world there are certain things that the law does not allow. There are penalties if you break the law of the world, and there are penalties if you break the rules of the house. It is my responsibility as your father to communicate that to you.'

If a child has been told the rules, and given the reasons for them, a penalty has to be imposed when the rules are broken; as they surely will be, because every child must learn from experience. If the penalty is not imposed, there is no authority in the house.

The best way to determine the penalty is to let the child say what it should be. If he is old enough you simply ask: 'What should the penalty be for what you've done?' When you can let the child fix the penalty, that's real authority and real justice.

'I see that I did do something wrong. I did do that. Yes, then I think I shouldn't watch television for two days.'

'Good. That is so. Then you shall not watch television for two days.'

In this case the child is able to look at the situation clearly because the parents don't blame or accuse him — they don't exact an emotional penalty. But a child who has not been treated with justice will not know how to be just or true to the situation, and therefore will not know what his punishment should be.

*

When Simon was six he started to question authority, as every child must. He didn't want to do what he was told.

'Why have I got to do what you tell me?'

'Because I've got the power.'

'Why've you got the power?'

'Because you can't pay your way yet. You've got no money. If you can't pay for your room, your food, the electricity or your clothes, you can't do what you want. The person who pays for those things has the power to tell you what to do. When you go to work and earn money to pay your way you can do what you want. Until then I've got the power. And you've got to do what your Mum or I tell you.'

He went away for a few minutes and then came back again, with a frown on his face.

'Barry, that's not fair.'

'Yes it is. It's fair because we pay for you and look after you until you're old enough to look after yourself — until you're old enough to pay your own way.'

Again he went away, and I found him sitting on the step, with his head in his hands.

'All right Simon, what's wrong. What are you thinking about?'

'Running away.'

'Oh. But that would be silly wouldn't it? It will be dark soon. You'll need some food and somewhere to sleep. And anyway, we love you and I'm telling you that you can't go.'

He was a bit relieved at that, but still rebellious: 'But why can't I do what I want?'

'I told you. You don't have the power yet. Until you can pay for yourself and look after yourself, I've got the power.'

Silence.

I had another go: 'Do we look after you?'

'I suppose so.'

'Do we love you?'

'Yes.'

'Good . . . Someone's always got the power, son, even when you're grown up. There's always someone with the power to stop you doing what you want. That's how it is right through life and you'll have to remember that fact. There's always going to be some authority over you which you will have to obey. If you don't accept that, then something will happen to land you in trouble.

'There are always laws and if you don't obey the law you can expect to be punished, because authority is always likely to catch up with you. There is a law for driving down the road. If you drive on the wrong side you might crash into another car, and then you might be fined and not allowed to drive again, or if someone was killed in the crash you might even go to jail.

'Without laws, people would go around hurting and killing each other all the time. Policemen are there to stop that. That is their authority. Often people break the law and are not caught. You might get away with it, but you might not. So you have to ask yourself: Do I want to take the risk? And the answer is: No, not really, unless it is very necessary, because the law gives the police the power to restrict my freedom.

'In the first instance the parent has the power, and in your case that means your mother or me. Because of my experience of life I know what is best for you. You might think differently from time to time, but finally you will have to accept that I am the authority here. What I say goes.

'You know that I love you and I will always endeavour to be honest with you. And as long as I have your love that is sufficient for me. I don't have to exercise my authority, except when my experience tells me it's necessary. Sometimes, because of your inexperience, you don't know what you're asking for and then I have to step in and make the decisions. But generally I don't have to exercise the power — not as long as we each contribute our love to the house.'

*

You have to exercise authority with firmness. If you don't know what you're doing, your children won't know what they're doing either; there will be a certain slackness between you. You have to be firm enough to convey that you will stick to your guns and be resolute; (although when the situation changes you must never stubbornly hold your position).

To teach your children right authority, you must know the rightness of your stand — even though you may be weeping inside at having to deny them something they very much want. To give them a right psychological basis for life your endeavour must be to communicate the justice in authority and to show your children the right use of it. They are going to copy you and learn from you.

The parent has to assume authority over the child and justice must not only be done but seen to be done. The just parent must rule like those kings and queens of olden days who truly ruled their kingdoms. Sometimes they had to order the punishment of a beloved subject who had broken the law. When you face a difficult situation and justice must be done it's no good judging the situation from the armchair of modern society, stuffed with its 'liberated' opinions of what might or might not prove to be best.

A certain way of behaving will be imprinted on the child, one way or another. Every brain is programmed, and programming it is an inevitable function of raising the child. It is better that this be done through the parents' love of fairness and truth than through some religious or moral code that the child will not be able to live up to in later life, and which will therefore cause confusion, guilt and uncertainty.

*

Both parents have to be true to the situation and must be together in facing it. If the child is to be punished, both parents must be agreed: one must not contradict the other and there must be no relenting. We are human and the emotions will rise but provided we are undivided as a partnership, we will not betray the child. If we contradict each other while exercising authority, the child will become confused, unhappy and devious.

I suggest that as parents you make an agreement: 'We are in this together. We must not contradict each other in front of the child. If ever we do that, it will mean something is not straight between us. If we are in conflict with each other, one of us will break off and make sure we sit down together and get ourselves straight. Only then can we deal with the child.'

Would you want to display your disagreement in front of a developing consciousness? Of course not, but inevitably it will happen and from time to time children will drive us to distraction. But as parents consciously endeavouring to act with justice you get things straight as soon as you can. And you discover how wonderful it is to be together in this endeavour.

'Let's agree . . . We're together in the raising of this child as the situation. It's agreed that if one of us is absent and the other punishes or penalises the child we will support each other. If necessary we can talk it over when the child's not in the room.'

In bringing up Simon, Kathy and I always supported each other. Since we were ourselves endeavouring to live in truth it was easy for us to be united in dealing with him. One day

I walked into the house to hear loud voices. Kathy was chastising Simon for spilling his poster paints over the bedroom carpet. She was being somewhat severe because he'd done it before. He had been told that he must not paint in the bedroom but only at his desk or the kitchen table. He was close to tears.

As I entered the room he looked at me pathetically, alert for any sign of sympathy. Like all of us, children are survivors; in a tight situation we all look for a quick way out. He was appealing to my love of him to overrule my love of justice. But that's not on. My love of him would let him escape the situation, which was there for him to face up to. He was resorting to the old trick of divide and conquer and it would destroy his mother's authority. Justice comes first.

'What happened?' I asked, and they told me. I said to Simon, 'Don't look to me for sympathy. Your behaviour has been unacceptable. Your mother is correcting you and telling you why. Now you attend to her and listen.'

Occasionally Kathy would go over the top in exasperation, as all parents will. She would hand out a punishment, some sort of deprivation, that was just too much for her comfort, my comfort and the comfort of the entire house.

'Simon, I told you not to do that and now look what you've done! I warned you and now I am going to punish you. You are not to watch television for one whole week!'

I used to advise Kathy against being too extreme in the punishment; for instance, a couple of days without television, but not 'one week'. The point of a punishment is its impact; its message has to penetrate. If it goes on too long the message is likely to be lost in the hurt that it causes.

There are times when you have to be very clear and insistent: 'No. You can't go to the birthday party. That is your penalty and I am not going to change my mind.'

There are other times when it is best to leave yourself some leeway: 'It's very doubtful that I will allow you to go to the party on Saturday. I'll let you know, but at this time I'm inclined to phone your friends and say you won't be going. If your behaviour improves over the next few days — and I see that you have truly listened to me — I might allow you to go.'

If the behaviour doesn't improve, you will have to stick to your guns. It is most important that you do what you say you're going to do. Children will not respect you or themselves if you don't, or if you waiver.

When the parent is occasionally unjust (and we must accept this is going to happen) it can be corrected. He or she is taken aside by the partner, shown the injustice and can then apologise to the child. This in itself is a demonstration of justice which the child will appreciate and retain. Such honesty will not reduce parental authority but enhance it.

For example, when Kathy sent Simon off to his room and sentenced him to 'one week, no television' the conversation went something like this . . .

'Kathy, we'll have to talk about what just happened. Seems you might have been a bit harsh.'

'Well, you know what it's like. In the moment, I just overdid it . . .'

'Okay. Well, let's see how we can deal with it.'

Together we went into Simon's room and I said: 'Your mother's told me what happened. And she's told me how you accepted your punishment. We have been talking about it and because you have not complained about the penalty that had to be imposed, and because you have shown your love in your lack of reaction, your mother and I have agreed to reduce the penalty. You have shown that you're a young man who can behave rightly. So we are able to take the pressure off you.'

The situation of justice is retrieved by the partnership working with one aim — to bring the child up rightly in the moment. The object is not to make the child true to anything, but true to life. That is, to discern what is right in any situation and grow up to be what we call a true man or woman.

*

I find that parents often do not know why it's necessary to smack a child. Some don't agree with it at all and others who do smack their children get disturbed about having to do it. This is because they don't know the reason for it.

You smack children to bring them back into the body. When they are wilful, angry and moody they are endeavouring to get out of the body. All you need to do is give them a smack on the legs. The sting brings them back into the body and then you can speak to them. That's why children have to be smacked. Or did you think it was to punish them?

The perspective of our human mind always gets it wrong. Everyone is out of the body. The only reason anyone suffers in the spiritual process towards God is to get them back into the body. That's why we all get smacked one way or another by life or God.

Most parents are sentimental about their children, even those who live a life of truth. The heart is sentimental; but on the way to truth the heart must be purified of its sweet memories and bitter pangs. We have to get out of our sentimental hearts (our attachments) and into the whole of the body. When you are fully in your body, and can remain there, you will never suffer emotionally again. Life won't need to smack you any more.

As soon as a child is back in the body the smacking should stop: it has served its purpose. When a child is in the body often enough, there will be no need for smacking at all, just the immediate communication: 'I see you are being wilful and unhappy. Now what are you going to do about it? . . . That's right. Give it up.'

If you deal with children as you deal with yourself in the truth, they will start to respond and become responsible for their own unhappiness. Then they will be able to throw it off more quickly. The only reason any of us suffer is because no one ever taught us how to give up suffering. We were never taught that we are responsible for our own unhappiness — or responsible for its absence, which is the good. How much more just and right it is to teach the children to deal with their own incipient suffering.

*

'The rule in this house, as you know, is that when any of us is unhappy we do our best to deal with it. We say what's causing it. If anything can be done about the problem, we do what we can to solve it. Otherwise we have to give up being unhappy about it. Now, do you know why you are unhappy?'

'Yes.'

'Is there anything you can do about the problem?'

'Not now.'

'Where do you feel it?'

'In my stomach.'

'What's it feel like?'

'Rotten.'

'Okay. It's there. You can feel it inside. You're containing it and dealing with it. It might feel bad but you've just got to face up to the pain while it's there. Do you know that?'

'Yes.'

'Good. And you seem to be handling it okay. Are you?'

'Yes. It's . . . it's all right, I suppose.'

'Now, come on! "All right" is not good enough, is it? Come on . . . Give it up.'

'But I can't!'

'Okay. Stay with it, and feel the good in your body at the same time. Life is good, isn't it?'

'Oh yes!'

With a smile, the gloom begins to lift. The longer the unhappiness is left, the more painful it is and the longer it takes to shift. But the more I face the fact that my unhappiness is in my body, nowhere else, and although it's a pain the sensation of my body as a whole is good, then the quicker I get rid of it.

If from the earliest age you have taught your children to keep 'Piggy out', it will be easier for them to handle their unhappiness in this way. But you must remain vigilant as unhappiness insidiously creeps into them. Always remind them of the first rule of the house: No unhappiness.

What a different way of life I'm proposing . . . a world in which I am responsible for my life, right from the moment I am born.

*

Mother: Our little boy is just beginning to toddle around and he gets into all the cupboards and climbs into the fridge, pulling everything out onto the floor. He isn't old enough to understand why he can't do it. We try to teach him the limits of what's acceptable but it seems he has to go on breaking the bounds. I get afraid that sooner or later he will hurt himself. He's intelligent enough. He knows he's not allowed to do it. But he keeps on doing it.

There is that experimental stage where young children play with everything in the house and you always have to have your eye on them. You will have to let him do it a few times and accept what happens. That's one of the situations of being a mother or a father.

How do you deal with it?

Mother: I keep my patience as long as I can. Sometimes I get irritated. I try not to get angry or shout at him. Usually I just keep going over and moving him away from the cupboards, saying 'No!' What else can I do?

I suggest you encourage him to play with his toys instead of things from the fridge. But you have to face the fact that he wants to explore and experiment. At some point he's going to try to turn on the television, isn't he? — even though it's forbidden.

Mother: Fortunately he's not big enough yet.

Well, when he is, you can take him over to the TV and show him how to do it.

'Now we're going to turn the television on. I'm going to show you how to turn the television on and we're going to push the On button.'

Show him and do it like a game. Allow him to do it several times, in your care, and then, when you want the television on, get him to turn it on for you.

'Where are you, son? Come here, please. Would you turn on the television please? Yes, that's right. That's the right button.'

He's got to have a go at pushing every button in turn, but then he will get used to pushing the right one.

Mother: And what should I do when he breaks things?

He has to experiment and offences must come. You can tell him to try not to break things around the house and you can give him toys to experiment with instead.

'I want you to be more careful with the things in the house. Play with your toys and if you're going to break anything, break one of those. But don't break it deliberately or you won't be able to play with it any more. It would be a pity to break it and not be able to play with it.'

When inevitably something gets broken it's an opportunity to learn more responsibility.

'Stop crying and come over here. It's broken. I know you enjoyed playing with that, and you want to have it back again, but now you have broken it, you see, and if you break something you can't have it again, except in its broken state.'

In this way you teach him that it's better not to break things.

'But if you want to hammer something, you've got this rubber hammer I've given you, and these wooden blocks, and you can hammer those.'

The endeavour must be to take appropriate action, without being too strict.

*

Father: Barry, sometimes the only way to get through to a child is to shout and be angry. Is there such a thing as 'right' anger?

No, but in some situations a force will arise in the body which you could call 'right anger'. Anger is distinguished by my being attached to it. So if a situation calls for that force, or 'right anger', I must be able to drop it at any moment, as the situation requires. Say I have to chastise a child and I ask him to stand up. As he pushes back his chair, he stumbles and is in danger of falling. I am immediately able to attend to the situation: 'Be careful. Are you all right? Take it steady. Good.' And then I can proceed and be rightfully angry again. That would be a demonstration of lack of attachment to the anger and its momentum.

But we should always address the first question. In this case, why would you be angry with your child?

Father: Well, I would say that it's mainly when I feel my authority is threatened . . .

And usually that is when you're being manipulated by the child's emotions and you can't get a handle on them. The emotions are so slippery that they will not face you. So you get forceful and angry.

All you can do is endeavour not to be attached to the anger. And of course, as always, try to find out what the child wants: 'What do you want that is making you behave in this way? What do you want?'

The emotion doesn't know what it wants, except that it wants to be angry, demanding or manipulative. So the child possessed by it doesn't know either. But in your wisdom and love, and by talking to your child as I speak to you, you eventually make him responsible.

*

Mother: How would you advise me to deal with the sort of situation that happened to me yesterday. My children did something that made me angry and I felt I had to make a really forceful complaint to them. But then they got upset and as a result I've been disturbed about it ever since.

First of all, remember that there are always situations in which you have to be forceful. Sooner or later everyone faces situations in life where a forceful protest or statement has to be made, and this is especially so with children. You might appear to be angry. You might get hold of them, sit them down and address them with force — and they might be quite frightened by it.

Children are often so excited or emotional that they are impervious to what you say. Their momentum drives them forward at such a speed that there is only one thing to do: you have to restrain the momentum, break it and penetrate the imperviousness. You have to suddenly bring them to their senses. That takes forceful but disciplined action. Then you can speak to them intelligently about why you are being forceful.

'I am very, very forceful at this moment. But I am not angry because I am not attached to what I'm saying. I am speaking to you like this to interrupt the momentum of your disobedience and excitement which is going forward like a train. You know how difficult it is to stop a train once it gets going? I have had to use something like the steel buffer at the end of the line to stop your train, because you have been wilfully disobedient. But now we have stopped the train. So now you can hear me and I don't have to be so forceful. Now we can get it straight.

'You have to do what you are told, although if you want to do something else you can always tell me. But you have to accept that if I say no, then you cannot do it. I am the power around here. But I will do whatever I can to give you what you need. So let's get rid of this momentum that's been in both of us. Let's be loving. Come here so I can give you a hug.'

We have to face the fact that we are sometimes driven to use force. But anger only becomes angry when you think about it. Remember: to be angry is to be attached to anger. When you said 'I've been disturbed about it ever since', it means you thought about it and probably you felt guilty. The only way to deal with the situation is to attend to it at the time with the child. Get it out in the open. Clear it up.

Don't blame yourself because you think Jesus didn't get angry or some psychologist said you should not shout at your child. The fact is that sometimes you have to use force. But don't be attached to the emotion as a continuity.

Twenty minutes later you might say: 'Come here and sit down while I talk to you. I want to tell you there is nothing in me about what happened between us. And I trust there's nothing in you because we love one another. Now, is there any problem? No? Good.'

Because you loved the child throughout there's no hurt left and you won't have any remorse afterwards. You must have no remorse in you because that makes you feel guilty; the guilt attaches to times in the past when you felt guilty and then there's no getting clear of it.

*

Mother: Often, when Ben gets excited or emotional, it's quite a while before we're able to calm him down. He can get very distressed when we stop him from doing what he wants. We have to give up whatever we're doing to be with him so we can address his emotion. But we don't give up on it. The trouble is, the longer it goes on the more self-doubt comes into us, because we start to think we're being unjust. But then suddenly his emotion will clear. He'll be free of it and back in his sweetness.

You must not consider yourself. Your self will want to be sorry for him and start to doubt. He'll look so beautiful and innocent and you'll hear yourself say: 'Oh, how can I do this to him? Am I being too harsh?' But you must look inside: Are you being unjust? Or are you doing what you have to do? As partners you must guide each other, not considering your feelings but only doing what is right.

This consideration for each other is in all of us. In truth all consideration is emotional — a demand put on the situation and based on feelings conditioned by past experience. There should be no consideration. But this is a life of human feelings, of compromise. The feelings will always be there, yet we can be guided by the situation to reduce them so that self-consideration doesn't influence our actions in justice or truth.

Mother: One rule we have is that Ben can't have what he wants until he stops demanding it. We are also trying to teach him that he may or may not get what he wants (depending on what it is) because sometimes it's not actually possible for us to give it to him when he wants it. Something else may have to take place first.

That is so. Some things can't be done because something else has not yet happened. So you show him that, explaining what you are doing and why, step by step, so that nothing is suddenly imposed on him. That's how you make him straight, and how he gets a sense of justice.

*

Father: I don't seem to be able to discipline my son's wilfulness. He is always running around and he gets so excited I can't get him to stop. He won't listen to me. We have a good relationship. I spend time with him and play with him a lot, so I don't think he is just reacting against me.

It's good to play with him, but don't give up your authority in the game. In other words, don't become child-like yourself. You are father and son, and he must not forget that.

When the games are over, and at a time when he is calm, sit with him and speak to him as the father. Pick your moment, when you yourself are still. Look into his eyes, and speak with him about anything he wants to talk about. But speak to him as his father, so that he gets a sense of the Father.

*

Mother: One of the biggest problems with my children is sibling rivalry. They get very unruly and competitive, and I find it very difficult to be around them when they are fighting. Can

I just let them sort it out by themselves?

No, they have to have guidance. You've lived a life of experience and from that experience you've gained in wisdom. The point of your experience is to impart your wisdom and guidance to your children because they lack it in themselves. You have to lay down the rules and stick to them. You have to explain to them why rules are necessary and that they must contribute harmony and not discord to the home, because you all live in it together.

Now, as I've said, the rules must apply to everyone in the house, so you have to follow them too — and not just when it suits you. In this instance I suggest you instruct your children by explaining what the rule is for yourselves as parents and partners.

'We endeavour not to argue with each other, and not accuse or blame each other. So if we suddenly find that we are beginning to have an argument, we stop and ask each other why we are arguing. That's our rule. Then we address the problem until we get rid of it between us.'

That can become a rule of the house for the children too, to the extent that they are old enough to be instructed in this way. So when they start fighting you can step in like a referee and say 'Stop!' and remind them of the rules. The more right instruction you've given them, the less likely they are to go on squabbling. Because they are developing intelligences they will respond to your straightness.

Then you can get at the situation: 'Now, what were you fighting about? Whose turn was it? Who is not being straight here?'

When the facts emerge, the parent must be the judge. You must be the point in the house that the children refer to for the truth. They have to be able to look to you for justice and honesty. They have to know that you will always endeavour to be just and fair but that you have the last word.

With your guidance and by your demonstration, your children must learn that they themselves are not the authority in the house and that they must accept that what you say is right for this moment. They must know that they are given to you to raise as best you can, and that is what you're doing.

Remember that there's no perfection in this imperfect world. These fights between the children are going to happen. Can you give an example of a situation where they might squabble?

Mother: They'll fight over which TV programme to watch. And the younger one, who's only four, will pick a fight with his sister if he feels she's getting too much of our attention.

Each of them will naturally have very distinct and particular areas of interest and this has to be faced. The younger one, the boy, will be more self-orientated and therefore more selfish, because of his years. He has to be informed that because he shares the house with everyone else he does not have the right to do just as he pleases. So the rule is he has to share the television with his sister. This has to be addressed before the eruption of any rivalry. You have to lay down in advance which programmes it is okay for him to watch and which ones he can't because his sister wants to watch something else.

You also have to instruct him that he's not allowed to try and get your attention when you need to give it to his sister. You have to tell him it's unloving and selfish of him to do that.

'You are loved and we will give you the attention as and when it's necessary, but you are not allowed to demand it because your sister is also a member of this family.'

You must say the same to your daughter so that it becomes one of the rules of the house.

*

Mother: Something I insist on is that the children put their toys away themselves. What do you say to that?

Putting the toys away should be routine and no effort for them. But you have to insist that they do it properly and not in a desultory and half-hearted way. You can't afford to let it slip and then make a fuss about it when visitors are coming. It confuses a child when the parent is not consistent.

I would put it to them as a rule of the house: 'You have to tidy up your own toys after you've been playing with them. You have toys to play with and they are yours to look after. When you want to play with them you go and get them from somewhere, don't you? Where do you get them from? . . . Over there; that's right. Well, when you finish playing with them you've got to put them back in the same place. At the end of every day you tidy up. That's the rule.'

*

Mother: I try to encourage the kids to do jobs around the house, make their own beds and clean up after themselves. It's a bit of a struggle to get them to co-operate. Do you have any tips on how to explain the need for these things?

Yes, I would say this: 'You are learning to live in the world by living in this house; and this is how you do it. You have to do certain jobs, like the rest of us. We have all got our jobs to do. You want to live here, so therefore you've got to work. That's how it is in this world. Everybody has to work.

'It's no good saying "Oh, no! I don't want to do it!" I don't want to hear any more of that nonsense from you. You have to make your contribution to the house, just as I have to make mine. You will take your share of the responsibility and you will make your own bed. Otherwise I'm going to suggest that I get you up a bit earlier in the morning and ask you to do a couple of my jobs as well. I have to do those things, and I don't say "Oh no . . . I don't want to do them" — because they are part of my contribution to the house. So you can have your choice. Do you want to do my jobs as well as yours? Or are you going to stop this nonsense?'

*

If you indulge your children and do not make them responsible for their lives, they will cause you future unhappiness — no matter how much you love them.

You have to start teaching them responsibility when they are very young. By the time they are teenagers it will be too late. They won't respect you. They will want to get away from you. When they eventually leave home, they won't even want to come back and visit you — except to stir up a bit of excitement now and again when they're bored. They won't be able to just sit down and be with you in love. They will not respect you because you did not respect them by loving them rightly and making them responsible.

It is a privilege to have a child in this world. But to have a child in love you have to be responsible for love. The reason homeless children are sleeping on the streets of our cities in the West today is that their parents have not learned how to love. Otherwise they would know how to take responsibility for their children.

*

Mother: My daughter has got to the age where she wants to go out a lot (she's nine) and needs to socialise. She really enjoys it and has a need for friends. I like to see that and encourage her. I've never set a time limit on her being out. But the other day she was gone all day and didn't come back until eight o'clock. She had gone past the time when she should have had her meal, and came back 'hyper', wound up and excited. I have never wanted to put too many limits on her, but I see now that her level of excitement is quite a good guide to how much experience she can take.

A nine year-old must have some freedom but there have to be limits, and you must say what the limits are. You did not say when she should be back, so she went too far. Both of you had to learn from the experience. But that's how we all learn, isn't it?

Your daughter knows that she went too far but the more you talk to her about her experience, and how hyperactivity comes into the brain or the body, the more she will be able to see it happening in her. It might seem that children don't heed these lessons, but at a deeper level they do.

As her mother you have to be vigilant and watch to see what is best, using your own experience of life and truth as your guide, not what you want or don't want for your child. While a child is not capable of setting the limits, the parents have to determine them in their wisdom, which is their experience of life purified of any personal desire, ambition or fear for the child.

*

Teenagers have to test the limits of their independence, and this of course often leads to conflict in the home. How can this be handled? I say that until your children can earn their own living and live independently, they live by privilege and need to be reminded of that.

This is what I would say to a teenager in my house: 'I love you. And it is my privilege to love you. You love me and it is my privilege to receive your love. Because you show love to the household, to your mother and to me, you are welcome to use the house as your own. It is absolutely yours to use as your own and that is your privilege. But you must understand that if you do not show love, then you start to forfeit the privilege.'

Everyone has to be made responsible. Teenagers must be informed that there's no such thing as a free lunch — even for them.

*

Mother: I'm a single parent and my son is now twelve. He's fast growing into a man and I am still besotted with him. He's not a little boy any more and I'm less able to give him the discipline he needs. It's not a big problem but I feel I would be doing the best for him if I could find a way of being very firm while still being loving.

If things do get out of hand, he starts to look very unhappy. If I had some way of really stopping things before they get out of control it would be a lot easier for both of us.

Then the question is: Where do things get out of hand? And why? What does he want to do that you don't want him to do?

Mother: There's actually a lot of wanting . . .

If it is a right wanting as far as you are concerned, you probably allow him to have what he wants. But when your experience sends up a warning signal you stop him. As he enters his teens, he is going to start looking for more experience and testing himself against what for you are the acceptable limits. So there will be these conflicts . . .

I hear that you are endeavouring to get a balance between 'firmness' and 'being loving', but I don't know that there can be any such balance. Are they alternatives? Or are you firm when you are loving and loving when you are firm?

Mother: I suppose the most important thing for me to

remember always is that as woman and as mother I am love — that's what I am.

Yes: 'I am love. And I am not attached.' There has to be intelligence in the love. Where there's attachment and emotion there's consideration — lack of intelligence. As soon as you consider him you will start to lose your power over the situation. You have to be careful of your consideration. Such as: 'I don't want you to be unhappy . . . So, alright, you can do what you want.' Be very careful of that sort of consideration.

Mother: It's hard for me to say no to him, especially if I know how badly he might want to do something.

To be true to the situation you've got to see why you're not allowing him his freedom; and then you must explain why you can't give him his way. Do you already do that?

Mother: I try, although often I long to be able to just say 'No! . . . No. And that's the end of it.' But maybe he's passed the age when I can do that?

Yes, that time may have gone. The explanation is important. You've got to be open with him. For there to be justice, a man has to know why he's being denied what he wants. His intelligence has to acknowledge the situation: 'Yes. Okay. That's fair enough.'

At the same time he has to be reminded who has the power. You have the power to say what the situation is and you will have the power until such times as he has it himself.

The rule for your son is: 'Until such times as you can work to support yourself I have to take responsibility.' His intelligence can see the rightness of that. The same goes for any teenager who is taught responsibility from an early age and not allowed to escape into unintelligence.

STRAIGHT TALK

I n a real family there is real communication between parents
and children. This means that as partners you can be straight
and honest with each other and as parents you can speak to
the children about the fact and truth of life; and when someone
is emotional you can address the situation without getting
emotional yourself.

When as partners you speak the truth to each other, you
affirm the love in the house. Doing your best to live the truth,
you contribute psychically to everyone who lives with you.
As you clean the unhappiness, anger and resentment out of
yourselves you change the psychic space in which you live.
By your very presence you emanate love, truth and honesty
to your children and in that way dispel some of their pain
and ignorance.

Mother: We try to live the truth in the family, but at the same
time I know that Ben, my son, will have to have pain. It seems,
oddly enough, that in my love I have to allow him to go out

into the world and hurt himself. He has to learn the hard way. Perhaps, knowing that, I sometimes let him get away with things . . .

Of course he has to go and make mistakes, do things that won't turn out as he wanted them to. You must allow him to experience life but you will not deliberately allow him to hurt himself.

Mother: Well, I sometimes doubt I'm doing the right thing. It comes up in small things. For instance, for his birthday Ben wanted a computer-game like his friends have, and I wasn't happy about buying it because to me it was another bit of the world coming into our house. But he said he wanted it. So I got it for him and then, after a couple of days, I noticed he stopped playing with it. I think my attitude probably spoilt it for him.

First of all, your doubt is not about the whole way you're raising him. You only have doubts sometimes about particular things. See that and you will feel much better. And don't be too hard on yourself, or on him. Then you'll be able to see more clearly whether you are imposing anything on him or not.

In a situation like the one you mention, you have to have a straight talk with the boy. Go over and ask why he's not playing with it any more. Get him to communicate his reasons. But don't demand to know them or put any pressure on him. This has to be done openly and easily, so that he can speak from his own space and not just give you an excuse or tell you what he knows you want to hear. Endeavour to get him to come from the deeper cause. He may just say one or two words that will be enough to inform you and confirm that you did indeed make him feel bad because of what you said about the computer-game. Or that may not be so.

You said you let him get away with things. Like what?

Mother: It's mainly when he's emotional about something. I will start off trying to stop him, or get him to give it up. But he goes on and on . . . and I tend to give up and say I won't talk to him any more.

The most important thing to remember is that you must act as soon as you see the first sign of emotion rising in him. If you can get to him in time, sit down with him as quickly as possible and speak to him. You have to be very straight and persistent.

'Now, what's the problem? Tell me what's making you emotional. What is it you want? . . . What is it you can't have? What do you want to do that you can't do? . . . Come on, speak to me about it. It has to be something you want and are not getting. It has to be something like that . . . Now tell me, what's the problem? For if you can't say why you're emotional, then you're not being true and honest. Everybody on earth can say why they are emotional, unless they are being dishonest.'

As you know from this teaching, and as everyone knows who is willing to look at the truth in their own experience, it is dishonest to say 'I don't know why I'm unhappy'. I cannot be moody or angry for no reason. As I am the one who is moody and angry I must be able to say why. Yet everyone in the world is allowed to get away with it. That's why it's so important to teach your child this truth from the earliest age.

There will be times when he continues to be moody and you can't communicate at all. He has so much emotion that you can't reach the root of the problem. You endeavour to reach beneath the unhappiness but it's too late. Dishonesty has seized him; the selfish one has taken possession. Then you have to say, 'I can't go on talking to your emotion. When you get rid of it, come and tell me and then we will go into it together and see what we can do about it.'

Mother: It does get quite bad sometimes. The more I try to talk to Ben the more stubborn he gets. I get emotional and then it's hopeless. But just the other day there was a change. He was refusing to do something I'd asked him to do. At first I got a bit angry with him but then I saw that I was actually imposing what I wanted on him. So I apologised . . .

Well, that's honest. But then I would speak to him — without emotion or demand — to open up the dialogue again. You have to get him to speak from the more profound place underneath his excuses or reactions. He must have been feeling some reaction or he would not have been stubborn. The source of his resentment may not be immediately apparent. Allow him to express his resentment and get it out. Listen carefully to what he has to say. Then there's more chance of real communication between you.

*

Father: The problem I have communicating with my son is that sometimes he just can't speak straight. When he gets excited he runs all his words together. It's not because he's too young. He's six and quite capable of holding a proper conversation. But when he's emotional nothing sensible comes out at all.

There's a build up of excitement in him which creates this momentum and then he hasn't got the ability to say what he wants to say quickly enough. So you've got to slow him down.

You and his mother must agree that you are both together in this. Then you have to introduce him to a game of 'slowing down'. You can find different ways of doing this. For example while you are all having a meal together you can deliberately slow down your conversation. Or use the opportunity of a car journey to deliberately speak very slowly. Always make it a game.

By slowing down the normal conversation, you will put more pause into him and in that way attack the build-up of emotion.

*

Mother: How do you deal with children when they are lying? My daughter said she had a headache so I let her off school. During the day she seemed fine. As evening approached she said she felt ill again. I asked her if she was saying this because she didn't want to go back to school again tomorrow. She got very upset — because, she said, I didn't believe her. I'd like to be able to deal with her in a straight way so that she can tell me the truth without getting emotional.

We've probably all played sick to get out of something we didn't want to do. We don't like doing what we don't want to do, so we lie. As children we find it's best to lie; we see that everyone around us lies and that way we can get what we want.

This is what I would say to your daughter: 'I asked you if you were lying because everyone lies sometimes and, as we both know, you have lied to me in the past. So I can't believe you. But there is no need to be angry about it. It's the way of the world that everyone lies. It is best not to lie any more than you have to. Endeavour not to lie so that eventually you never have to be dishonest.'

It's a good idea to open up the whole subject of lying with the children so that we can all see what lying is and whether it is necessary. The more we look into something like that, the more it drops away as a need. So you might say, 'I'll tell you what I'm willing to do. I will endeavour to tell you the next time I'm about to lie. And you can endeavour to do the same. Is that all right? I'll do it first, so you can see what I mean. The next time I'm moved to lie I won't. Instead I'll tell you that I was about to lie and we'll see why I was going to lie and whether it was really necessary.'

We've got to stop our children harbouring their secrets, if possible. And we have to get rid of our own secrets. Having secrets makes everybody unhappy.

Are there things inside of you that you dare not tell anybody? The sooner they are told, the sooner you'll be free. But who can you tell your secrets to? That's the question.

Are your secrets necessary? Many of them are not, but you hold on to them for emotional support. Secrets are only necessary because nobody wants to hear the truth.

*

Mother: I try to be open and honest with Ben but I wonder sometimes if I'm transferring my anxieties to him by talking about them too openly. When something is disturbing me, he will probably notice it and because we are together I will talk about it. But I don't want to put my worries into him.

Where is the line between protecting him and being open with him?

The line is: Don't tell him what he doesn't need to know now.

There are many things that Ben doesn't need to know because he hasn't yet got the experience to deal with them, and you could create anxieties in him by saying too much.

Don't jump ahead with children. When a child asks a question, don't assume the next question. Answer the first question and then let it be. Don't try to enlarge on your answer and don't answer a question before it's asked.

Father: Our tendency is to want to explain things to him as much as possible. Are you saying this is not right?

It's us, the adults, who feel the pressure to explain, the need to elaborate. The need is in us, not the children. It is best not to elaborate. Just answer the question that's being asked. Then the child can receive the answer before coming back with the next question, which as a general rule he will do later on. In this way, what you say will be right for the child to receive and you won't have to elaborate about matters that really don't concern him.

Mother: There are situations where as partners we discuss things that concern us, and Ben is in the room. I feel I don't want to exclude him. There are quite a few things that concern me and I feel I want to be open about them. For example, Ben's schooling. He knows I am anxious about him going to the junior school next term . . . although I don't want him to feel worried about it.

Why would you want to tell him your anxieties? Your anxieties are not the fact of the situation. It's important to tell him the fact. For example: 'This school is different to the school where you've been going, but it will be a new experience for you. There are a lot more children there . . .' and so on.

Speak to him about the fact. There's no anxiety in that, is there?

Mother: No . . . But is it not right to mention everything that worries me?

No, not everything, not in his presence. Don't discuss in front of him what he does not need to know. There are things that are not for his ears. If it's a conversation between you and me, it's not a conversation between Ben and me, or you and Ben. If you're going to speak to a child, speak to the child. If something is worrying you and you need to speak to your partner about it, speak to your partner. But you have to choose the moment, because the child will be listening and likely to get an impression or false notion of the fact.

Don't just let children overhear your conversations and pick up impressions of what's going on. Let them sense that Mum and Dad are being direct and straight with them.

Mother: I remember from my own childhood that many things weren't spoken about in front of me, although I knew that something was wrong and it was very disturbing to me not to know what it was. So I thought it was better to be honest and open with my own child.

Indeed you should speak to Ben about what's going on. But tell him the facts of what he needs to know and speak to him straight, treating him as an adult in a young body with young experience.

What is the underlying problem in the family that you want to speak to him about?

Father: We are very short of money at the moment.

Money is so often a fundamental cause of anxiety, but you can speak about it to him in a straight way — without making a problem of it for him. Tell him how the world works with money and what the family situation is.

'We don't have a lot of money at the moment, but somehow we always manage to get through. Daddy works hard and I support him and we do our best to manage with what we've got. That's why we don't waste our money. We can't always have what people with more money can have, but it's all right. We're always going to get through.'

You can talk to him in that way, in practical terms that he can understand. That way is right and honest, isn't it?

Mother: Yes, but I see that I have been talking too much to him about things that are worrying me. I remember he had a nightmare after we had been talking about whether we could afford to send him to a private school, which might mean selling the house. This conversation must have left quite a deep impression on him, because in his dream we did not have enough money and were leaving the house.

That's a good example. I can relate something similar from my own life. During the Depression, when I was a boy of five or six, my father didn't have much money. He had to get up at four o'clock in the morning to help train some race-horses. There was talk about why Daddy had to get up so early and I took it inside myself. In my conscientiousness I couldn't sleep and I would wander into my parents' room in the middle of the night, shaking them: 'Daddy, is it time to get up?'

We all have these concerns about money, and they inevitably get discussed, but it's wise to avoid speaking about them when the children are listening.

Mother: I think my anxieties, whether they are about money or whatever, have a lot to do with being afraid that something will go wrong. It's as if my fear is quite close to my love. I get quite stressed when Ben goes out to play in the street, in case he gets hurt somehow.

As adults we all have to learn how to handle anxiety — how to face the situation as it is without undue stress. Remember: the anxiety is not the fact.

Here's the adult sequel to my childhood experience . . . My wife Julie was dying of cancer. We discovered that there was a special clinic where she could possibly get help with a special diet, but we lived in London and the clinic was in Mexico. So we made a great effort to find the money to get there. We booked a flight to Los Angeles, with a connection to San Diego. We arranged for a car and driver to meet us there and take us down into Mexico. All the arrangements were made.

We got to the airport in plenty of time and were waiting at the boarding gate. Then I discovered I'd dropped the Mexican visas somewhere. I rushed back to Immigration Control checking the floor all the way — unsuccessfully — and charged back to the gate, just in time to see the aircraft door slammed shut.

I shouted, 'You can't close it!' (I took absolute responsibility on myself). 'You can't!' Using a very explicit expletive, 'You can't . . . do it! Open that door! She's got to catch the plane!'

They said, 'We can't sir. That's the end of it.'

And Julie said — she was quite cool about it — she said: 'And all his racehorses died at once.' Which was true.

I flopped down. Yes, it was true. All my racehorses had died at once. I'd pushed it as far as I could. I'd done everything I could do and now I just had to die to it, immediately.

Although we all do everything we can do, finally we have to face the fact that life in its wisdom closes the door on those we love.

*

Grandfather: I think we tend to keep the children innocent as long as we can, protecting them from the adult world. And there's a bit of self-interest here, because of our pleasure in their innocence . . . I enjoy playing 'Let's pretend' with my grandson . . . I think we want children to remind us of our own childhood, when we didn't have a care in the world and we could all go on pretending, you know, that there is a Santa Claus . . .

Well, of course, where I come from, a child should be informed very early on that there is no Santa Claus and Father Christmas does not come down the chimney. It's just a story. Father Christmas is not real.

Grandfather: And how would you explain that, without taking away the fun?

I'd say: 'Santa Claus is as real as the Man in the Moon and though people enjoy pretending he exists, they know he really doesn't. He's just for fun.'
Tell them the truth from the start.
'The idea of Father Christmas is based on a very old fact of life that few people have any knowledge of these days. That is: we are given gifts. We have so many gifts given to us every day, like our food, the air we breathe, a nice warm house; but we forget about those gifts. So we put all our gifts together once a year and call it Christmas. And the imagination of all those gifts is put into one exciting figure, Father Christmas, who comes along with all our gifts in a bag. It's not true. It's just a story. But the wonder of all the gifts we have — the beauty of life and all the little creatures and all the birds in the garden — that's real.'
I say that you will not ruin a child's life by revealing that there is no Santa Claus. I say you're going to ruin the child's life by lying to him — because one day, as happened to me, he will have to be told there's no such person.
As you say, the child is innocent. So he believes what you say. But what do you think happens when you turn round and tell him: 'Well, there is no Santa Claus. It's not true' — having told this lie for years? The bottom drops out of the child's innards. It's a betrayal. But people think that's all right because

they are betrayed all the time. They're betraying love and betraying everything with double standards.

The young child quickly accumulates emotions and forcefulness but still has the innocence to believe in things. People love to pamper that belief. And they'll say: 'Oh, how awful to tell a child there's no Santa Claus!' Well, I say it's an awful thing to tell a child who believes in Santa Claus that it is a lie. That's the crime.

*

The grandparents, aunties and uncles arrive and lavish lovey-dovey attention on the children. They spoil the children with sweets and gifts. They appeal to the demand in the child and play up to it. Then they depart, leaving you with repeated demands. The way to deal with this is to have a straight talk with them. All the relatives and everybody else who comes to spend time with you should be told the rules of the house. They should not be in any doubt about the way you raise your children.

With your own parents you have to get it straight that you are raising the children in your way and not theirs. You don't want the rules of the house subverted or contradicted, no matter how well-intentioned their words or deeds.

'This is my son and he will be brought up as I see best and not as you see it. That's how it is. You had your chance with me. And if I represent anything, I represent your way of raising children. If you don't like what I'm doing then you don't like the way you brought me up. So why should I listen to you?'

'But I'm your mother . . . You can't talk to me like that!'

Well, perhaps you can't talk to her as I would, but somehow you must get it straight with her. Many young parents are not able to stand up to the apparent or assumed authority of their older relations. The parents-in-law are often even more difficult to deal with; and in their case of course you need the support of your partner.

You should be able to listen to any advice you are given but at the same time do what you know is right for your child and the situation. If the relatives disrupt the harmony of the house you have to make it clear to them how you are raising your children and why. Don't give in to their demands or emotion especially if they accuse you of being unkind or harsh. Only if they are prepared to look after the children day and night can they determine what's right for them. Otherwise they must not interfere.

Father: I found my Mum and Dad's advice very helpful, especially when the baby was born. They'd been through it all themselves. Problems only come when the practical advice gets mixed up with an opinion of some kind, or they start going into the past.

Yes, the grandparent should be guru. That is what we are supposed to be in the eventide of life. I do not mean that every older person should become guru or teacher as I am. My task was to experience practically everything a man can experience so that I could express the truth of it to many men and women and so help them bring more love and honesty into the world. But all older individuals, according to their lights or predispositions, should be doing the same thing in their own way, and be the wise ones of the family.

Once upon a time Grandfather passed on the wisdom of his years and told the children the truth of life. He had learned the lessons of experience and was now in touch with the Godhead. One with God and one with a life of experience, he was able to pass on that knowledge to the younger ones. But because humanity has lost contact with the state of God-realisation, it is generally only experience of the world that grandfathers pass on to the next generation.

Once upon a time Grandmother was the quiet woman who had loved man and raised children and therefore could instruct the younger ones in all matters of love and the family. Now so many older women are too emotional to give right instruction and their love is mixed with sentiment.

The great majority of older people I meet or hear about can't hear the truth because they want to live in the past. Of course they enjoy being with the little ones, but they are likely to substitute them for their own children and start to depend on them emotionally. Grandparents who try to live through their grandchildren will make themselves and everyone else unhappy. Something often happens to stop them seeing the grandchildren as often as they would like.

Mother: My mother and father are very generous people and it's hard to get them to understand that they are not to indulge the children. I do speak to them as straight as I can, but I realise it's too much to ask them to take on my values. I can't expect them to even want to listen to the truth as I see it. It's enough that I just love them. And I've learned not to quote Barry Long!

So many parents tell me about the conflicts they have with their own parents and the reactions they're likely to get when the words 'guru', 'spiritual master' or 'realised man' pop up, or my name is mentioned. Immediately assumptions are made and the listener goes hard, tense inside and emotional — instead of listening to what I say to see if there's any truth in it.

So many older people have a very long tail. It doesn't show but trailing behind them is a tail of emotion. You have to be able to be straight with your parents and relatives; and not let them pin their tail on you.

Having made something of a mess of their own lives, older people endeavour to tell the next generations how not to make a mess of theirs. But if I have not learned the lessons of my life, am I fit to tell you how to live yours?

I'd say: 'Look, Mum and Dad, your life is your life. And you got through. My life is my life. I thank you for all your help and support and experience. But please, don't expect me to live my life for you. And please don't expect to live your life through me or my children.'

Father: In the family we do our best to live according to your teaching and it pervades every situation in the house, but neither of our children express any interest in it. I do not see anything wrong with this and I do not wish to press anything on them.

There is no need for the children to be interested in this teaching in any overt way and certainly no one should impose it on them. As you say, it pervades the situation in the house and the communication is done through your example and by speaking to the children openly in honesty, truth and love.

It is not 'the teaching' that's important, is it? It is what the teaching is in you that's important, because you are the one in charge of the children.

*

Mother: I find that living with my twelve year-old son keeps me very much alert to the truth of things. He has a very sharp way of questioning me. For example if he thinks I'm not speaking the truth, he points it out. Or the other day, when I quoted something you had said, he knew it wasn't coming from me (I wasn't living it) and he picked me up on it straight away.

That's good. And it's good for him if you acknowledge that straightness in him and he can see from your response that his perceptions are right (if they are).

He is showing himself to be man. Man is supposed to question you, to get rid of your ignorance. No matter what his age, if he's asking the right questions, he's man asking you questions to make you pure, or make you purer for God. That's man's job; and because he hasn't yet taken on too much of the burden and ignorance of the world his questions are likely to be good and straight, as you say.

Once he's taken on the burden of the world his questions are likely to be obscured by what he has been thinking about, his worries and sexual secrets. At present the young masculine energy of puberty flowing through him remains relatively pure. But that same divine energy will later strengthen the unhappiness in his body and corrupt him. When sexual cunning is in him he won't be able to be so straight. You might then find that he doesn't ask such good questions because they might reveal him to himself.

Mother: I am beginning to see the change in him. Sometimes I see it in his face: 'Oh, no, there she goes again . . .' The look that says: 'Don't tell me. I don't want to know.'

And in that situation are you answering his questions? Or are you trying to teach him something?

Mother: Well . . . I suppose usually I'm trying to teach him something.

It's fair enough to try and point something out; but he has to be able to relate what you are saying to his own experience or interests. He will go, 'Oh no!' unless you make it real for him. And as he gets more into his adolescence he'll go 'Oh no!' more and more, because he'll be tracking out into the world of experience. He'll think he's running towards the truth, but he will be running away from it.

What sort of questions is he asking?

Mother: Sometimes his questions are about truth. Such as, 'How can you take on what Barry Long says is truth, when most of the world doesn't hear it as the truth?' He is questioning why the truth for me is not the same as the objective, scientific truth of the world.

That's just his challenge to you. It can be easily explained to him that the truth I speak is concerned with the inner life, the life of love, and not objective science. They're two different realms. What makes my teaching real is that everybody dies. I concern myself with the reality behind death, which science of course can never address.

*

Father: I'm afraid I have reached a point with my son, who is now sixteen, where I can't have a talk with him without him instantly reacting. He just doesn't want to be told anything, however friendly or fatherly I am. A couple of years ago I'd have gotten reactive about that kind of behaviour. Now I see it does no good. I can't persuade him of anything. It's his life. Of course I'd love to have him come and ask my advice, but I guess it's up to him, not me. I can only be there for him if he wants to come and talk.

Yes, that's the message for all parents who might try to live their lives through their children — who try to tell them what to do and what not to do.

It would be sheer self-indulgence for you to get emotional with him. But you can still speak to him without wanting anything for yourself.

'It seems to me, son, from my experience, which is quite considerable on this earth, if you follow the path you're taking, one way or another you're going to regret it. But your life is your life and you'll probably come out the other side, because everybody survives, mostly.

'You've got to go and do what you must do. I did all the same stupid things that you're probably going to do and I came out the other side. So you'll probably be all right. Of course, I still say it would be better not to go and do it, but if you do, then there are a couple of things you should watch out for and I'd just like to mention them, if that's okay . . .

'Okay, son. I just wanted to tell you that. Now go your way.'

Man: Every teenager sooner or later has to start leading a separate life from the life of the family so isn't it inevitable that there will be a breakdown of communication? — whether the parents are living the truth or not.

Whatever you are doing with your life is the truth of your life. The reason teenagers grow apart from their parents is that the parents don't tell the children what they are doing with their lives. They haven't involved them from the beginning in the family situation. So the children, as they grow up, don't involve the parents. When I was a teenager I never told my Mum and Dad anything. And my father used to to say: 'Uh, uh . . . here comes the Secret Society.'

Here is a letter I received recently. It's from a woman in Melbourne.

Dear Mr Long,

I've never written to anyone like this before and I don't know why I'm writing to you. I'm just desperate. I thought perhaps you could help me, but I understand if you can't. My son is twenty-five and he's living in Perth. He's been there for five years. He doesn't work and he lives in a shared house. My husband and I have tried to get him to communicate with us and he won't. I'm desperately worried for him. I love him but

I don't know what I can do.

There is pathos in the letter and the true love of a mother for a son. But how can the parents expect to communicate with their son if they didn't communicate when he was young? — if they didn't talk about love, God, life, truth and death; if they only talked about money, or Grandma and Grandpa, or who's going to win the election?

That's the tragedy of this terribly ignorant planet, as represented by the body of mankind. The communication is lost between mother and daughter, father and son because the parents don't talk to the children about what is really important.

What is more important than love? Yet in so many homes the subject is studiously avoided because of sexual dishonesty and embarrassment.

I was invited to talk about the truth of love and sex to a small group of teenagers in a high school near where I live in Australia. They knew why I was coming to speak to them and they had their parents' permission to be there. But they'd never met anyone like me before. There were five girls and one boy, all aged sixteen or seventeen. A couple of the other boys had dropped out for fear of what their friends would say.

I started to talk to them precisely as I talk at any teaching meeting or seminar and I went at length into the difference between love and sex. They loved it.

'Why can't we talk to our parents like this?' asked one of the girls.

'Well, why can't you? It's a good question. The reason is that I treat you as man and woman. I don't try to bullshit you. You are man and woman. You are as intelligent as your mother and your father. You're as intelligent as I am. The only difference is in our experience of life. Although you lack experience, you are intelligent man and woman but adults usually treat you as if you're not.'

I had asked them to stop me if anything I said was not true, or to confirm it if it was the truth for them. So when I asked them: 'Am I telling you about love, just as it is? Is what I'm saying right? Is it the truth?' the girls all nodded. The boy said 'Yeah' and grinned from ear to ear.

FEAR AND THE DARK

Young children are always afraid of something, particularly the dark. What is there to be afraid of? Where does the fear come from? They are afraid of a dark, inexplicable part of their self, deep down underneath the conscious mind. This fear of the self is inside everybody.

Children are fascinated by horror stories and ghosts; yet they are terrified by them when they're alone. Popular children's stories, films and toys feature monsters of one kind or another. The latest craze might be some horror film about dinosaurs. From a very young age children are exposed to many images through their friends or television to reaffirm the fear.

Mother: This happens with my four year-old boy. He has his own bedroom but he doesn't want to sleep in it. He'll play there during the day but at night he comes back to sleep in our room. When we ask him why he won't sleep in his own bed he says he's scared of monsters . . . I show him around the whole house so he can see there's nothing there. But he is still scared.

Yes, it is good to walk around with him and reassure him. Look into all the cupboards to see that there are no monsters there. But of course rationality is not going to deal with the fear. You're not going to be able to eradicate it completely.

He's too young to talk to about the fear in the subconscious, the things in the psyche that threaten us all; you just can't address that with young children. (It would be different if he actually saw a ghost or some psychic phenomenon. Then you would have to speak about it rightly, according to the questions he asked.)

Just try to help him through it. When he is exposed to horror stories or films, smile and say that if these things exist then they don't exist around here. Show him that there is nothing to be scared of in this house. And you can tell him that the dark is a lovely place to be.

'Let's go into your room together in the dark and we will lie there and feel the sweetness of the dark as we lie on the bed together before you go to sleep.

'See how sweet the darkness is? See how quiet it is?

'There's nothing in the darkness. There is never anything in the darkness. It's a sweet state to lie here with me, isn't it? Every night, when the darkness comes, all the night-time creatures who are asleep during the day, like possums and bats and owls, wake up and enjoy the night. And the mice come out to play in the fields and it's a very sweet time. It's a time when the trees really come to life. All the time their leaves are breathing in the carbon dioxide and stale air from the breath that all the animals and human beings have been breathing out in the day, and all night the trees are out there in the dark absorbing these gases and turning them back into oxygen and lovely fresh air. And that is another contribution to us of the night; for when we open the window in the morning the lovely fresh air comes in so that you can smell it, and breathe it in, and feel the freshness of it. And the night is the time when the dew starts to fall, to refresh the flowers and the plants. At night the temperature drops because the sun is gone, and then little droplets of water in the air, too small even to see, condense and form the finest mist. And because the droplets are cold and heavier than air, they fall as dew, descending very gradually onto the flowers and blades of grass. That's the dew we see when we wake up in the morning; we'll see the little drops of dew on the plants before the sun gets around the garden and warms it up again. All these things are because of the night.

'The night contains all these beautiful things that are a part of nature. And the night is the time when we can go to sleep and be refreshed.

'So, see how lovely it is as we lie here? It's very beautiful. So be comforted by the night and the dark. The night is very sweet and there's nothing in the dark.'

*

Mother: Our little boy sleeps in our bed with us and when it's his bedtime we take turns to read him a story and cuddle up with him. Or we sing to him until he's asleep. He has never had any difficulty going to bed and usually falls asleep easily. When I wake up in the morning he's usually cuddled up to me. Now he's getting older, the question arises about how long this should go on. Perhaps we are creating some sort of attachment to us. I've been talking to other parents about this and some of them express their doubts about whether it's right to share a bed with a child. But I have not yet heard of a young child who wants to sleep alone. It seems to be something that has to be enforced and then you get tears and resistance.

There is much to be said for giving a child and particularly a baby as much physical contact as possible; for example carrying the baby around with you so that there's nearly always some physical contact with mother and father. You want to give your child all the love you can, and your motives in keeping him close to you as long as possible are absolutely virtuous. But our desire and duty as parents is to equip children with the ability to cope with the world. The longer you keep him in your bed the more difficult it is going to be.

You will have to start breaking him from the habit of sleeping with you. If he won't go to sleep unless you sing or read to him you will have to break that habit too. Cuddling him is fine, but if he can't go to sleep unless you're cuddling him it has become habitual cosiness. You must do what you see is right, but I say you should start preparing him to sleep in his own bed, in a room of his own, and then move him into it as soon as you can.

As for any disturbance it might cause, children have an extraordinary ability to adapt to changed situations and go through certain phases. Suddenly they get through that stage and the experience of it just goes down into the subconscious; you don't encounter it overtly again.

I am reminded of something that happened with my own baby daughter. Her grandparents came to stay for a week and they would nurse her all the time and walk her around before bedtime for half an hour or an hour. And all that time the grandfather would jog the baby in his arms. Jog, jog, jog, jog.

When they went away at the end of the week, the child would not go to sleep. It was a terrible time for us. She would just cry and cry. One night in desperation we put her in the car and drove her around the block. That worked. The motion of the car simulated the jogging of her grandad's nursing. For some time the only way we could get a night's rest was to take her for a drive before bed.

Given what I know now I'd tell the grandparents 'no thanks'. I'd take charge: 'You can nurse her quietly in your arms but don't continually jog her up and down and stimulate her like that. She will become attached to it.'

*

Mother: Something happened the other night which scared us all. Tom (who is four) was getting ready for bed when he got his penis caught in the zipper of his pyjamas. He was very freaked out. It is difficult not to panic in a situation like this. It was very frightening. We would like to know how to deal with something like that.

It's important to inform children, as soon as they are able to understand, that because they're in a physical body they are likely to hurt themselves, just like the rest of us. We are likely to stub a toe or accidentally cut ourselves.

So in your conversations with the children you will have informed them in advance: 'Should you ever hurt yourself, and feel frightened, know that Mum and Dad will do everything they can to make it right as quickly as possible. If ever anything happens and you are hurt, Mummy and Daddy will look after you.'

Inevitably the child falls over and scrapes his knee, or gets into a distressing situation, like the one you mention.

'It will be all right. Just be still. Everything's going to be all right. We're going to fix it up. Now be quiet. Be still. We're attending to it. We know what to do, so just be as quiet and still as you can and it will be all right.'

*

Mother: About an hour after Ben goes to sleep he gets up, eyes wide open. He walks around in circles on the bed and cries out 'I want Mummy' but he doesn't see or hear me. He goes downstairs and again walks in circles, very fast, but not treading on any toys or bumping into anything, and saying things I don't understand. After ten or fifteen minutes he wakes up and doesn't remember anything. Is it best to leave him in this state or should I try to wake him?

The child walking in his sleep is being controlled by an area of the psyche beyond our understanding. My advice is to do what I recall my mother did. She would come over to me as I walked, or whatever I was doing, and speak softly to me.

'Hello darling, it's all right. It's all right . . .' And she'd gently put her hand on my shoulder or take my hand. 'Are you coming back to bed now?'

She would gently lead me. If the child were to resist you would have to act according to your response in the moment, but I don't remember ever resisting my mother's loving action as she took me back to bed, and gave me a kiss and said, 'It's all right. Good night now, and see you in the morning.'

That's the only advice I can give you. Bring the child back to bed through the loving communication of the voice and the touch, leading him as quietly as possible. And in the morning don't refer to the incident unless the child mentions it.

*

Laura is eight. Her parents recently moved with their two children from America to England. Laura was finding it difficult to adjust to the change. I asked if she would like to speak to me about it and she came to see me with her mother . . .

Laura: When I go to bed at night I get upset and I can't

sleep because I miss my home in America.

Now, the important thing is not to miss anything, not to think back . . . You left one home and now you are in another. The secret is not to think about America — so that you don't get discontented. When you are ready to go to America again you will find yourself there. Meanwhile you are here. And you've only just arrived haven't you, not long ago. So you're going to be settling in.

I always say that when we move house it takes about three months to start to settle in. Give it a little bit of time and you'll find new friends will come to you, or you will find yourself back with your old friends sooner or later. But you've got to live your life where you are now, or otherwise you'll become unhappy.

Laura: But I loved it in America.

If you loved your life in America you can just let it be and it will come again. But it's best not to think about it, because that will make you unhappy.

Do you know, if you really love something, you don't have to think about it? Sometimes, to make this point to people, I say: 'I love you too much to think about you.'

Do you know how many countries I've lived in and been in? Australia, India, England . . . I've been across America and all around the world, I don't know how many times. Once, when I had to leave Australia for the first time, I thought my life had ended. Just like you love America I loved Australia. But after many years away I ended up living in Australia again.

So always make the best of it. Don't think about what you haven't got, and everything will turn out right.

Laura: Can I ask you something else? About dreams . . . Why do I wake up in the night with a bad dream? Like last night . . .

Can you remember the dream? (She shook her head.) Can you still feel the vibration of it in your tummy? Do you feel anything from it still inside of you?

Laura: No, I was just frightened. I went back to sleep.

Well, I can tell you what happens when we have a bad dream. An energy comes up from deep down inside our bodies. It comes up like it's on a piece of vibrating wire. The images of the dream go but the vibration inside me stays and sometimes I can feel it's still there. I don't know what the dream's about but I can still feel it in me.

Mother: I think I was more disturbed by it than Laura was. She woke up and was obviously having a bad dream. I asked her at the time what it was, but she just fell asleep again.

Well, whatever it was, it disturbed her subconscious and vibrated in her. Meanwhile images that her memory could not hold have been informing her subconscious.

When she wakes disturbed by a dream, the thing to do, of course, is reassure her. But do not distract her from the energy of the dream. Allow her to feel it, but give her a cuddle at the same time.

'It's all right, Mummy's here. There's nothing to be frightened of. You were dreaming and now you are waking up and Mummy is here.

'Do you want to tell me what was happening? Can you feel what's happening in your tummy?

'It's nothing to be afraid of. Can you feel my arms around you? It's all right. You can go back to sleep now.'

Speak in that way, and see that you do not convey anything

of your own disturbance to the child.

Mother: I do tend to get disturbed if I see that she's having a nightmare. I think I used to have bad dreams a lot when I was her age.

Then you can see in your own experience what dreams are and what their purpose is. Sometimes a nightmare wakes us and even though there's no image, hours afterwards we can still have the feeling of it, vibrating in the subconscious. Something from the deep depths of human experience inside us has risen up through the world of the dream — the intermediate world or subconscious, where these things happen. It doesn't reach the conscious level, except that it wakes us and we get a feeling of dread and a knowledge that something's going on.

Whatever a dream is about, it has to do with re-living past experience in order to confront it. The past is being faced with an intelligence in the subconscious, and something is being done there. In dreams I am facing the past in myself. But it is not necessarily my immediate personal past, or even the past since I was born, but the past of the entire human race and of the earth out of which we came.

We must not see our selves as 'personal', any more than we have to. We are as vast as life itself. The more we become that vastness the less we identify with our little person and its likes and dislikes.

The past in my self is as deep as the earth. Right to its core, the earth represents the past that is in every one of us. It represents my self as the past life of all the species that have ever contributed to life on this planet. Things that are absolutely beyond my ken rise up in me from the past of the species and some of them can be very disturbing. This is the basis of nightmares.

Because all this happens in our psyche, there can be the sense of a psychic presence around us. This can be very disturbing because these psychic presences have no body. Every dream is disembodied.

*

Father: What would you say to a child who says he sees things moving around in his bedroom at night? I don't want to alarm him by talking about ghosts.

Where do we get the idea of ghosts? — from people who know nothing about the psyche. If our children could only hear the truth of the psyche they wouldn't be frightened by ghosts. But our stupid society excites them with spooks, and frightens them with notions of the bad or fearful, instead of giving them the truth, which is the good.

This is what you must communicate to the child: 'There is another place called the psychic world. Sometimes things from there travel here, to our world. But theirs is not a physical world so they have no actual existence. If you ever meet anything like that in your bedroom at night remember it cannot do you any physical harm. Nothing that ever appears in a vision in front of you can ever touch you. And you must not be afraid of it, for if you get emotional you will give it strength from your fear.'

Most people (scientists particularly) know nothing about the psychic world because they're too busy with their mortgages and their computers to discover the truth about love, life, truth, death and God. If the media and the scientists were not so ignorant of the psychic world, the people would be much less afraid and would not pass on so much fear to their children.

Have you ever seen a ghost in your room, or anywhere? Have you ever seen a vision at the end of the bed? Such things are much more common than people generally admit. I was in England, but I'd been staying with my mother in her flat in Sydney a few days before. Her heart had been giving her a bit of trouble and she was concerned about it. She walked out of the kitchen and looked over at the chair in the corner. There I was, as clear as day for her. She was so shocked to see me there because she knew I'd already gone to England. Then suddenly I disappeared. Her heart didn't bother her again, she said. The pain just left.

Now did my mother make that up? Or is that sort of thing happening everywhere in the world, all the time?

Why would you want to be afraid of the marvels of the psyche? Don't you want to see what's happening? Why not introduce yourself to a world that is so extraordinary it defies description? Then you may be able to say (as I did when visions in the night appeared before me), 'No, I won't switch on the light. Let me see. Let me see what's happening here.'

The vision comes from the intermediate place between this physical world and eternity. It appears in your psyche but it cannot appear in physical form. To actually come from out of existence and take physical form is very hard and time-consuming, as we all know. The psychic entity still has to come, however, moving at a speed beyond our conception. But it cannot stay for very long.

There it is, very clear. Then it disintegrates, just breaks up — because it cannot maintain its presence in the physical world. It's your mind that sees it and it can't live in the past of your mind.

The mind is so confused — 'What's going on here? Let me get around this!' While it's trying to get around the vision, the thing remains. But after a few seconds the mind collects itself. As soon as it moves into memory or tries to think about what's happening, the thing disappears.

Such things always disappear because we put too much past between them and us. That's why scientists can't recognise them and why they disappear in front of researchers and journalists. And that's why children, with more open minds and less past in them, are much more likely to witness psychic phenomena.

LOVE COMES FIRST

M an and woman must put love of each other before love of their child. Otherwise partnership and family will collapse, sooner or later. The parents grow apart but try to go on loving each other through the children. With little love left between them, the children become their chief reason for staying together. Keeping the family together without love is living death — not life together. Whether the mother and father care to admit it or not, family life becomes a barely concealed misery, with occasional spells of relief but no hope of real harmony in the home.

All is well when the common aim is to live together with the minimum of disharmony. If man and woman put love first and live in right love together, everything else is looked after and the children are in their right place. Everything is always in its right place when man and woman are united in what is right and true.

Love is not restrained by considerations of comfort or convenience or what is morally acceptable in society. Putting love first means that if the parents leave love then one of them invariably leaves home. In the agonising stress and conflict of this situation love must continue to come first. If there is love enough, love can resolve every concern about the long-term consequences for the security and wellbeing of the children.

*

A split family can still be a real family. By living the truth of the situation and with sufficient love, the difficulties facing the single parent and the pressures felt by all parties in a split family can be overcome. Living this way is certainly not easy. But if you put love first you'll find it works.

Right from the beginning of the new situation, it is important to speak openly to the children about what has changed. And where there is a split family, or the children are not with their natural parent, it is even more important to establish the house-rules for your life together.

In speaking to the children remember the main points:
— Tell them the facts of the whole situation and include them in what's happening.
— Answer their questions but without anticipating anything.
— Inform everyone concerned about what you are doing with your life.

When you take on responsibility for the children of a new partner:
— Establish that the common aim of the family is to live in harmony without unhappiness.
— Make it clear who is in command of the house and that certain rules are necessary. Everybody must make a contribution to the harmony of the home.

'We are all going to be living together so it's important that we have a talk about how we are going to arrange things. I want you to know a few things about me, so I'm going to tell you about my life and what's important to me. And you can ask questions about anything you don't understand or are unhappy about.

'First of all, you know I am here because I love your mother. Love is why I am here, and because we love each other this will be a house of love. My life is about finding a greater truth or love in myself. That means I have to endeavour to be honest and to be more giving and true to the situation every day.

'You will be in my care as well as your mother's, and I must demonstrate justice and responsibility to you. If we are not brought up in justice, truth and love we grow up confused and unhappy and then we become a misfit in the world.

'When I talk about justice I mean that there cannot be one law for you and another one for me. What we agree as the rule of the house must apply to us all. Now, if we are going to live in harmony, the one rule that we must all endeavour to live is that this house is to be as free of unhappiness as we can make it. And it would be silly not to agree about that, wouldn't it?

'From time to time we will sit down together and have a talk about how things are going. Because your mother and I are both endeavouring to live in this way, you might notice some changes in the way things are done but they will be for the good, provided we all remember that the main thing is to not be unhappy and the purpose of being together is to contribute our love of life and love of truth to the harmony of this house.

'We are going to be a family. To be a family means that we're all in it together. We're all going to endeavour to live free of unhappiness, as best we can. I'm going to get rid of my anger and moods as quickly as I can and so is your mother. But it's no good us doing it if you don't. So will you endeavour to give up your unhappiness when we point it out to you? We'll all fail sometimes, but we will do our best.

131

'We're not doing it for ourselves. We are going to do it for all of us together. That's what makes a real family. And that's our purpose in being a family.'

Man: In that situation, isn't there a danger of causing a reaction? Most youngsters will resist someone 'preaching' to them. Would they have to be 'converted' to your teaching?

The truth, like love, is demonstrated by living it now. For those in your care you can be the example of a man who in a practical way can address the truth of life as you know it to be. By lacking emotionality you can demonstrate the possibility of freedom from unhappiness. And in your availability, honesty and giving you can demonstrate love. Never try to change anyone. The love you are, or the truth in the situation, or life itself, makes the change.

All you ask of your family is that they do their best to live together in love and honesty and truth, and at the same time you help them to live their own lives.

Man: Well, that makes sense. I sometimes encounter a bit of reaction in people. There's a man I work with who keeps questioning me. He likes discussing things but he's very sceptical about truth.

You could say: 'All I'm doing is telling you how it is for me. I am endeavouring to find more truth and love in my life. But that doesn't mean that this way is for you. Nor does it mean you don't have love and truth in you. You might have far more than me. I'm not accusing you or blaming you or defending anything. I'm just answering your questions the best way I can, which is with the truth as I see it or know it to be.'

You must be more straight in the world so that you are not put under pressure by emotional people. It is emotion, the absence of love, that makes man dishonest and argumentative.

In the family, if not in the world, you can endeavour to keep the emotion out. If there is emotion in you at home, you have to be honest enough to say what you are emotional about. Then you can face your partner or child and get rid of it.

Remember: no emotional demands can be tolerated in a house of love.

Mother: I find I get very torn between my daughter and my partner. She's six and a half now, and John came to live with us nearly two years ago. But the three of us don't seem to be able to be blissful together . . . There are more demands from both of them than I can handle.

Be careful of that word 'blissful'. It suggests something that is just not real. 'Harmony' is a better word.

Nobody can handle demands. It doesn't matter how much love you have, it cannot fill demand — because demand never ends, never gets enough. If you tolerate demands being made on you by your child or your partner, it will ruin your life.

You will have to get that straight with them. I suggest you start with your partner.

Mother: Yes, I hear that. One of the problems is that John and I have different ideas about how to be a good parent.

If there was only one way of doing it, why would it take two of you?

If you and your partner can come together in love you can look to see what is best. If you are split in how to do it, you'll present a divided defence against your daughter's emotion. Then she will take advantage, playing one of you off against the other. So you've got to come together. You have a common aim — to teach her to stop being restless and demanding.

What's the difference between you and your partner in this?

Mother: The level of patience we each have, seeing how long it takes for her to learn.

If you've been indulging the demand in your daughter then it will be in her flesh, getting its satisfaction. And it will take a good time to reverse this. It's going to take time and patience. You must be persistent and refuse to allow her demands. You must never give in, until she undergoes a change, which children can do very quickly. You will have to tell her every day if necessary what demand is, and what love is.

'You have to understand that you have no right to demand anything. John is living with us now and he and I are doing everything we can to provide a home for you. We go out to work to earn the money. We clean the house. And because we look after everything, we are responsible. So you have no right to demand. However, this is a house of love. Although John works hard and I work hard, it is our love to give you everything we can. In exchange you have to give us back your love.

'It is not love to demand, so John and I have agreed to stop giving you what you demand. This is going to disturb you. You will get frustrated. You will find it is better to give up your demand. And as you give it up, you will find that there is harmony in this house. Then we will be pleased to give you the things you need.'

*

Woman: I am a single parent and I live with my thirteen year-old son. I find some of his questions difficult to answer and wonder if he is missing something by not having a male father-figure in the house.

It is a fact of his life that he doesn't have his father with him. His father is elsewhere and so, necessarily it seems, he obviously cannot live with his father. That's how it is.

Life is its own sufficiency. Somehow or other the situation is serving his development. That doesn't mean things are always going to stay as they are, because life is surprising in what it turns up. But for now things have to be as they are.

This is not to deny that you as his mother see that it would be a good thing for him to have the example of a man to grow up with. However, I ask you to look and see if there is not also some need in yourself — the desire for a partner? If you are seeing the situation through your own desire, you may be projecting on to your son a need of your own.

*

Man: I haven't got any children of my own, but my lover has a boy and a girl. We don't live together, although I am at their house a lot. The kids see their father at weekends sometimes, but I am becoming more like a father to them. What advice do you have for me in this situation?

Do you love the woman? Do you know there's purpose in your love? Do you know that you're fulfilling a purpose in giving to each other and going deeper into the partnership together?

Man: Oh yes! And I am thinking about moving in with her. But I'm not sure I want to be responsible for the two children.

She comes with two kids. That's the situation. It's no good thinking about how the children might limit your freedom. Don't allow yourself to think: 'Oh, but what if . . .'

Why not take them all on? Why not move in with them? And if you do, then go all the way. No reservations.

If it doesn't work out, what have you lost? You might gain something that will last. Take them on and move in. Give, give, and give again. And make a real family together.

*

Mother: I had a child when I was very young. I didn't know how to look after him. I wasn't capable of being a good mother and the baby was taken away from me. Now everything is different. I am with a man I love and I would like to have another child, but I often feel fraught with guilt when I think about my first.

What's happening to make you feel guilty about the baby? Something in your life now is making you think about him. It might just be something you associate with him in your mind. I suggest you look inside yourself for the connection. You probably know what it is. But whatever it is, the way to deal with the problem (the guilt) is to know that whatever is in your mind is not now.

'I love my son. I do not know what's happened to him or where in the world he is. But I will stay with my love of him, which I can feel within me now, and if it is to be, life will bring us together somewhere in the world, or I will be moved to go and find him.'

As cruel as it may sound, you have to keep out all reference to the past or it will disturb you. As soon as you start to give the guilt any life it will grow. It will feed on your vitality and you will feel more and more guilty. And as that bit of your self gets stronger and stronger it will come between you and your new partner. When you are making love it will rise as a shadow and cut you off from your love. You must get rid of it.

You must not indulge in thinking and dreaming about your son. The world of dreaming and thinking is a very strong magnet, pulling you towards it. It wants to exist in you because it's possessed by an entity of unhappiness that feeds on misery. The way this entity gets inside people is through sentiment. You don't need sentiment. You love your son and that's the end of it.

Not to think about him is to love him, because then you leave him in God's hands, or you leave him to life. That is love — impersonal love.

Every time you or your lover asks, 'Have you been thinking about me? Have you missed me, darling?' that's personal love. To want to make anyone cling on to the past is personal love.

Every time a parent, grandparent, auntie or uncle says to a child, 'Did you miss me?' the adult is teaching the child to hold on to the past, to sentiment, to personal love; and introducing the prospect of unhappiness.

Stop clinging on to your past. It is finished. Over. Do not give in to your guilt any more. Stay with the love you are now.

*

Mother: My partner has a four year-old son from a previous relationship, who comes to stay with us at weekends. So I'm a part-time mother to a boy who is not my own child and who spends the rest of his life in a family where the way of dealing with him is quite different. This leads to some confusion for him and for us.

A difficult situation; in the other home he is not being taught that family life is about getting free of unhappiness and not being shown how to contribute harmony to the house. When he comes to your house, you do your best to instruct him. Then, when he's back with the other family, they say to him: 'What on earth are you talking about?'

All you can do is continue to be true to the situation; and do not in any way criticise his natural mother. She's doing her best.

When a conflict or question arises in the boy, you might say something like this: 'Come and sit down and let's talk about this situation. Now, when you are with us we instruct you as we do, and there are certain rules in this house. When you go back to your other house, your Mum instructs you in her way and that's between you and her. But here we instruct you in another way and I trust that what we say is true for you.

'Whenever anyone says something is true for them you should examine whether it is also true for you. And that will be a good thing for you to do throughout your life.'

That's all you can do. Then you leave it to God, because life has put the boy into that divided situation for its own inscrutable purpose.

All you can do is be true to what you are responsible for, without blaming or criticising another. If in this case you blame and criticise the other woman, you will divide the child in himself, in his heart, and that would be disastrous.

Father: The difficulty comes when I take him back to his mother. Quite a few times he's demonstrated quite strong emotions; that he really wants to stay with me. Most of the time he happily goes in, but sometimes there's this clinging on to me and I have to turn him round and put him inside the door, almost forcibly.

Life makes these situations and all we can do is our best.

As he grows up, go on telling him that he has two families and there's no need for him to feel divided. It's right for him to be at his mother's house, because he's loved there. And it's right for him to come and be with you because he's loved here too.

As much as possible, endeavour to break down any feeling of isolation, any 'damming' of emotion that might build up in him in any particular instance.

*

Mother: I am separated from the father of the children, and they go to him for weekends and holidays. They come back so excited, it takes all week to get them back to themselves again. It's getting worse as they get older. They pick up things from him that undermine me. Is there anything I can do about this?

First of all, if the father loves the children he will see the truth. Can you speak to him about it? Will he hear you? Or is he too resentful? He may love his resentment of you more than he loves the children. But even so, you've still got to deal with the situation as best you can.

If after separation one or both of the parents remain resentful, the children will pick it up psychically. A resentful former partner cannot resist surreptitiously undermining the other parent and the children will carry that in them. They will start to have an attitude towards their mother or father. Sooner or later, when there's any problem at home, especially one concerning discipline, you'll hear one of the children say to you: 'Well, Dad says you're such and such. You did so and so!' For them to say anything like that would reveal a disgraceful lack of love on the part of their father.

If I was the father, I would have to get rid of the resentment in me. When I am unhappy there is no love or beauty in life, only a clenched fist that will suddenly lash out as a cruel deed or word to bruise or lacerate. No matter what you had done to me, I would have to give up my resentment and die to it, for my unhappiness would be polluting my love, my children.

139

Can your former lover hear this truth? Can he see that he's psychically poisoning the children? Does he know that while he resents you he will not be free to really love another woman? — that he will carry his resentment and unhappiness on into his next partnership and make the next woman unhappy? Then, when she's unhappy, he will become even more unhappy. That's the story of the world.

If the father of your children cannot hear the truth of this, all you can do is go on communicating your love to them. When the house is quiet and there is love between you, tell them how you see it, making a point of not blaming the father for anything.

'Look, this is how I see it. When you come home from your Dad's, you're usually more hyped-up and excited than before you go away. When you come down from the excitement you get unhappy. That's the truth, isn't it? Isn't that what happens? Within forty-eight hours you are likely to be upset about something and crying.

'So may I give you some advice? If you don't want to be unhappy, don't let yourselves be so excitable.'

In the case of older children and teenagers, a period of excitement will be followed by a period of distinct restlessness. Whenever they come up against some authority, or are prevented from doing what they want, they get tight and resentful. All sullen adolescent resentfulness comes from having been too excited. Excitement always comes to an end, and that's the problem.

*

Man: I am stepfather to a teenage daughter, whom I love and I think she loves me, but she is just seventeen and having trouble emotionally. There's a communication problem. No one can get through to her. Her mother gets frustrated and the natural father doesn't have much understanding, it seems, and isn't any help. So I would like to do what I can to explain things to her. Do you have any advice?

At seventeen our children are developed individuals and in many of them there is already much emotional disturbance, anger and frustration. If she was not instructed in the spiritual life from a young age it will be difficult for you to address her problem. If she doesn't already know how to free herself of unhappiness, what can you do? If she won't confide in you, then you can't participate in her life. And yet there is no other way of discovering what her frustration or anger is about.

Where there's been a separation from the natural father, very intricate and complicated emotional forces can act in the subconscious. The separation was nobody's fault; but she may be blaming her mother or blaming you because you're not her father.

You can only do your best to open up a dialogue. It is a split family but there is love and that is wonderful. The fact that she loves you and you love her is the hope in the situation. You may be able to sit down with her at the right time, have an intelligent conversation and talk about what's disturbing her.

Just encourage her to get the problem out and let her know that you will do anything you can to help her deal with it. But don't adopt any kind of spiritual attitude or come down heavily on her. If you try and tell her how silly she is you're likely to turn her against you, or create more anger and frustration.

As much as possible you should join her in what she sees as important. The difficulty in communicating with young people arises only because they get isolated from the adults closest to them at a time when sexual tension is building up in their bodies. To communicate with them we have to participate in their lives enough for them to know that we are interested in how their individuality is developing.

*

Man: I've already brought up a family and they've all left home. Now I'm older and wiser (I've been listening to you) and I have to stand and watch while my grown kids go off and do all the wrong things . . . And the irony is, of course, that I was their teacher in the first place. Sometimes this is difficult to live with.

Wrong things . . . meaning things that are going to lead them into unhappiness. And as parents in our ignorance we encourage them!

For thirty-one years this body of mine was pretty ignorant. I was married in my twenties and raised two young children, a boy and a girl. And like you with your children, I taught them the wrong things. Later, when I started to get things right inside of me, I had to leave them.

I endeavoured to communicate with the children but it was too late and now they are not particularly moved towards anything I say, as far as I know. I hardly ever see them, but there is love there, which is all that matters. When we have more knowledge of life, and more love in us, we have to live with the knowledge that we are not the man or woman we were yesterday.

Life is supposed to be a process of growing in wisdom and truth. Someone had to teach your children their ignorance and you were as good at it as anyone, weren't you?

Youth is forever optimistic. There is no death for youth. When we're young, it's never going to happen to us. So youth plunges further into ignorance and tries either to achieve or reject the values of the mothers and fathers, not knowing that they are all wrong precepts anyway — because that's the nature of the game. We all have to be immersed in ignorance, emotion and pain. It's dreadful, but that's the way it is. We have to go through the tunnel of life because that's the only way to experience living.

Angels (if there are such beings) are without the experience of life as man or woman and therefore cannot realise God. Man and woman are angels who have fallen into the experience of good and bad, right and wrong. And our children, like us, have to go through the tunnel of life until with knowledge of good and bad, they come out on the other side.

In the life of experience what was once good is now bad. Only when we cry 'God help me!' can life send us some truth of our own. We never leave our experience behind but we start to see through it. Then we climb out of the tunnel.

You may not be able to help your children now, but you will be there for them when they lose something dear to them. Dad will be there, a wiser man. They will be able to come to you as guru and ask for your help.

Then, when they go back into the world again, and make the same mistakes again, and maybe even go mad, don't despair. Just wait. A Dad who loves his children just waits in his wisdom and knowledge.

'I am always here, my son or daughter. I will interfere as little I can, but I'm always here and if the time ever comes when you need me, know that I will be here.'

2

EDUCATION IN CONSCIOUSNESS

Doing your best for the child

The Karmic Debt – The Developing Personality
The Price of Excitement – Giving to the Child
The Developing Imagination – Telling Stories
Going to School – Parents as Teachers

'I've done you a picture,' said little Tom.
'You've drawn me a picture? Good. I'll be very pleased to see it. Will you show it to me? I'd like to see your art.'

He comes over and presents his drawing, a swirl of yellow crayon with a blue blob in the middle.

'Thank you Tom. Thank you for your picture. I see you've selected a lovely golden colour, a very nice colour, the colour of the sun. That's the colour of Leo the Lion, which I happen to be in my astrological sign, so it's a lovely colour to me. Is it a picture of a lion?'

'It's a drain,' said Tom very gravely, 'And it has all the water inside.'

'Ah, yes,' I said, 'Going down the drain . . . That's a very nice picture, Tom. Thank you.'

THE KARMIC DEBT

There's no perfection in parenting. You can only do your best and you can't help making your mistakes. Everybody has what is called their karma, a predisposition in existence that is the shape of their lives, and although it can be changed here and there by love, presence, wisdom and truth, our children still have to live their lives. We can't save them from what they have to do.

Ours is a society of dishonesty and ignorance. The karma of society is in everybody from birth. Our own parents had to express that karma, each according to their lights. But still they went to work to earn the money to look after us and feed us; or stayed home to be with us when they would rather have been out on their own. When we were sick they took care of us. They sacrificed what they wanted and gave to us.

All this activity in the family of man is the expression of impersonal love. Although our parents loved us personally, and their personal love made them emotional and brought unhappiness to the family, yet still they did their best to love us. That is the action of God in each being as service to another being.

Since everybody is taught dishonesty and ignorance from birth, how can we blame any parent for passing it on to the children? You can't blame your mother and father for getting things wrong. It wasn't easy for them, was it? They did their best. And many times to serve you they had to die to themselves.

Do not judge your parents. Always acknowledge that whatever they did, they were always doing their best in the situation and even when they were dishonest and emotional or hurt you, they are not to be blamed.

*

In my seminars I usually endeavour to get people to give up their unhappiness and take steps to get their lives right. Many hundreds of people of all ages and from different countries have spoken to me from the audience about what was troubling them. Whenever I ask questions to reveal the problem it frequently turns out to be a conflict with mother or father. If the parent is alive then I recommend what I call 'an intelligent conversation'.

'Mum, Dad, can I tell you what I am doing with my life? I'm endeavouring to keep unhappiness out of myself and my home. I've found this means I have to be more honest and there are a few things I need to clear up with you . . .

'I realise I can't blame you for my unhappiness. I know you love me and have always done your best for me. Whatever you want to think about me or my life, I don't want to have any anger or resentment of you inside of me. I just wanted you to know that, and to hear what I had to say.'

You have to show your parents by your words and actions

that you are responsible for your own life.

In an extreme case of conflict it may be necessary to say: 'If you persist in making me unhappy, I will have to stay away from you. I acknowledge all that you have done for me and I will always be open to visiting you or being with you, because I love you, but I can only be with you as long as we are able to keep any unhappiness from coming between us.'

*

The source of the trouble may be far in the past and beyond the memory. It may have been an act of violence, separation or sexual abuse. Many people, both men and women, in my seminars have reported a childhood incident when they were sexually abused and say they still carry the guilt, confusion and hurt of it. I do not ask them to forgive the perpetrator. I ask them to give up blaming him and to stop holding on to the pain.

We can't blame an individual for the sexual ignorance of man. Is the individual responsible for the world's sexual dishonesty? We can certainly do our best to get it straight with those who have hurt us, even though they may have great difficulty in hearing what we have to say. We can point out their dishonesty. But man's dishonesty is endemic. It will appear sooner or later and it usually arises in sexual activity. As a general rule in this society, man lives with terrible sexual frustration and knows nothing about the love of woman. In an extreme case of frustration and unexpressed emotion a man can be driven to molest a child. Such a man usually knows that he is no longer responsible for his actions — which only compounds his self-inflicted guilt.

No individual can be held responsible for the sexual dishonesty of the human race. But as individuals we can be responsible in ourselves. We can each endeavour to be more honest and more true. In that way we break the otherwise endless cycle of ignorance repeating itself on earth.

＊

Woman: I always resented my father and I was very unhappy as a child. I don't think he ever abused me, but he was never really there when I wanted him. Now he's dead. I feel he failed me. Sometimes I think in some subconscious way I'm passing on the resentment to my own children, because I have a fear of failing them. I get depressed. I get angry around the house for no good reason. I have been in therapy about my problems and I wonder if there is anything you can say to me about it?

Yes. Stop judging your father. If he 'failed' it was only because of the pain inflicted on him by society and his own parents. And they couldn't help doing whatever they did — any more than you can.

The way to get rid of any hurt is to be positive and take action. If your father was alive you could go and have an intelligent conversation with him. But as he is dead you have to put it straight with him inside yourself.

Can you see all the good things he endeavoured to do, despite his pain? Can you see that whatever his failings he made sacrifices for you and provided for you? He gave you all he could, for he could not give you any more.

When you hold a resentment against anyone you make a prisoner of them. Your Dad is a prisoner of your anger, in a jail you've built inside you. The jail has become part of your self. Now you must let him out. Let your prisoner go.

You don't need to be in therapy to do it.

Here is something for you to do as a meditation: sit with eyes closed, go inside and locate the resentment. It is a specific feeling in the area of the stomach or lower abdomen. Then be aware of the surrounding warmth or love or life in the sensation. Your pure sensation is good, isn't it?

You might or might not feel any love for your father but you know the sensation of love inside you. So be that sensation. Love frees everything. Love leaves me open. Love frees my pain — without a therapist.

Now, open the prison door and let your prisoner go in love.

(If you need more help with this, I suggest you listen to my audio tape, 'Start Meditating Now', where I take you step by step into meditation and specifically deal with 'freeing your prisoners'.)

To get rid of any hurt you have to take action. If someone should harm you, do whatever you have to do to get it straight. Take him to court if necessary. But don't ever hold anything against the man emotionally, because that would make him a prisoner and a part of your unhappy self.

Jesus is supposed to have said 'Love your fellow man as you love yourself'. I tell you not to love your self, because your self is always unhappy. I say love 'me', the intimate truth and sensation that everyone recognises in their own body as 'the real me'.

Whatever your father did to you, or didn't do, it's in the past. The pain is always in my self — the past in me. There is no pain and resentment in me or what I am now. So I say: Do everything for me. As much as you can, give up your past and refuse to give in to your self.

By the law of karma, the past must repeat itself. The only way to stop it is to take responsibility for life now. The past only repeats itself if you hold on to it. If you hang on to resentment, anger and heartbreak, then the emotion is held in your self as your past and must be repeated in your life in other circumstances. So you will have to face the same pain again and again until you let the resentment and anger go.

Learn the lesson of life. Let everything go. Don't hold on to anything.

Woman: Thank you. I understand what you're saying, but when I'm angry it's very hard to just let it go. My husband tries to help. He's a good man but I take it out on him. And the children suffer, which makes me feel even worse. Is there anything we can do together that would help?

Yes. When you are angry, it is always because of something in your current circumstances, not because of something your father may or may not have done thirty years ago. To take responsibility for your emotion you have to be able to say why you are angry now. It can only be because of a person or an event. Look for the immediate cause of any negative emotion. Talk with your husband about it — as long as you are not both emotional, not accusing, blaming or judging the other or the situation. Have an intelligent conversation. Be honest to each other.

The solution of course is love. Anger comes up in man and woman when they are sexually frustrated. If you and your partner can learn to love each other more, neither of you will be so sexually frustrated and you will be able to deal with the difficult situations of life without getting so angry.

Woman: I'm sure that's right. When things are good between us I'm much more open. But we get separate and I'm drawn back into my past, somehow or other. At the time there always seems to be so much mess and I'll never get out of it. But now I get the feeling I'm not entirely a hopeless case!

No, but you will have to stop judging yourself and the situation. And, as much as you can, practise giving up the past. In that way you will become more true and more responsible for your life.

Remember that living a responsible life always comes down to simple little everyday things. The past is given up in simple ways, like not reflecting on the movie you saw last night, or not thinking about the little things that happened yesterday. You don't need to hold on to them. And you do not need to think about what you're going to do next weekend. You will find you can do without a great deal of your thinking. Whenever you need to be reminded of something, the thought will simply rise up into your mind from inside you.

And don't forget to pause in your busy day and acknowledge the good, as the sensation or being inside your body and wherever you see the good in life.

Whatever you have heard as true, that is the truth for you. So start with that. Live it and it will start to unravel your complicated life.

Woman: Thank you. I will. I don't want to go on inflicting myself on the children, or on my husband. He is very patient with me but sometimes despairs at the mess we get into.

He has to be responsible for what he once wanted. Many men feel trapped by their situation: job, house, car, partner and kids. That is why so many men and women are unhappy. But the situation they complain of is the one they made and once wanted. The man who got the job, made the children and acquired everything was not the man he is today. We are all different today. But what we wanted or did in the past we must now take responsibility for.

*

Mother: My child is six months old. I have been talking to him in the way you suggest from the moment he was born. I see that raising him in the right way will lessen his suffering;

although he must still live through his karma and pain. We can see it happening already. He tries to stand up on his own, falls down with a bump and cries.

That's right. While he's learning to stand on his own feet, he is going to fall down and cry. But as a true parent you will be giving him a foundation for life and for love. While he is getting his experience he will still have your love to fall back on. He will be able to turn to his mother whenever he is confused.

He's certainly going to be confused when the sex energy starts to enter him. Ten to fifteen years from now he's going to want to love and will be drawn to love woman. But because you will have informed him as much as possible about love, he will know where to turn. Along with all his cronies and his friends he'll think he knows everything, until he runs up against something that he knows nothing about. Then he will be able to come to you: 'Mum, my girlfriend is really upset. And I really didn't do anything. I only said I was going fishing with Charlie. Why did she run off like that?' And then you'll be able to speak to him and tell him a bit more about man and woman.

Mother: Should I tell him about what his self is going to do to him?

No. It's done by demonstration, in the moment. When he is angry, you can teach him to know that anger is his self, for example, and that he can't always have what he wants. Then you can teach him the difference between wanting something and needing it. You can demonstrate to him that when we give up wanting we start to see that we get what we need anyway; and then a great strain disappears from our lives.

Mother: Until I had my own child I didn't realise how

painful growing up is. Even though my boy is only six months, we can see what an effort it takes.

That's the way it is here. But the trick is to be the intelligence behind it all, and not climb into the picture.

The whole world is identified with the picture. We have to stand against the world: 'No, I'm not going to identify with this painful existence.' When you are not identified with it, you're impersonal.

And then the world turns on you: 'How cruel! How heartless!' — because a personal world cannot understand impersonal love.

*

Children attract the experience they need, whether it be the cruelty of a bully at school, the hurtful word, or the pain of sickness or accident. Behind every baby at birth is a negative potential. It is this that attracts the broken nose, the broken home or broken heart. Everything a child needs is already a potential waiting to happen.

You cannot save your children from their karma. All you can do as a parent is prepare them for life as it is. You cannot protect them from their ignorance. You can't save them from having to go out into the world to collect experience — along with the attachment to it. Nor of course can you save them from coming to the point in later years when they must detach from experience and free themselves from ignorance.

Of course you always endeavour to do and be the greatest good for your children. Whenever difficult situations arise, you look to see what you should do and then you do your best. Everyone is doing their best to live as good a life as they can in the circumstances. Yet as we see around us there is a great deal of cruelty and ignorance in the world and very little love.

We all have to be instructed about love. Otherwise lack of love and ignorance are perpetuated. We have to continually demonstrate love and justice to our children. Out in the world they enter the lovelessness. We have to take the world out of them every day when they come home from school. But despite all our good work at home, they pick up the rational and scientific explanation of what life is about. All sorts of wrong notions are instilled into them. They mix with other children and adults who habitually substitute emotionalism for love. They are introduced to excitement and taught to be emotional. The passion for life that is in every body turns into excitement — and excitement always ends in crying and pain.

To be a real parent is to be courageous for love and stand against all the forces that will corrupt your child — not only in the world but in your own self and those closest to you; your partner, your own mother and father or the child's aunties and uncles. If you indulge anyone who continually puts the world into your child, both you and the child must suffer.

That's not to blame anyone for anything. Everyone is acting for different forces of ignorance in this world. Everyone does what they do, really thinking that they're doing what is right. So don't blame anyone, but always endeavour to be true to the situation.

*

Teach your children: 'Don't hold anything against your enemies'.

Christians say Jesus taught us to love our enemies. But how can your child love the bully who just pushed him over in the schoolyard? He can't. The love the child knows or experiences is not up to it. It's impossible. You can't love your enemies, but you can give up holding anything against them. Doesn't that make more sense to a child?

Tell your children: 'Everybody has pain put into them through being hurt by others. They can't help taking that pain out on someone else. That's what makes people cruel. People do unkind things. But there's no need to hold it against them. Don't join them emotionally. Know that people have pain in them. But don't hold their pain in you.'

*

Man: It must be the karma of society that we have to live with the world's corruption of the children — juvenile delinquency, anti-social behaviour, drugs etc. If all our parents (and theirs before them) had actually tried to live the truth, surely the children of today would be more contented and creative. But I suppose their individual karmas would still lead them astray?

Yes, but any tendency to excessive or erratic behaviour can certainly be counterbalanced by an intelligent approach to parenting in the early years; instructing them what love is, explaining what life is about and telling them the truth behind the normal world and everything they learn at school.

The parents' job is to continually destroy the developing world in the child by explaining and demonstrating life as it is — how people in the world make themselves unhappy by trying and wanting; how they never talk about the present or about love, God, life, truth, or death. We all develop in truth by seeing for ourselves how people live in excuses and delusion.

Do not allow your children (or yourself) to judge or blame people for their ignorance or delusion, for they know not what they do. But teach the children to look for truth and to endeavour in their own lives to be as true as they can to what they know; without foisting it on others, unless they are asked.

Parents who truly love their children undermine the world in them, and the result is the wisdom that comes from seeing the truth through the false.

Man: What would you say about the parent's job if you were talking to a young son?

I would say this: 'I am here as your parent or guardian to give you the opportunity, as much as I can, to address the world in a right way so that you are able to cope with the various anxieties and forces that you are inevitably going to meet throughout your life.

'I have to teach you to cope with the world and I have to tell you that the world is very demanding and unkind. At the same time there are people in the world who are kind and have love in them, and I also teach you how to be with them. It is my job to teach you the justice and discrimination that you will need to be a loving man in the world.

'The world is filled with ignorance and lies; and people who live a lie, which means they say things they don't do. What we endeavour to do is not live a lie. So if I say I love you, to be true to you I've got to live my love of you, haven't I?

'Let's see what I actually do. I look after you. I endeavour to stop you from getting emotional, because my love says that if you're emotional your body will get all tight and then the emotion will make you feel a bit sick. My love stops that.

'So, you see, my job is to tell you the truth of life and to love you.

'Now, you tell me if I am I being true to why you are with me . . .'

THE DEVELOPING PERSONALITY

G azing wide-eyed from the cot I am still in touch with the warmth and wellbeing of the womb. But now my passion for life is uncontained. Excited by the stimulus of the world I start to explore this amazing place. Reacting to pleasure, discomfort and constant change, I start to get experience of my self. Crawling and toddling around, I test myself against the shape of things. I discover my limits. I find out that the world is often a place of strange coldness; where love is sometimes suddenly removed from me. By the age of two I am learning how to survive without getting hurt. I am discovering how to get what I want. My personality is being defined.

To consciously follow the development of your child's personality is a process of self-observation as much as vigilant parenting. To illustrate this, here is a conversation with a mother, held on a few occasions over a period of more than a year, during the critical time when her son's personality was beginning to show itself.

Mother: Sam is just fourteen months old now and is still a relatively blank slate. But we are starting to see the beginnings of a change in him. There are a few examples of this that I'd like to mention.

The first is when we play music on the cassette machine. He will stand and watch the lights flashing on the graphic equaliser. We can almost see him coming out of his eyes as he does it. His body changes, almost imperceptibly, like he's temporarily left it. We covered up the equaliser and now he just dances again.

It is true: he will leave his body when he comes out of his eyes like that. It is good that you are able to get him dancing and back in his body again.

As we see all around us, our children and youth are more and more being forced to come out of their eyes and ears through visual stimuli, video screens and the loud thumping beats of recorded pop music. In a world that worships anything electromagnetic, technical, and rational, it is extremely important to encourage children from an early age to participate in natural activities such as dancing, drawing and working with their hands. It is very important for them to inspect the products of the earth, see the insects, look at the dogs and cats, make observations about the birds and all natural things. Let them see for instance how the lustre of the blackbird's wing is the natural sheen produced when the bird preens its feathers. This kind of close observation of nature is all we have to counter the headlong rush into the world of the electromagnetic mind.

The idea is to produce a balanced child, as much as it can be done in this existence, by balancing the experience of the world with experience of the earth. To give our children that equilibrium we must encourage them to stay or be in the body.

The body has no problems. I can tell you this, for I am the body. Behind the sensory projection which appears to be my body I am profound and there is no end to the depth of what I am within. That is what I am and I am where my body is. I am not trying to be some other body somewhere else or in some other time. I am one with my body. I am my body. And if I dance in this state, I am dancing in this inner place of joy, the equilibrium inside me.

It is the same for your child when he is in that state. He is dancing with all his limbs and senses — the body dances. So encourage him in that, and when appropriate, join in and gently dance with him.

Mother: Another thing I've noticed is the way he's starting to copy other children's behaviour. We take him to a child-minder a couple of mornings a week and he plays with a two year-old girl there. She is being brought up in a very different way and has a certain 'face' that she puts on. Sam has started to copy it, and it looks ugly because it's not him. He's picked up her vocal mannerisms too. I know he must be copying us as well, but I can't see that as clearly because I am with him so much of the time.

I watch him put on different faces, look for reactions and explore the feelings that they create both in himself and us. He's aware of doing it, just as I was — I remember doing the same thing — but he can drop it in an instant and immediately come back into his body. I'm not so conscious of when I'm doing it myself, but I see it happening in Sam most clearly. He really is my teacher.

Yes, children do try out the expressions they see on their parents or playmates' faces. They entertain themselves and then eventually identify with the entertainment.

Mother: I was working on the computer at home and was trying to achieve something, so I wasn't paying Sam any attention. I was getting irritated with his interruptions so I let him know it and I thought he'd gone away. Then I turned round and saw him making faces at the mirror. I watched him let them fall and then try them again. He was observing his self very closely, with great interest and with obviously mounting excitement. So I stopped trying to achieve things, and we went out for a walk.

Yes, that's the way. Always try to break the hold of 'the intermediate world'. This is the world that stands between what you see in front of you and the reality of life within your body. It is the world of wanting, trying, visualisation and imagination. Its ground is emotion and its field is thought.

In the intermediate world the wellbeing inside the body becomes contracted. So when you were trying to achieve something on the computer you were getting irritated with Sam's interruptions. You were in the intermediate world of mental pictures and you'd left him. For company he turned to the mirror where he could see himself and get the attention he wanted from his own reflection. In other words, he joined you in an intermediate world of his own. You were looking into the computer screen; he was looking into his self. He tried on a mask, let it fall and then he re-made the mask in a different form. It's something the child does around this age.

Mother: I don't like getting irritated with him.

We mustn't be idealistic. Everyone gets irritated at some time or other. But when for instance he interrupts you in the middle of doing something that you need to do, instead of getting irritated, turn round to him, sit him down and immediately get it straight.

'I am doing this work that I need to do. I am not leaving you, but I have to do this. You have your own things to do. You have your toys. They are there for you to play with while I am doing what I have to do. So you sit here beside me and play with your toys while I do my work, and if you allow me to get it finished I will be able to come and play with you or we'll go for a walk.'

Although he may seem to be too young to understand, remember that it is important to address him with the same straightness and intelligence that you would use with an adult.

Mother: On the subject of talking to him; a few weeks ago he started to whine when asking for things. As he can't yet say 'please', I taught him to say 'Mama' when he wants something. After a few days of relief he started to whine the word 'Mama'; so then we had to teach him how to say it cheerfully, without demand. He does this now, when we remind him. Sometimes he doesn't and the agitation still prickles under the surface. But it's interesting that it is possible to convey specific things like that to a child of his age. I suppose he's still so close to his being that he can understand it perfectly and do it easily.

We use the word 'cheerfully' to describe the way to ask for what he wants. Is there a better word?

No, that's the way to do it. And whenever you or his father ask for something, of course you must also ask cheerfully so that you actually demonstrate to the boy what you mean. Although it's practically impossible to always do it, in front of the child you must endeavour to always do what you tell him to do; because that's how you communicate what is best or required, and right parenting means trying to find a right way to communicate.

When for example during a meal you ask your partner to pass something across the table, speak sweetly or cheerfully and look at Sam with a smile, so that he becomes part of the action of your asking; his participation is implicit. Then, by your demonstration, he will understand what 'cheerfully' or 'rightly' means.

We have to remember that every child is a copier. And it's not only facial expressions and inflections of speech; everything is copied by our children in their earliest years.

*

Mother: I'm interested in how Sam's language is developing. I thought it would be useful to write down the groups of words that he learned first.
1. Food — the words are cooking, juice, biscuits, cheese.
2. Dada, Mama.
3. Animals — moo, baa, cockerel, blackbird.
4. Objects — window, door, tree, sky.

That's a good illustration of the way we develop. It may not be exactly the same for all children, but that's the pattern as a general rule.

The first concern is with the needs of the body and things of the senses. (Sam might be particularly attracted to food — his list of words is quite impressive!) The first thing we want is food and drink, represented initially by a demand for mother's milk. We can see in this our first selfishness; the need for immediate satisfaction of the body's desires.

The second want is the comfort and security of mother and father's company. So Mama or Dada are our first words as we reach out from the senses to connect with others. The words represent a mental link that has now been made to the warmth and security of the parental embrace or presence. Uttering the words reminds the child: 'I am not alone in existence'.

Next we reach further out into the environment and name what is seen. In Sam's case (as I am pleased to hear) this is the naming of the animals that are always around the garden or the immediate vicinity. They represent the earth and anything to do with the earth represents being in the body. As he watches the

166

blackbird he is brought back into his own body; you'll see the stillness in him as he observes what the bird is doing. You will see the correspondence in that moment between the bird and the boy because they are both the product of the earth.

At the fourth stage his words describe objects in the wider world — window, door, tree, sky. He's starting to name things that are more distant from his body. This stage represents the beginning of the intermediate world of mentality, where we name objects and eventually learn to string them together to form the rational world that we all live in.

*

A couple of months later: there's now more emotion in the relationship of mother and son . . .

Mother: I have a few observations about the emotion I see in Sam, and in myself. For instance there were several people with us in the house and they each asked Sam for a kiss. He kissed them all but when I asked for one he turned his head away and wanted something else. I realise I was taking this personally but I wonder why he refused me.

Whatever the reason, it is obvious that he is learning to manipulate you — because you wanted the kiss. The others were not emotionally attached to getting one but there was a certain wanting in you; perhaps to keep up with the others. A child will psychically register this emotion and say 'No!' or turn away and wander off.

You are being manipulated because you are trying to get something. He will learn manipulation from your example. That is not to blame you; we all do this at some time or another.

As you say, you took it personally. You demonstrated that you were attached to his kiss. In the impersonal life when what I ask for is refused I am not attached to it.

Mother: Living with Sam certainly tests our attachments. But more and more I think we are realising the importance of not holding on to anything.

There was an incident the other day, when Sam broke a pen-nib. It was an accident but he'd been told several times not to touch the pen, so he was reprimanded. It was his father's, and had some value to us, so we were cross.

We let go of our emotion quite quickly but Sam cried and tried to keep the momentum going, to avoid being responsible. We told him it was all finished; we had let go of it and now everything was okay. He stopped crying, looked his Dad in the eye, apologised and carried on doing something else. Next day he remarked, after seeing the pen, that he'd broken it. He had no fear of mentioning it. There was no sign of any emotional residue.

Good. That's how to handle that sort of situation. If we, the parents, can only let go rightly — and show the child that we've let go — then he will let go too. For he gains his reflection from his parents and the adults around him.

Mother: It's not always like that. There are times when I get unreasonably angry with him, when he won't do as he's told. For instance, he kept pulling a jar of raisins out of the kitchen cupboard and he wouldn't stop. I did my best to tell him not to do it, and told him why he shouldn't, but every time my back was turned there were the raisins, upset on the floor again. Something like that makes me absolutely furious.

I had a look at what might be behind this and noticed that I'm looking for a formula for good parenting. If I was a good parent Sam would be a responsible, loving, obedient and unattached child. I get quite discouraged when he misbehaves and I see my limitations, weaknesses and failures. This self-criticism and wanting to be right is the flip side of a self-satisfaction which seems to be very strong in me. I'd like to know what I can do about it.

Also, there is a fear in me that Sam will be disobedient. Is it right authority that causes a child to be obedient?

Yes. A child who is rightly obedient knows the reason for obedience because the parents have communicated it. But every child is going to be rebellious and behave in the way you've described. This is not bad or wrong; it is simply the flexing of the muscles of self. It's irritating, at times infuriating, but there's nothing you can do about it because the child has to develop a sense of self-assertion.

Sam is exercising his ability to control objects and manipulate people through his behaviour. When he gets a reaction it gives him a sense of his developing power. This is an unavoidable part of his development. It is also, as you have seen, part of your own self-discovery. You will have to practise putting more pause between the irritation and your reaction to him; that will help you to deal with the situation.

You have to keep bringing justice and rightness into every communication and association with the boy. The key to every question of authority or obedience is: 'We are all endeavouring to keep this house free of unhappiness and contribute harmony to the house. So why are you disrupting it?' The more this is inculcated into him, the less troublesome he will be. When inevitably he is rebellious, he will be able to drop it more quickly. The more he sees rightness in your actions the more he will know why it is right to obey you, given the situation. There will be no suppression in his obedience.

There's no perfect child. You might have an over-expectation of Sam because he is your child and you feel responsible for him. You have to overcome your self-doubt and sense of failure. You can only do your best, and know that like all children he is passing through a stage of development that you and everyone else passed through in their turn. All these things pass. In my experience it gets easier after the age of two when there's more understanding and communication is easier.

Just endeavour to communicate the rightness of life as you see it, leaving him with as few scars as possible. And when he's frustrated, don't forget to take him by the hand or pick him up: 'Come on, let's have a game now. Or let's go for a little walk.' Do something like that to distract him from the frustration.

Mother: I do that, but I notice that if I am playing with him I have to be really there and not get distracted myself . . . I might be reading or singing to him, and I realise that for a long while I've been thinking — I've left him. Sometimes I might not notice this directly, myself, but I will see an agitation in Sam. If I'm conscious enough at that moment I realise he's stressed because he can somehow feel that I am not really with him.

Yes, even dancing or singing with him, if you're thinking, he'll psychically register that you've left him. This may not be easily seen in every child, but as a general rule it's what happens. That's why, as parents, we have to be so careful. We have to know that much more than we ever realise is being registered by the child.

If you're going be with your child, be absolutely there. That's love. Just as when you're making love with your partner, if one of you drifts off or starts thinking it will disturb the psychic field of the other.

Mother: Yes, I see that. But I don't seem to be able to let it go. I realise I've been thinking and I am not really with Sam any more, but then I'm likely to feel guilty so I try to do something to make up for it. I start to look for reassurance from him, which of course I shouldn't.

Why not say: 'Come here, I want to tell you something. While I was singing to you I was thinking about something else. That meant that I wasn't quite with you, and that's why you were a bit agitated. Now I want you to know that all the time I am endeavouring to be with you, as I hope that you are endeavouring to be with me. So let's sing the song again.'

Why not tell him? And then he can learn from your honesty and humility.

＊

Sam was coming up to his second birthday. With every month that passes, a child's individuality is more evident and the parent is aware of increasing separation.

Mother: I have noticed lately that I'm getting even more unreal and unconscious in my responses to what Sam is saying or doing. I am tending to fall into a formula, or set patterns of speech. And when I read to him, it's getting increasingly difficult to stay engaged in real communication.

As much as you or anyone would like to remain completely conscious with your child, you're not going to be able to do it all the time. And as for formulas of speech and behaviour: we get into habits which continue for a while, but then there's a change and we start to relate again in a new way.

Don't judge yourself. It is very difficult to bring up a child and you have to stop trying to be perfect. Remember, you can't be a perfect parent. You can only do your best.

You must also face the fact that you are training a robot. In every child there is the great creativity of Life The Divine. But it is divine life in a human robot. Although you and I have been inspired by a greater creativity to live a more conscious life, we are still robotic matter. Our job is to introduce a more conscious element into it, but the robot of course resists any change of consciousness.

171

Developing self-consciousness or individualisation brings an immediate robotic response, such as the desire to demonstrate independence and to exhibit an ability to make decisions or force decisions from others. This is standard robotic behaviour. There are certain patterns of resistance that are present in matter from the beginning, even before the body is born. And as a parent you are endeavouring to overcome this resistance in a body that is not even your own . . .

Mother: He is certainly more independent now. Instead of deciding everything for him, I've started asking him what he wants or what he would like to do. But is this a good idea?

I might ask him, 'Would you like to go for a walk?' Most of the time he answers happily but sometimes he'll say 'No! No!' quite forcefully, and he will look sulky, repeating 'No!' Then a few minutes later he says or does something to suggest that he would really like to go for a walk after all, but he is still upset and looks confused and unhappy.

It is best not to give children too much opportunity for liking or disliking. With a child of this age, it's better to make the decisions for him: 'Come on, let's go for a walk.'

The sulky look will have been picked up from some other child or adult. The contrariness is another example of the perversity of children as they flex their egoic muscle. The opportunity to defy your authority gives the child a stronger sense of individuality.

I can't tell you what age he should be before he makes his own choices. Some would say it's important to begin early but I say that discovering the ability to make choices allows the personality to assert itself, so it's important to limit the opportunities he has for 'choosing'. There is increasing choice in the western world and the tendency will be to give children more and more opportunity to decide between one thing and another. Until they are capable of making choices rightly, they will take the opportunity to like and dislike, accept and reject; and, when they don't get what they want, they're likely to get disgruntled. So, in the early years, the less children get the opportunity the better; and only later, according to their development and as the parents see fit, should they start making some of their own decisions.

Mother: You mentioned the perversity of behaviour as individuality asserts itself. We often notice it in Sam. Sometimes he gets agitated when his father and I are talking; it can be about any kind of subject. First he whimpers briefly. Then bangs his spoon on the table; or something like that. When we ask him what's the matter, he just makes a sweeping gesture, without speaking, towards something he wants from the table. And he can want one thing after another. When we give him what he seems to want, he just says 'No! No!' and turns aside. At first we thought this was his demand for attention, but we are not inattentive and as a rule I see to his needs promptly. It seems he's just being perverse and disruptive.

Yes, this is his need to get attention, but not any particular form of attention. He wants you to give your attention to him and not each other.

His behaviour is all part of the process of individualisation which leads to more and more independence.

*

Mother: I'm interested in how Sam's use of language is developing. One thing is that he always talks in the first person, even when he is referring to someone else. So, for example, when he asks me if I want a cup of tea, it comes out as 'I would like a cup of tea, Mum?' Or, if he needs me to help him with something, he will say 'Shall I help you?' So he speaks for the other person, as it were. This is amusing but seems quite logical as his experience of the world is still very subjective.

He hasn't yet learned to twist his mind from I to you. By putting a query on the end of it — 'I want a cup of tea, Mum?' — in his own mind he feels he's communicating what you might want. He will grow out of it, but at present, as you say, he's still close to the subjective world. Coming from the very point of subjectivity, out of God's womb into existence, he hasn't fully made the mental shift in the psyche that would completely objectify his existence.

I will explain the truth behind the objective world and say what subjectivity really is; relating it to Sam's development.

We live in 'an objective world', which is a mental existence. The whole aspiration of rational culture, as represented by scientists and schoolteachers, is to be objective. But the reality and truth is that life is subjective.

Subjective reality has no past in it. Our mental 'objective world' is totally in the past. Although everything in this world is done in the present, there's no objective 'present' in any of our communications; we are always speaking to each other from a point already passed.

Man thinks the universe is an objective reality, but despite the rationality of the scientists, I say that in truth the universe is not objective because it has no past. Time only began with life on earth and only applies to life on earth. In the universal or cosmic, beyond life on earth, there is no time, no past. The universe has always been, and always will be, precisely as it is now.

Objectivity would endeavour to show that the universe is changing. But what changes is the objectivity, not the universe. Any shift seen by the objective or rational mind is due only to its own aberration, its projection of itself. The universe is always the same because it is subjective — meaning it is within me now.

Having entered objective existence and become an expert in being objective, it is possible in the spiritual life to make the objective world secondary; to return to the subjective life in which everything is inside of me — where there is only one I in the universe.

Evolution in the objective world is our progress away from subjectivity. Even quite recently we were more subjective in our experience of the earth than we are today. For instance, it was harder for man to be objective about the planet when he could not see it from space. First he had to conceive what it might be like, then he had to draw his notions of it and only recently could he photograph it from a satellite. All this progress, culminating in what the astronauts see with their own eyes, is the result of the rational thought processes of man over a considerable period. So it is with our whole evolution as mental creatures. We steadily learn to objectify the world and in the process our rational minds are conditioned to see and imagine the world as 'objective reality'.

In the same way, Sam is leaving subjectivity behind and quickly being conditioned to live in the world of time and objects. He is becoming absorbed in the world of you's, where 'you' and 'I' are separate. He will soon lose touch with where 'I' come from — beyond the womb — and forget that reality until, much later in life, reality or God is consciously revealed to him once more.

THE PRICE OF EXCITEMENT

O ur senses allow us to enjoy our life. They also put us in touch with pain. As children growing up, our sensual life is steadily dulled. The natural passion for life sinks beneath the excitement and disappointment of living in the normal world.

In our earliest wonderful days, not long out of the timeless womb, our senses are fully open to receive the glory of life and the earth. The place where we first take breath and sense our love of the earth, has a deep significance. Where we were raised, or were loved very much, has profound meaning in our senses: the smells, sights, colours will always resonate in us. Today, walking down the street, a particular colour will catch the eye: we won't know why, yet often it's associated with that blessed time when our senses were so innocent and open.

Not far into time, the pollution and corruption begins. It is only hours or days before the negativity of existence starts to enter our bodies. In those first days the parent should communicate the wonder of life to the baby, speaking to the intelligence in the infant body.

'You have come here to this world and it's often an uncomfortable place. It is a temporary life here, but we do our best to live without unhappiness. Where you are there, in the sweetness and peace of your own body, where it is warm and beautiful, that is the truth.

'Now you are coming out of peace and beauty into disharmony. That's what this existence is. The only one who can make it into a harmony is you and you do that by staying in touch as much as possible with the nothingness, the sweetness that makes you gurgle and smile at me with your bright little eyes.

'I will do everything I possibly can to keep you connected with the beauty that you just left, the beauty beyond the womb. Throughout my life, I will endeavour to prepare you to experience living in this physical world. But for now, just stay in that place of beauty. Don't be seduced by the excitement that seems to be out here.'

*

The baby looks out of the awareness of being, with apparently vacant eyes, in wonderment. Meanwhile everyone is working very hard, cooing over the cot, waving things, shaking rattles.

'Look at Mummy. Look! Look! Look! Mummy is smiling at you, isn't she? Can you see the big smile on my face? And Daddy's smiling at you. And here's a rubber duck.

'Oh and look! Here's Auntie Nellie come to visit you. Now what do you think of that!'

Bewildered now in the wonderment, the baby gazes back: 'What on earth are they doing?'

They are trying to teach you to think, Baby.

'Oh! And why do I want to think?'

Well, Baby, you've got to think because you've just been born into a world of ignorance where thinking is worshipped.

Thinking makes people unhappy, and this is a world that loves unhappiness, so you have got to be taught how to join in with Mummy and Daddy who do lots of thinking and love their unhappiness. Sorry, but that's how it is here.

Mother: Every mother wants to be happy with her baby and enjoy his reactions. I don't see it's got anything to do with 'thinking'. I really like to see the intelligence in my little boy.

Of course you do. We are born as intelligence. But we are not born thinking. Your intelligence knows the difference. The way of thinking is to go on thinking about something and that means excitement or worry leading to unhappiness.

We have to learn to think. It took a lot for humanity to come out of the earth and eventually start to think. It was a tremendous effort to learn how to do it. And it is the same for every child. Now, of course, as adults in this world we have to learn how to stop thinking.

Mother: Are you opposed to giving rattles to babies?

Yes, if the rattle pulls the baby's attention away and distracts the consciousness from being in a place of peace, just gurgling in the pram or cot. Parents, aunts and uncles, always waving things, pull the baby's consciousness out into the world.

And yet rattles have a right purpose: to exercise the infant's sense of hearing. It is essential to give a baby as much experience of the senses as possible, but your endeavour to do this should always be balanced by your recognition of the inner life. It is when that balance is missing that children can get possessed by the negativity that comes into existence through their bodies.

*

Excitement seduces us and draws us out into the world. We must do what we can to help our children to remain in their bodies as long as possible. We have to reduce the excitement before it escalates.

As children get worked up with feelings of excitement their expectations build — until a peak of hyperactivity is inevitably followed by a decline into some form of depression. They whinge. They can't sleep. It is difficult for you to relate to them.

Watch for the first signs. Listen for the words: 'Oh that'll be good! I'm looking forward to that.' And then do what you can to bring the child back to the present.

Woman: Having a high means I end up with a low — I think I've discovered that in my life! — but I don't understand how you can be so against normal feelings. I've been with various spiritual masters and teachings and probably the main thing I've learned is to go by my heart and not my head.

The trouble with normal feelings is that they are not natural sensations. Feelings are always effects of something that is not now. Feelings are always looking backwards or forwards to some experience; such as anger, discomfort, sadness, jealousy or excitement. If you go by your feelings, you will go on exciting them. Feelings always look for excitement.

Natural sensation is just the being of the body now. I enjoy the pleasure of just being in my body. When I go to the beach or am swimming in the sea, how good it is; how beautiful . . . I am in the sensation of beauty.

The beauty of being is not a feeling; it's a sensation. When we say 'It feels good,' we are simply endeavouring to describe the pure sensation of rightness and goodness. The body is sensation. My body loves being in the sea because it is sensational. Love, joy, beauty are sensational, always.

You might have observed that even so-called 'spiritual people' often go to spiritual masters to excite themselves, despite what they may think. They join spiritual communities for social excitement. They get pleasure from talking to other people about love or the truth instead of living it now by not thinking and not having feelings.

Do whatever you want to do without having feelings about it or thinking about it. You will not make a problem of any activity as long as you don't think about it, or get emotional or excited about it.

Woman: But there's always something new to look forward to. That's part of the fun . . .

What? What do you need to look forward to?

Woman: Well, I was looking forward to today — coming to see you!

Fair enough . . . But if you're looking forward to going anywhere tomorrow, remember you might drop dead on the way!

This teaching is about living a balanced life. Give up living with highs and lows. Give up looking forward and enjoy life as it is now — that's equilibrium in the spiritual life. Otherwise you will teach your children to live by excitement.

I say that an excited child is heading for unhappiness. Do you want unhappiness? Do you want that for your child? Or are you going to be an intelligent parent?

The truth of this has to be demonstrated to children, just as I am endeavouring to demonstrate it to you.

'You have to be intelligent. You have to know that when you get excited, within a day or two or a few hours, you will be crying or unhappy.'

'Oh no I won't!' comes the reply, 'I don't believe it. I'm enjoying myself. I won't get unhappy.'

'Okay, let's see what happens. And if I see that you are unhappy tomorrow, may I point it out?'

181

All parents know this story. The kids get excited. They run around. They can't eat their food. They want this; they want that. Tomorrow comes and what happens? They're moody. They're restless. They don't know what they want. They grizzle. Up today — down tomorrow: that's the law. If we are unhappy today, it's because yesterday we were out of balance. We broke the law. We have not been intelligent. But that's how we learn self-knowledge.

So, as a true parent to my children, I must not get excited about anything. I must deny my self, so that I might die to my self for my children. That's love.

How does that sound to you? Is it true?

Woman: Well, you've certainly shaken my expectations. It sounds true, but I don't feel very happy about it. I'm not sure what I think of you. I'm sorry — I don't like your teaching very much!

In the truth there is nothing to like or dislike. There is just what is. Equilibrium comes from denying yourself the right to like or dislike anything.

The identification with attraction/repulsion creates an emotional pendulum inside of us, swinging from one side to the other: 'I like this . . . I don't like that . . . Oh, I do like this . . .' You hear it going on all the time, about everything in life. Cars, fashion, food, everything. And it all begins in the cradle, as parents actively encourage the child to react automatically with liking and disliking. Everything the child is exposed to in the world will continue to encourage this reactivity of attraction and repulsion. There is no point of balance in it.

If we can refrain from using the words 'like' and 'dislike', we might start to get rid of the liking/disliking in ourselves and introduce more equilibrium. And give the children a wonderful demonstration.

'Ugh! . . . Don't like it!' squeals the child, pulling a face.

'Never screw your face up and say you don't like something.

Just say you don't want it, thank you. Everything has its existence, which doesn't depend on whether you like it or not.'

Woman: That was me — screwing up my face. I've always been like that.

Well, we're all grown-up children. Now as the adult you can see that it's just not necessary to say you like something or don't like it.

When you are in equilibrium there is no judgment in you. If all the time you judge things with a like or dislike, you will also judge people. Those who are continually critical of others are uncertain of themselves and usually have low self-esteem. So judging others you judge yourself and tend to feel doubtful and unworthy, or a failure. This self-judgment develops with the swing of the emotional pendulum in childhood, from excitement to disappointment, from liking to disliking, from attraction to repulsion. Because we are all grown-up children it is best to nip it in the bud.

*

Always do what you can to take the excitement out of your child's experience of life; although of course this is not easy to do in a world which thrives on excitement.

At kindergarten the teachers will excite the young ones with such things as the celebration of birthdays . . .

'Who's birthday is it today? It's Billy's birthday! Isn't that exciting, everyone! This afternoon we'll have a party and a cake with four candles . . . ' So all the children get excited because Billy is four today. Next month it's your son's birthday; his excitement has already started.

Don't excite children about their birthdays. Acknowledge the birthday and let your children have a celebration, just as their friends do. But take the excitement out of the party. Nanny, Grandpa, Auntie, Uncle and the mothers of the other children may say: 'How can you do that? How unkind!' But having indulged the children, they can all decamp and go home, leaving you to deal with a hyped-up child.

'We're going to have a party on your birthday and we are going to plan it carefully and do everything necessary so that you and all your friends will enjoy it. But first I have to say something important to you. We must be very careful that we don't get too excited about it. If we get excited and look forward to it and something was to go wrong, we would be disappointed. So let's make our plans and preparations and not get excited about it. Then we will all enjoy it.'

Denying excitement doesn't destroy the joy of celebration or the enjoyment of being with friends and companions. Neither joy nor passion contain excitement. I am joyous because life is good. I am joyous because I love. Being joyous is a steady passionate state. It has no peaks and troughs; and no end. It is pure fulfilment. Excitement on the other hand requires satisfaction. That is its end — satisfaction of the mind and emotions. A child brought up on excitement is a child that gets bored very easily.

'Mum, when is it going to be my birthday? Is it tomorrow? When are we having the party, Mum? When is it? When, when, when?'

'Next week, on Friday.'

'On Friday, on Friday . . . Mum, is it Friday yet?'

Don't let the child look forward to anything. Keep lowering the level of excitement.

'Now sit down. I've got something to say to you. You are beginning to get excited about the party. And there's no need to get excited. If you get excited now you'll be unhappy later. We're going to have a party — if it happens — but let me tell you a story . . .

'There was once a little girl who wanted to have a birthday party with a barbecue in the garden. She got very excited about the idea and for two days before the party she couldn't sleep properly. She spent all day blowing up balloons and tied them to all the trees. But just as everyone was arriving it started to rain. And it rained and rained. They moved the party into the house and everyone went into the kitchen, except the little girl. She went to her bedroom. From her window she could see the balloons bobbing about in the wind and the rain. It made her feel so sad that she started crying and she went on crying until everyone had gone home.

'Now why do you think she did that? After all it was the same party with the same friends. She got unhappy because she looked forward to something that didn't happen the way she expected it. People usually get unhappy if they get themselves excited like that.

'We can't be sure that anything is going to happen as we plan it. Nothing is certain in this life. But as far as I can see we're going to have a party, and we're inviting all your friends and we're going to enjoy ourselves. But we mustn't look forward to it.

'Now, we need to buy some candles and some icing sugar for the cake. So we will go out to the shop this afternoon and buy everything we need. And we will enjoy doing that, won't we? — as long as we don't get excited by looking forward and thinking about it.'

*

Mother: Is there something to be said for allowing children to let off steam? Sometimes my boys will get themselves very excited and just yell and run around. Do they actually need to go wild and be so noisy? Should I stop it or allow it?

They do have to have spells of wildness. It usually starts while they are playing games, doesn't it? If you can't get any peace and the noise starts to make you unhappy you will have to do something about it. There will have to be a rule about not playing noisy games or running around in the house. Send them outside and let them go wild out there, where you can still keep your eye on them. Or, if it's raining, the game must be over when you say so.

You will also have to explain the rule of the house to any of your children's friends who happen to be there. They may come from a family where they're never told what's happening or why, and they may feel you're very odd, but still you have to tell them how it is in your house.

'Now calm down a minute . . . I have something to say to you all. There's a rule in the house: No noisy running around indoors. It's okay for you all to play and have fun together, because it's good to be together. But there must be no running through the house. And I'll tell you why. It's because children running round corners can run into each other and get hurt. Or you might knock something over and break it. A house is not for running in. A house is for living in. You are contained in a house. So play in the room together, play with the toys, have fun, but stop running around.'

Mother: And why do they need to go wild sometimes?

Because that's the way the world is. They have to experience the excitement and the momentum, apparently.

It begins with children's games, getting excited and going wild. Then it shows up on the football field, and in all sports where they can really hit balls hard, kick things, be aggressive and throw things around. The next thing is to go to stadiums and gather together in hundreds and thousands to cheer and make a great noise. That's the easy way to get excited — be a spectator and let the poor fellows on the field take all the knocks. Or even easier, sit at home and watch it on TV. All these grown-up children, identifying with what's happening,

186

going 'Oooh' and 'Ahhh', get excited and have their spell of mass noise; followed with absolute inevitability by come-downs and bouts of disappointment. That's how life is on this planet and the point it has reached in its evolving maturity.

All kids get excited at some time or another, and often they get excited about nothing at all. But where there is excessive excitement, you can point out to them what happens so that they see for themselves how depression or unhappiness always follows.

'And you know, if you don't get too excited as you run around, you might not fall over so much. You watch out for that and then come and tell me if it's true.'

GIVING TO THE CHILD

Quick-fix parental love in our times is based on giving things and opportunities rather than giving of ourselves; on doing what we think is right or good for the child rather than what is right or good.

How do you give yourself? Not by giving what you have to do anyway, such as going to work to pay the rent, providing food, money, entertainment or picking the child up after school. Giving of yourself is giving of your time, convenience and perhaps comfort. It is reaching out to young people through what they perceive as their need, and not only through our own notion of what they need.

The most important thing for parents to give a child is their time. It's often the hardest thing to do, but being a parent means spending time with your child. You've got to have time to speak with them, play with them, sit and help with the homework, hold the pencil and encourage them with their drawing. You have to sit there and be prepared to take an intelligent interest in whatever they are doing. Don't just let them get on with it. Give up your own time. That's love.

Then, having given them your time, give them your sweet nature. For there to be harmony in the house there must be ease in giving to each other and a shared knowledge of the rightness of it. By being easy and giving you demonstrate your sweet nature to the children; and they will reflect it back to you. Giving your sweet nature is an acknowledgement of the beauty or rightness of life. And it's amazing how it is reflected back to us when life is truly acknowledged.

The law is: What I acknowledge I get. If what I give to life is my anger or the lack of openness of my contracted self, then that is what will come back to me in the circumstances of my life, my family and the people around me. But if I give my sweet nature I get sweet nature back; although I won't get it back everywhere or from every person. When we give rightly, we don't do it to get anything back.

*

Because of the developing self-centredness of young children (roughly between four to seven years old) there can be a tendency to ignore others and live in their own world. You can help them overcome any tendency to become withdrawn. You do this through the everyday demonstration of your own giving and sweet nature.

Here's an example. A small boy is playing contentedly at home when someone comes to the door. The mother welcomes the visitor into the house and he turns to greet the boy. No response; the boy goes past, into the next room, and does not reply or give any acknowledgement. Later on, when it suits him and the adults are deep in conversation, the boy brushes past and says hello, or gives some little indication of acknowledgement. This kind of behaviour is not good enough. If habitually repeated it will add experience to an aspect of his personality that will make him suffer in future years, appearing in his love-life, his job and in self-doubting moments in the middle of the night. Although people may put up with his dismissive behaviour now, when he's older they'll turn away from him. Then he will relate to his cut-offness as loneliness. He will feel depressed and have to compensate by projecting a personality that will not be his sweet nature at all but a defensive mechanism likely to hit out or become habitually moody.

Some children are of course by nature less extrovert, but a child who is becoming habitually withdrawn has to be instructed to open up and give his sweet nature — because that's what he wants others to do to him. You can only give the necessary instruction when the child is receptive. But having communicated the point you must not let up. So if for instance he ignores people or fails to greet them, you have to go on reminding him to say hello. Don't come down too heavily on him. Always endeavour to lighten the situation and make a game of it.

'Let's play a game of opening up. And the game is, whenever anyone comes to the door we're going to be sure to smile at them and say hello.'

'No. Don't want to.'

'Okay. Well then, I have to ask you this. When people come over to our house do you want them to ignore you and not speak to you? They won't want to talk to you if you don't want to talk to them. What about if it's someone you really want to be with? You see, if you don't want that person to ignore you — because you wouldn't like it, would you? — then you have to open up. So come on, let's practise it now. I'll go outside and then I'll come back in and you can say hello and give me your sweet nature . . .'

Sometimes the adults are at fault for indulging the child. For instance, in a social situation they might allude to his 'shyness' as though it were an attractive trait of character, and smile knowingly at each other thinking it's cute. This is a denial of the right development of the child. He should not be congratulated for being withdrawn but instructed that it is not entertaining.

Adult social behaviour can be confusing to children, but they have to learn how to handle situations, just as they have to graduate from using a spoon to a knife and a fork. For instance, shaking hands as a greeting is not natural to a child and so when a boy is suddenly confronted with a man putting out his hand to shake hands, he might pull back and feel self-consciously awkward. Here is an opportunity to take the boy aside at the right moment and explain why we shake hands. It makes a good story.

'You know why people shake hands? Because in olden days, when men wore swords, it was a simple, quick way of saying "Hello, I bear you no ill-will. See, my sword is still in the scabbard. My sword-hand is outstretched towards you. I greet you and I am open to you." That's where shaking hands comes from, and although now it's mostly done out of habit, its real meaning is still that the people shaking hands are open to meet and be with each other. So you might remember that, and not just put out your hand out of habit. Instead you can make the gesture a living reality by being open to the person you are meeting.'

Encouraging your child to be open and giving is one of the finest gifts a parent can give.

*

Mother: What advice do you have about giving presents for birthdays and Christmas? In our family we tend to make presents for each other. Simple little things, usually. I think many children get given too many toys and expect too much.

I hear the good sense in that. Toys are important but a constant cascade of them may give the child too much choice.

When you give a child a toy or game, take an interest in it. Tell the child how good it is to see him playing with it. Join in sometimes. This associates you and your love with that toy.

Mother: When the relatives come over they often bring presents. They're very generous. We don't have much money, but we try to give something back. So I get the kids to make some little gift or a birthday card. One of them got upset the other day, after his birthday, and didn't want to do a thank-you note to his Grandad. I couldn't get any sense out of him and wondered if I was asking him to do something that was not right . . .

Well, first of all, when the relatives give your children toys or gifts, you will have to watch to see that they do not get too many. Or, if there are too many at once, you could keep one or two back and give them later.

The little boy who got upset has some resentment in him, which you would have to speak to him about at the time. But you can also speak to him about why you were asking him to acknowledge the gift.

'Tell me, why didn't you want to write to Grandpa?'

'Well, I didn't want to.'

'All right, but I feel you should acknowledge his gift and thank him for it. Of course I'm not you. So if you don't want to do it, that's all right — as long as you're open to what I'm endeavouring to say.

'You see, we can't just go on taking all the time. We can't go on getting presents and not giving something in return, even if it's only a thank-you. I'm endeavouring to teach you that and to get you to give something back for all that you receive. I'm sure that in your own time you will be more giving because I know you hear what I'm saying.'

*

Mother: I celebrate my daughter's birthday but I don't give her much at Christmas. There's just her and me and I suppose I try and see it as just another day. But I get the feeling that she might be missing out somehow . . .

You would have to talk to her to find out if she sees that something is absent. If you don't celebrate Christmas together, can she handle it when her friends talk about what they've been doing? Does she feel isolated from other people?

You can tell her how you see it: 'You know the reason we don't celebrate Christmas as something very special is because we can have a celebration any time we like. It doesn't have to be Christmas. We can go out and have fun together any day and it's another day of joy.'

Should the opportunity arise for her to participate with others in Christmas parties and celebrations, I wouldn't deny her, but I would of course endeavour to take the excitement and hype out of it.

Mother: The only real problem she's had is when some other girl came and stuck her face into hers: 'And what did you get for Christmas . . . ?' proceeding to give an endless list of the presents she'd got.

You give her gifts from time to time? Of course you do. She mentions she wants something. You go and get it for her and when she comes home from school there it is on the kitchen table. 'How lovely!' she says, 'That's just what I wanted. Thank you very much Mum!' And you say, 'Yes, this is how we celebrate life and our love for each other, isn't it? We don't need Christmas to give our gifts, do we? We can surprise each other and buy or make something lovely without needing a special day of celebration. We don't need a special day for loving one another because we love each other every day.'

*

Mother: My mother insists on bringing sweets for the kids, although I don't like them to have too much sugar. Is it right to give sweets, or not?

Why do we give them sweets? And why do they love them so much? Why do children want money to buy sweets and then, as they grow up, gradually lose interest in them? Is there some physical demand in the young body for a constant supply of sugar? Or is it a conditioned gratification?

You have to see how many sweets your children are eating or being given. Are they needed, or not? Observe whether there is demand in the child. Watch the situation.

You will have to explain the situation to your mother and ask her to help you by not giving the children sweets without your agreement.

*

Father: As I see it, there's a natural desire to keep giving to children, but obviously it can be overdone. People say that giving children everything they want is 'spoiling' them. What's the right balance here? And how can we tell if a child is being spoiled?

A child who has been spoiled is a child who has plenty of toys but hangs around saying he's got nothing to do.

'Toys are given to you to play with. If you've got a roomful of toys and you say you have nothing to do, it means you have more toys than you need.'

When the child pleads with you to go and buy that special toy and says he really wants it, you have to make the point that if you go and buy it, he has to play with it and not put it aside.

The balanced approach is to see what the child needs and explain the situation.

'You can have what you need, but you can't have more. No one can have everything they want in this world, so you're not going to get everything that you want from me. But you're certainly going to get everything you need.

'If you want something you can always ask for it and we'll look and see whether you can have it or not. But you have to understand that you won't always be able to have it.'

'Well, why not? Why can't I have it?'

'Because we are here to help you to grow up in a world where nobody is able to have everything they want. We will gradually show you that it's impossible. To start with, look at the fact that there are millions of people in the world, all wanting lots of things. How could they possibly all get what they want?

'If you think you should get everything you want, why shouldn't everyone else? If you want to go to the beach, why shouldn't everyone? — because there wouldn't be room on the beach for all of us. They might all want to stop work and go off to the beach in their motor cars, but if they did who would be at work? No one would be making the motor cars and no one would be earning the money to buy the motor cars!

'You see, it's impossible for all the people to have all they want all at the same time. Sometimes we have to do without what we want so that other people can have what they want.'

*

Mother: I sometimes find myself bargaining with Karl, my little boy. He can have an apple if he will have a bath. That sort of thing. Do you see any problem with that?

Striking bargains is a part of life. It's a compromise that we live with in this world, so there's a place for it; but only if it's already been established that you, the parent, are the authority in the house. He must know that he has to have his bath anyway, if you say so. But I don't see why there cannot be some bargaining, if you see that it's appropriate or necessary for his process of individualisation.

Mother: And what about giving rewards?

Give rewards by all means, but don't allow any expectation of reward.

Don't make promises. For instance, don't promise the boy something if he is good.

And never give him sweets or toys as bribes; because that will lead him to try to manipulate you emotionally.

Mother: I understand that it's not right to give a reward if it's really meant as a kind of bribe. But I don't see what's wrong with making promises.

If you make promises, you will teach your son to make promises himself, and then he will learn to believe in them. Every promise exists to be broken. As soon as a promise is broken we blame the one who made the promise. Then we get unhappy

197

with ourselves, with the promiser and with life. Is that the truth?

Mother: Yes, but it's quite a difficult one for me. What would I say for instance to my sister who has promised Karl that she'll take him out at the weekend?

I suggest you take her aside and tell her the situation: 'Please, don't promise him anything. By all means tell him what you want to do or intend to do, but don't hold out any promises, please, because we don't make promises in this house.'

Later on, say to the boy: 'Auntie wants to take you to the zoo and if it turns out that she can, it will be good, won't it? But don't get excited because you know, people sometimes make promises they can't keep. And that leads to disappointment. So it is best not to believe in what anyone promises you. It might happen; it might not. We'll have to wait and see.'

Don't underestimate the importance of teaching children about promises. Start young. Then perhaps in later years, when they are captivated by the dream and fervour of youth, disappointment will leave less of a mark.

'I promise to be your friend for ever and ever . . . Be mine, I promise I will love you forever.'

Why would anyone believe it? You don't know how long you'll love anything, do you? It is enough just to tell me you love me. 'Come to me every day and say "I love you" and I will be able to see whether indeed you love me. It will show in what you do. But you cannot promise to love me forever.'

*

Mother: I want to ask you about possessiveness. My daughter is already showing signs of it, although she's only five. She'll have a tantrum if I stop her playing with something and take it away from her. How can I get her to not mind when I do this, so that we avoid a battle?

You're not going to avoid the battle. It's a stage in her development. Perhaps it doesn't arise in all children, but generally speaking they will hang on to something and not want to give it up when the parent says so. Or when a playmate comes over, there will be a tendency to hold on to a toy or a doll and not share it. Or the child will persist in spite of an imminent accident that you can see coming, but she has not the experience to foresee.

You have to endeavour to deal with the situation as gently as possible. Don't get locked into it. Do the best you can to encourage her to surrender the thing, and don't give up on her until she has. But be gently persistent and don't allow yourself to become irritated or forceful. She will pass through this stage and then you'll find there will be a change.

A sense of possession is a practical necessity in life but it is not born in us. We have to acquire it from our parents, relatives, friends and the society around us. It is only when we emphasise the sense of possession as a right or a virtue that we are likely to become possessive. In other words it only becomes a problem when we become attached to things and hold on to them as 'mine'. Then, inevitably, in the school of life the attachment to what's 'mine' must be broken.

I recall an incident many years ago when this was brought home to me. I was living in a country cottage in England with Julie, my second wife. My two young stepsons were visiting us. The small bathroom was festooned with bath towels. Despite my fastidious, churlish efforts to keep my towel dry it was always wet — and grubby too. I was murderously suspicious that Jonathan, age nine, might have something to do with it. Apart from having his regular baths, he would frequently be in there obeying orders to wash his face and hands. I was amazed at the speed with which he was in and out glowing with the unsoiled look of the newborn. I waited my chance and dallied outside the bathroom. In he ducked and out he swanned.

'Jonathan! Wait!' The imperious command stopped him in his tracks. 'Which towel do you use, Jonathan, each time you go in there?'

'The driest. Why?'

Children are simple and logical. Things are perceived as they are. A dry towel is best because it dries you quickest and easiest. Who cares whose towel it is?

*

Father: Do you have any advice about giving children pocket money? Our boy is seven. We continue to buy him most of the things he wants, but we have started giving him a couple of dollars every Saturday. How would you help children to manage money?

When the time comes to start giving a little money, which might be around the age of seven, I would talk to the child and explain the situation.

'Your Mum and I think you're old enough now to be able to handle your own money. What we are going to do is to give you some money every Saturday. But first we have to ask you how you would like that.'

'Oh yes, please. That'll be great.'

'Good. Now you have to know that a responsibility comes with having pocket money. The money is so that you can buy the small things and sweets that you want. You are not to come and ask us for any more. This means that you will have to learn how to manage your money. Of course the bigger things are still our responsibility, like your clothes and toys which you cannot possibly pay for. So, starting this Saturday, we are going to give you two dollars a week and your job is to manage until the next Saturday . . . And no borrowing!'

I don't know how far two dollars goes with children these days but I would suggest that when the time comes to raise it to five dollars you say: 'We've got to have a talk, because we've reached the point where you've got to take more responsibility. Starting next week, your pocket money is going up to five dollars, but you will still have to be careful about managing it. And to begin with I'd like you to come and tell me what you spend it on. Is that okay with you?'

In this way you keep an open communication and at the same time prepare the child to be responsible in the world.

In the teenage years, when the need for money will be the mark of independence, the parent has to know that the son or daughter is being responsible for the money given to them. Adolescents are likely to ask you for money when they should be asking for your advice. So you must find out what they're doing with the money.

If you give teenagers money without making them accountable for it, they are likely to misuse it and indulge themselves at your expense. They will even be dishonest with you to get what they want. This is what happens, as a general rule, because of the independence that children develop in a loveless society. For independence follows lack of love.

Sooner or later the child or youth will run into a situation where money or lack of it causes conflict. Perhaps he is careless and loses the money he's been saving up. Or he wants something he can't afford and you're not willing to supply the balance. Whatever the case, the time comes when it is good to put the significance and importance of money in its context.

'Son, you will be taught in the world that the most important thing is money. That's what you'll find everybody talking about — because money provides enjoyment in the world. But we are devoted to an inner life, a real life where money comes second to love and harmony. We accept the way the world lives and what the world teaches us; and in the world it is right that money is the most important thing. But in this house we put love first and money comes second. When people put love and money the other way round, money becomes their love. And when that happens, they get unhappy.

'Money is very important, and we need it, but it is not as important as love. That's because love is vital to us, and money is only necessary.

'I'll explain the difference. "Necessary" means there is some action to be taken. You can't have money without someone having earned it through action. You can't know how much money you've got without counting it — that's an action. You can't buy anything without handing over some money — action. Money is a necessary part of the action of the world. But love is not an action. We know love when we are still, in harmony with the birds and the trees. Love is an inner state, where we are at peace with what we call God or life and can feel the sweetness or rightness inside of us. In other words love is "vital".

Money and love: If money was our love and we lost it all we'd get a feeling of great loss, a great unhappiness. That would be a feeling inside us, but it would not be love and it would not be true. Unhappiness comes and goes, like what's necessary comes and goes, depending on when you need it. If you suddenly got some more money your unhappiness would vanish immediately. So unhappiness is not true, whereas the love or truth inside us is always there, always vital, even when you can't feel it. That's what makes it true.

'All the necessary things could be taken away from you — your money, your home, the whole world — but you would still be able to feel what is vital in your body because when you take away what's necessary you are left with the vital, the sensation or being of love.

'It's like when you go to sleep and you lose touch with the world. You leave the necessary and slip back into the vital. Next morning you wake up and say 'Oh, what a good sleep I had.' That's because deep sleep is vital to us; we can't go on living without it.

'You know, all that happens when we die is that we slip into the vital world, only this time it's for good and we leave everything necessary behind. That's why you hear people say: 'It doesn't matter how rich you are, it's better to have love than money, because you can't take your money with you when you die.'

THE DEVELOPING IMAGINATION

One morning set the alarm so that the whole family can get up before dawn and watch the sun rise: 'Ah, look at it coming up over there. See the darkness disappear and all the colours as the sun brings us the light and the warmth. See? Isn't it beautiful?' And then in the evening: 'Come on, let's go and watch the sunset over the lake, where the colours are reflected in the water, and you can tell me all about the beauty you see.'

A child who's seen the sunrise does not need to imagine one. A child who has held a cat and stroked its fur does not need to imagine a cat. Better to discover the earth and the animals through the living reality than through cartoon films or talking cats in storybooks. A cat does not talk. Should a child be encouraged to imagine that a cat or any other animal can talk? Is that good? Is it a good preparation for life in a world where cats don't talk; a world which is not at all as people like to imagine?

Imagination is thinking about something that's not real, not here now. We should introduce children to the wonder of the earth as it is; not as we would like it to be, but as it is when we see it in the moment. That gets rid of the imagination. It also gets rid of worry. Imagination, pleasant thoughts, worry — they are all the same. You might be imagining nice, pleasant things but they are things that are not here now. Worry is thinking about unpleasant things that are not here now either.

I do not worry, for my mind is straight and clear; and the reason is that I don't imagine anything. I don't use imagination, but I am creative. If I go to write something, I write. If I make love, I love. If I go to do anything, I am creative. I don't think about whatever I'm going to do. I just do it. Or I look inside myself to see what arises.

'Looking' is not 'thinking'. I don't think. When I look to see what's arising, it's like looking into a room to see what's there. I'm not thinking. Thinking makes my mind discursive: 'looking' makes it straight.

True creativity has no imagination. All creativity is in the body. Nobody has ever done anything creative outside the body and no-one ever will. The creative genius works in the moment, now, without any imaginative thinking. The creativity of the body is always now. Imagination is the creativity of the self, the unhappy part of every individual that holds on to past hurt and wants life to be other than it is. All self is based on unhappiness or the desire to escape from it. If you have any notion of a 'higher self', forget it; it's the dream of a self that wants to escape itself. The child's desire is to escape the confined life of being in the body in a hostile world. The world of the child's imagination offers escape. But that same psychic space is a future world of fear, worry and self-projection.

So I question the popular idea that it's important to encourage a child's imagination. I know there are theories about the importance of imagination to children. But I have to ask: If it is true that the child's imagination is the source of future worry and fear, is it good to encourage it?

Everyone gets unhappy, including all the child psychologists and theorists. So perhaps they're just promoting more unhappiness. I recall that the famous Dr Spock changed his advice about giving cow's milk to babies after a whole generation had followed his ideas for more than twenty years: 'Oh, sorry folks, I was wrong.' Do you really want to believe in the theories?

The value placed on imaginative thinking in the education of children is another example of the corruption of this society. I am suggesting an alternative way of looking at it, and that allows you in the moment to be less imaginative, more creative.

Look creatively at these questions for yourself. I tell you I do not have to think or imagine anything, that I simply look and see straight. Will you now look inside yourself and see if that is indeed a desirable state? And if so, what are we teaching our children? Are we doing anything wrong?

Asking questions of ourselves — that's the beginning of raising a child in consciousness.

*

Man: I don't see how you can separate imagination from creativity. I don't know that there can be any creative solution to a problem without using the imagination.

Creativity is the root of imagination, but when we overlay imaginative thinking on real creativity we get a mix of the creative and the imagined. The imagined then separates out from the creative and imagination becomes the negative pole of the positive creativity. It is this separation that generates worry, discontent, disharmony and fear. Our imagination is creativity's creation of fear through imagining whatever is not the fact.

The power of real creativity only arises in me when I do not need to imagine anything. Then it can come through the straightness of the fact. Then I can actually be creative with authority and genuine originality. This real creativity is the truth behind the imagination.

Any creative writer will tell you that once you start writing, the story writes itself. You look into yourself and the characters and situations arise through your brain. It doesn't require imagination. People who don't write (and possibly even some writers) might think you would imagine a scene and then write it. That might produce a clever and even entertaining piece of imagination. But if you could do that (without your creativity intervening to change things) it wouldn't produce the gripping originality of a good story.

Man: I would say it's a genuine creative process when a young child paints a picture.

Fair enough. Let's say that both the adult writer and the child painting the picture are acting more or less spontaneously and free of fear — the creativity and the imagination have not separated out.

It's the separative projection of imagination as thinking that creates the problems. That's where the fear and anxiety come from. And the way to get rid of the imaginative element is to return to the fact.

A child afraid of the dark is imagining things in the shadows. So you have to go out at night and look at the fact: 'It's a dark night so we can't see what's going on in the garden, but there's nothing to be afraid of. It's just dark. There are patches of lighter dark in the blackness. There are shadows. And there are the stars. Do you see how black it is between the stars? The same darkness that is always there when the sunlight has gone. Do you see how soft and deep and dark it is? Like the darkness of closing your eyes when you fall asleep . . .'

There's something spontaneously creative in me as I speak to a child like that. I'm not imagining anything. I'm addressing the dark with fidelity, as a fact. I am being creative; not imaginative.

I'm not encouraging the child to imagine what's out there . . .
I am simply resorting to the wonder of the fact.

There is no fear in the fact. The fact is always in the moment.
There is no fear in the moment, even though the body might
tremble or run away. Fear is in the mind. Fear is imagination.

When we come back to the fact we get rid of the imagination
and the fear. In a non-imaginative world (such as the sensory,
physical world that we actually live in) there is no reconstruction
in the mind of what was, or what might be — only the fact of
what is now. It is a fact that I am sitting down now. What I can
see is the fact. The room is a fact. I'm not saying to myself, 'Oh
if only I could stay here a while longer . . .' or 'This is where
we used to come when things were so different.' Where I am
is the fact.

The fact of life inevitably leads to the fact of death. The
imagination cannot address the fact of death without imagining
what death means; and so it burgeons into the great cloud of
imagination — fear.

If I was talking to children about death I would take them
and show them the shell of a crab on the beach, or a shrivelled,
dead spider: 'Pick it up and weigh it in your hands. See how light
it is? It's got no life in it now, has it? Do you see? The creativity
has gone out of it.'

The creativity of the truth is in the fact of death; and in
being able to address it. It is to be able to see through the fact
of life by seeing the fact of death in everything around you;
for eventually you will see that there is no death.

*

Children in our times are encouraged to be imaginative
because they have to be taught to live in the past. Everybody

in the world lives in the past, and everybody in the world suffers. To be like everybody else our children have to suffer.

It is a dreadful thing that we all have to develop an imagination because that same imagination will one day make us suffer. Such as: my lover has left me for another man or woman and I can't get the picture of them out of my mind.

The imagination is fiendish. It is a devil that seeks to leave God's world (here now) to make another world somewhere else some other time.

Man: Do you suggest that in some way we should try to dismantle or suppress the child's imagination? Is that even possible?

No. Only later in life, when you have acquired all the experience you need and have suffered enough, do I say, 'Now get rid of your imagination.'

The imagination has to develop in children on their way out into the world. What we have to do as parents is balance that development by being practical and factual in our everyday interactions with them. We have to help them to find out about the world. We have to teach them to live in it without undue fear or suffering. And to do that we have to continually dismantle the past in ourselves. We have to give them that example.

There's nothing you can dream up that doesn't arise from the past. All imagination is the reconstruction of images from previous experience.

A child scared by monsters has heard of monsters. He has constructed a composite image in himself of what a monster is. Even though a young child might not be able to draw one very precisely, his drawing will represent an emotional response to all the images he's seen and things he's heard about monsters. His imagination is the ability to reconstruct a monster out of those past images and emotions. In other words it is a construction of self. And his primary motivation is the fear or fright in the self that has been stimulated by listening to stories about monsters.

The imagination is constructive. Like a dream, the imagination is the place where we are able to construct something immaterial. Since it is the only thing that a very young child can construct, imagination is our first independent creation.

Through our childhood the constructive force of imagination extends, harnessed to the energies of growth and development. If the energy expressed in the need to develop imagination is suppressed, instead of constructing things, it may wilfully destroy them. This explains some of the negativity and vandalism exhibited by children and youth. So the child's imagination must not be suppressed but balanced by education in consciousness; which means attention to the fact and truth of life through open communication with the parent or teacher.

As we grow into adults the imagination takes over our brains, constructing fantasies to entertain ourselves and fears to plague us. But in a conscious life the truth destroys whatever we imagine and finally, when we have suffered enough, we detach from the imagination. Then we can speak and communicate rightly with real creativity; and we trust that then imagination can sometimes be put to use to do something worthwhile to entertain and instruct us in this existence.

*

Grandmother: I've been encouraging our little two-year old, my grand-daughter, when she's imaginative. I thought it was good for her to use her imagination. Isn't it just natural for little ones? She has imaginary possums and frogs. She asks me to pat them and puts them in my pocket!

She's only two years old. Children of that age and younger show that sort of inclination. They are still innocent. They've only just come out of the intermediate world where everything is connected. There they can do anything and nature, especially, is so beautiful. That's why children love nature and animals.

The little girl is 'imagining' she's got a frog in her hand, but really this is a throwback to the world she just came from, where there are frogs and other lovely things — no hard tables and no having to put food in your mouth with a hard spoon; just a beautiful oneness with nature and a being in touch with nature's creatures. There's a great innocence in children. A very young child is drawn to young things and to the innocence of animals. But society soon gets rid of that.

We call what she's doing 'imagination', but is it? Or is it 'real' in the sense that she's still in touch with that beautiful, innocent state? As we know, some children can talk to what could be called spirits — because the world they've so recently come from contains all sorts of companions, all sorts of things that are not necessarily in their purview in existence. Where they've come from still makes a great impression on them.

That's where the imagination dawns. Then we tell children nursery stories and fairy tales. We start to give them our imagination and they put it onto their knowledge of the other world. As we tell the story, they actually see it enacted. We can see this in their eyes; they're rapt in wonder. They become imaginative themselves and begin to imagine their own stories. Then their imagination gets developed by society, in the anticipation of birthdays, imagining how it good it will be, and in silly stories about Santa Claus for instance. And so the imagination develops — because adults inculcate in children an anticipation of things, so that they imagine life, rather than see the fact of it.

Gradually imagination turns into visualisation and wilfully

thinking about things, which leads to worry. And eventually it leads to fantasies, especially sexual fantasy.

Imagination is the existential side of the reality within. Children should be told right from the beginning about love, truth and being, and reminded where they come from. As the little girl's grandmother you will be able to take her aside and tell her the real story.

'You've come out of a most wonderful world. It's a glorious place and it's a place of love. You know how you love these little creatures like your frog and your possum? Well, I know that those little things are in the wonderful world you've come from. You love that wonderful world and so you're repeating it in this one. In that world your animals are there for you immediately you want them to be. They're not here in this world, though I know you feel they are. This is a very different place where the little animals have taken form. There are frogs here, but not ones that you can just invent.

'The other world is the world of love. You know how you love these little things inside of you? Well, that's love. And it's the world of God. Do you see that the world of God is so wonderful because it's got such beautiful little things in it? Well, that world is still within you.'

If you start in this way you can introduce the child more and more to the world of God and love. As she grows up you will be able to remind her where she comes from and go on telling her about the other world so that she retains the knowledge of it. Then one day you will be able to tell her about life and death.

'In this existence all is separation, you know. We're all separate people here, whereas in the other world nothing is separate. The frogs and the possums and the people — everything — is just one thing. Existence is just like a tunnel. You come in one end and go out the other. When you die you go back straight into God's wonderful world where all the creatures are, except in that world they don't have bodies any more. They're just lovely vital energies. So that's what death is. Death is that life. Well now, where do you think you will go when you die? You'll go back into the world you came from, where everything is beautiful, right and true.

'Here, in this existence, there are so many things to do. And it's not easy to do them. When you're starting to walk you toddle and fall over and it's difficult. But you've got to learn to walk here. And you've got to learn to eat your food here. You know how you have trouble with the spoon? But you've got to use spoons here. That's the nature of this existence. In that other world you don't have to do any of those things, but as you're here, you've got to learn to do what we do here. You've got to learn things here, until such time as you finish your useful life. All lives are very useful because something very important is being done here. But when we get old we die — some die before they get old — but then we all go back to that beautiful state of the other world.'

If we told the children about the whole of life, we'd be telling them the truth. For death is life; and living is only a half-life.

*

Mother: I think imagination is an important part of play. All play is a learning experience and there's a real need for children to play imaginatively. They take things that haven't happened to them and act them out to get some idea of what those things feel like. So the child might act out a mouse being chased by a cat, and actually feel what that would be like for the animals. It's imagination, but it's a way of learning about things that are not actually experienced in real life. So I do not want to discourage imaginative play in my little boy . . .

I do not say you should discourage imaginative play. But

the sooner you bring him back to this world, the better. What I say is that the child's imagination has a deep significance for all of us because it must turn into a monster of momentum, worry and fear.

It is all a matter of educating the consciousness. I say the child is not really conscious of what he is doing when he's in his fantasy world. He does not know that he's pretending to be a mouse to find out what it feels like to have a cat on your tail. What is he is actually doing is entertaining himself subconsciously with fear. Whether or not this is useful in stimulating his 'fright and flight' reflexes, it is a subconscious and not a conscious process.

I suggest you join the child in his play and ask him to tell you what's happening in the world of his imagination. Then you can tell him what's happening to you in the world of actual fact. In this way you encourage a right balance.

Father: It's not so easy to share his private world. He gets deeply involved in what he's doing in secret. Sometimes we can hear him from the next room talking to himself and acting things out. If we suddenly walk in, and he's aware that we've been watching him, he gets embarrassed and awkward. He's likely to stop or tell us to go away.

All children do this and we all did it. But the truth is that this private fantasy world is the work of the devil in man; a separate creation. In our ignorance we praise imagination but can you see how it becomes an invitation to guilt and fear?

A child who disappears into a secret world, populated with imaginary friends, is seeking a substitute world under his own control because his parents, teachers and everyone around him are not making the actual world sufficiently conscious for him. So I say it is best to bring him back as soon as possible to this world, where you can talk to him consciously about life and what is actually happening.

You have to get him to open up and talk to you about it. Join the boy in the world of his imagination and then in your wisdom you may be able to see what's actually happening. Better to share his fantasy as the caring loving parent, than to have him dwell there on his own. Get him to describe what's going on. Then when you come into the room, you will be his friend in that world, not an intruder. At present he knows he can do what he likes in his fantasy world because he is its sole creator. He will be very suspicious of any intrusion because it's not his own invention.

To be able to go into a secret place inside ourselves and invent a fantastic world is part of our organism's way of protecting itself against the loneliness of being in existence. To be in a human body separate from every other body is a most isolated existence. None of us can really cope with it, especially as children, so we invent imaginative worlds for ourselves where all the things are part of one creation, our own.

The truth is that all things are one creation and if we were able to see everything that's happening on this earth now, we would see that we are all connected with everything else around us by an extraordinary psychic network or plasma. But to be denied that connection by the appearance of things, to have to fend for myself, when really I am connected with the movement of all things — that's very difficult to cope with. That's why imaginative fantasies arise.

TELLING STORIES

A ll children love to describe things and tell their own stories. This is part of the emergence and exercise of their creativity, mixed with the developing imagination. While sometimes their stories will be very imaginative, at other times you won't know if it's a story or actual experience.

Around the ages of nine to twelve you'll find they love to retell the story of a book or movie; everything that happened from beginning to end. Or they insist on telling you every detail of what someone did at school. This is part of the development of the memory. They want to name everything they see. They are learning to regurgitate experience and state it.

Woman: I'm a nanny to two little girls. One of them is two and a half years and she chatters constantly. It seems to go on all the time but especially when we're driving along in the car; she's naming everything she sees, asking questions, and never stops talking. I'm not sure what to do about it, or if I should just let her be.

This is a stage most children go through. One thing you can do is to get her to collect all her naming and random thoughts into a narrative. By encouraging her to give her experience some formal shape, you will help to transform the momentum in her.

'Here's a game. You tell me a story . . .'

'What shall I tell the story about?'

'About everything you saw when we went out in the car today. But to be a good story it must have a beginning, a middle and an end . . .'

If the story doesn't come to an end you can say: 'But you haven't told me the end yet. Now, what's the end of the story?'

What you're endeavouring to do is break her momentum. The storytelling helps her to give her experience a more conscious form.

Woman: I spend quite a lot of time reading stories to the children. Often just to keep them occupied. But I think some stories are good for them to hear. There's some educational purpose.

Yes, there is a purpose in telling stories to young children, which is to inform them about the world they are entering. It is a place of past and future and young children are educated to live in it through the stories you read them. As they grow up, literature and movies expose them to more of the world; and, as entertainment, stories help us cope with what the world is.

Mother: Do you have any advice about the best kind of stories for children? Before I read a book to a child I read it myself first, to ensure it's suitable. Sometimes I just don't know whether it's appropriate or not.

I do suggest that you are selective about the books and

movies that young children read or watch; and later on, you guide them in making their choices. I would avoid the fantastic, violent or sentimental and select stories that present the incidents of real life, historical and contemporary, as seen through a child's eyes. Or myths, legends and traditional tales that still have the ring of truth.

As a general rule, the best stories stay close to the truth of life and feature heroism, nobility and love.

Man: Myths and legends often deal with fantastic events. They appeal to the imagination. Do you make a distinction between myth and fantasy?

Yes. Myth is the only way the truth of life can be described. At a certain level of the mind myth can seem to be imagination. Sometimes I write or speak about something that may seem to be fantastic but really it is myth, because I am looking at a structure of reality or truth inside of me.

The truth is always seen behind the fact and the more we face the fact, the more we perceive the truth. I see the fact. Behind the fact I realise the truth. Behind the truth I see into the myth of things. I see into God's mind. I am no different in this from you. When you hear the myth of life spoken you see into it and you say, 'Somehow I know this. This is the truth.' So myth is the expression and story of truth.

This of course is demonstrated by the great world myths. The Mahabarata is the endeavour to express the truth of the story of the whole universe. The story of Adam and Eve is the endeavour to express the myth of man and woman and how the world began. Every great myth is an aspect of an idea in God's mind.

In God's mind there is no philosophy; no hazy, fragmented view of life such as we find in the world of philosophies. God's mind is not our human mind, filled with fantasies and half-truths; based in pain, love of suffering and defence of anger. The human mind is filled with everything poisonous and problem-making. In the myth of life the human mind is the smog of pollution you see over the cities of the earth, distorting the light of the sun over Los Angeles, London, and even Sydney. When I was a boy I used to notice a little bit of haze over Sydney harbour, but now when I fly in I am amazed how often there is thick smog over the city. Can we clean up the pollution? Well, I have no smog in me, no problem. There's nothing in my human mind any more. So I am able to look into God's mind.

So the difference between fantasy and myth is the direct perception of the fact or the truth. Out of that perception comes the knowledge which is expressed as myth. By taking responsibility for the children and for your life now, you can start to clear the haze of fantasy from the human mind.

＊

Man: Is there any virtue in telling children fairy stories?

The virtue is that it is entertaining. But we should inform children of what entertainment is and tell them that the stories are not true.

'This is a fairy story, but there are no such things as fairies — unless you can show me one. We need to be entertained in this existence. Your Mummy and I will watch television or a video when we want to be entertained, but we never think the video or story is the truth. The actors in the films are only entertaining us. Although we'd like to think the story is true, they're only acting it — they are not really doing it. The more we think it's true the more we identify emotionally with what's happening; and then we get tense. So it's important to remember that it's just a story, like a game. Then we can play the game and enjoy it, can't we?'

Man: There's a theory that fairy stories work in the subconscious of children and prepare them for the cruelties of adult life. For example, 'Little Red Riding Hood' and other tales of that sort contain an element of horror, a reflection of the horror in the world, presented in an acceptable and entertaining way.

There's no doubt these stories contain elements of horror, but is the horror introduced to the child in a right way? As you say, it works in the subconscious. Do the storytellers, or parents reading the stories to children, gloss over the horror? Do they run away from the reality of the fairy story, which is usually very violent? — 'The wolf has eaten Granny and is about to devour the little girl too. But I won't make anything of it. I'll gloss over that and leave it to the kid's subconscious to work it out.' Or is it better to say: 'Little Red Riding Hood is a most violent tale. I might have to look at this story which could frighten my child with its violence. Unless I can explain what it's about, I won't introduce it to the children.'

There's a strange psychic dichotomy in the story. We are asked to imagine Granny, sitting up in bed with her glasses on — a sweet, safe and reassuring gloss of the imagination. Set against it is the image of the terrible Big Bad Wolf who is impersonating her. 'What big teeth you've got!' It's a lovely little folk tale, with flashes of sheer terror.

What is the story really about? If I were prepared to go into it with a child, I would talk about what happens in the real world when children leave the protection of their families; they find it's a cruel and hostile place where civilisation is a very thin human gloss on the animal law of survival — eat and be eaten.

Any entertainment or story can be used to instruct and inform the child about the world.

Man: Is that right? What about the 'mindless violence' of so much popular entertainment, movies in particular? Obviously some things have more quality than others. But I suppose you can use anything to talk about the truth of it.

So much entertainment engenders simulated fear or characterises terrible violence — including children's video games and TV shows and even cartoon films made for the youngest age-group. We have to ask what the purpose is of all this fake violence and simulated horror. Is it because the entertainment makes the cruelty of the world acceptable?

Why are there always goodies and baddies in films? Is it because the movies are simplified pictures of what the world is really like? Increasingly people look at the real world as if it is a movie. They are more and more influenced by what they see on the screen. More and more the world is being run by movie actors.

So, yes, at the appropriate moment, talk to the children about it.

'I don't enjoy this kind of film at all. But I can understand that it entertains you, if it does. To entertain ourselves we always seem to need a goody and a baddy. You'll see them in every movie, in some way or other. The goody stands for what we think is grand or beautiful. The baddy stands for what is bad or evil. The goody tries to beat the baddy and usually does; but not always, because we're a quirky society these days and sometimes it's more exciting if the baddy overcomes the goody. Films like that are there to excite you. You should know that when you get excited there's likely to be a negative reaction of some kind. So it's best not to think about them afterwards. And what you should always remember is that the movies are entertainment. They are not the real world.'

GOING TO SCHOOL

You can remain largely responsible for everything that influences your children until they go to school. Whichever school they go to will put the world into them. You want to do your best for your children, but their schooling is to a great extent always beyond your control.

What can you do? Some parents, wanting to give their children a better start, send them to a special school where the standard of education is thought to be higher, or where there is apparently more understanding of truth and love. But it doesn't matter how good, true or real the teaching is, if it comes through schoolteachers who are themselves ignorant or emotional, there will be ignorance and emotion in the teaching. The Montessori and the Steiner schools, for example, are systems where certain precepts are laid down as a basis for teaching. I don't know in detail what the teachings are; I do not criticise them. But every teaching has to come through a person. This is a psychic life and it is the invisible psychic influences on us that work for good or do the damage. You have to know that the schoolteachers are doing their best but they are always the weak link, whatever the education system.

The reason children go to school is to get more experience of the world. What you have to do is face the fact of the situation and know that your child has to enter the world. You can do your best to send your children to a school consistent with your ideas about education, but to get a right preparation for life they might have to go to the local state school. Then every day when they come home again, you can do your best to take the world out of them.

Mother: Because of our reservations about the state education system we wanted to find an alternative for Ben but it's a hopeless task, especially in the area where we live. The only possible type of education that would be acceptable, we thought, might be in a Steiner school so we visited one and spoke to the teachers and other parents. But it didn't seem to be quite right for us and for various reasons we do not want to move to be near one of these schools. So when the time came we sent Ben to the local junior school. So far he's enjoying it but I am getting worried because he's learning things that I think are not important, and missing out on other things like creativity. His class teacher seems very kind but the attitude of teachers generally is not one I feel is right — not one of love. I know I have a tendency to want everything to be perfect for Ben, which is impossible. Perhaps I can make things better by getting involved with the school as a parent, but the fact is there just isn't a school that approaches life the way we do at home.

The general course of education in a state school system will reflect the condition of society. So state schools will teach the values of the world. That is not to demean the efforts of conscientious individual teachers who endeavour to impart what they know to be real and true. But it is extremely difficult for them to do it against the force of a society such as ours.

You have looked at the alternatives and, as you say, the most prominent system based on apparently spiritual values is the Steiner education. As I have heard, it involves the child in physical and creative activity associated with the harmony of the earth. [It is based on the work of Rudolf Steiner, a philosopher and spiritual teacher who died in 1925.] Presumably Steiner school teachers know the value of love and the importance of retaining that connection to the earth which I have said is so important in raising children. However, there are probably aspects of a Steiner education that conflict with the needs of children today because the teaching is based on out-of-date philosophic ideals.

Steiner lived and taught when materialism had not yet completely overtaken western culture and Christian belief was still all-pervasive. But we are no longer believers. Our society is materialistic, dishonest and has no spiritual values. As individuals we are becoming more and more empirical — working not on the basis of ideals or faith but from observation and experience. What is positive in this is that we now have the opportunity to see beyond beliefs and to know what is beyond the indoctrination of religions. We have the opportunity to perceive what is true using our own intelligence. This means we can be true to what is occurring every moment, as our own immediate experience — not true to a belief in anything or to feelings, convictions or any experience of the past. This is fundamental in my teaching and what I call 'being true to the situation'.

So we have to look at the situation and the purpose that the state school serves. It takes children into a microcosm of the wider society. They encounter at school what they'll find in the wider society. A Steiner education, in comparison, is likely to promote the protective cocoon of a model society which does not exist in the contemporary world. Being true to the situation, children have to have the opportunity to confront and be confronted by the world; provided they are also being introduced to the truth of it and continuously informed what the situation is.

'When you come home from school, I want you to come and tell me about your experience today. I will find the time to be with you so that we can talk about anything you want to talk about. We can talk about any situation that happened at school, with the teacher or the other boys and girls, and then you can tell me how you handled it. If necessary, we can look at it together to see how you might handle it better in the future; because you have to learn how to handle situations in life. The things that happen at school are the same kind of things that you'll encounter in the world when you grow up. You have to discover what society is like; that's one of the reasons why we go to school.'

The loving parent has to provide the other side of the story, the part the school will not teach (or cannot teach). If you see that there are things that are not being taught at school then it's your job to impart them.

*

Mother: Laura is going to school in England but she began her schooling in California where the system is very different. The method of teaching was more relaxed and there was more emphasis on creative play, less on discipline. Now she spends a lot more time working at a desk. There are more rules. And she has to go to a morning Assembly which of course is Christian. I am concerned about the effect on her of this sort of education.

The school Assembly with its emphasis on religion is part of the English system and you can't change it. Nominally it's a Christian society, although as everyone can observe, practising members of the Church are now a very small minority, which suggests that most teachers at Assembly are unlikely to be practising Christians. Because the state school system has to follow what's orthodox the situation cannot change until society as a whole rejects this dishonesty.

On the question of rules and discipline: right discipline (not hard or grinding, of course) is essential for children, just as it is in adult spiritual life. Without right discipline children become self-indulgent and unable to function adequately. As young adults they flop around like jellyfish, with no clear edge to them. They become restless and can't stick at anything for long. Unable to blend in with society they keep on the move and lose themselves. Such behaviour comes from lack of right discipline in younger years.

Eventually we have to be disciplined; and if we don't discipline ourselves, it has to be done for us. If parents don't impose it, then the world will. Children have to go to school and eventually they have to go to work. As a general rule we have to be disciplined to go to work and earn a living. We can try to avoid it, do things our own way and drop out of society — but only for so long.

There is a great reaction in the world to this need for discipline. So there are people who want a life where they don't have to settle down, a job where they can do things in their own way or time; where they can do what they might call creative work. But you will find that such people get depressed easily and lose direction. They start to feel bad if they're not really being creative; and they find that their love-life is not fulfilling. It requires great self-discipline to get your life right, especially your love-life.

You cannot be honest and true to the situation unless you are self-disciplined. You need to have had the experience of being disciplined to understand and value it so that it becomes a way of life inside yourself rather than one imposed by an outside order.

Mother: What about the emphasis on academic work at the expense of play and physical exercise?

If you see that the child is not getting enough exercise or play you can do something about it out of school hours.

The need for play changes as the child grows up. Toddlers during the age of physical identification with the world need to touch things, manipulate things with their bodies and be physically involved in their surroundings. As they get older they play with other children to get social skills. And later on games and pastimes help them to acquire the mental discipline needed to stay focused.

The ability to focus on a particular subject is an important part of the self-discipline that children have to acquire. I deliberately use the word 'focus' and not 'concentrate'. To focus on something is to get it in a right perspective. It is the ability to contain the perception so that it's not wandering off, restless or looking for entertainment and distraction. Concentration, on the other hand, requires a forceful and exclusive narrowing of the attention which eventually causes children to become emotional. Never teach a child to concentrate.

We all know that when we were at school we were taught things that seemed to have no practical use whatsoever — in my day, all those dates in history. Why did they teach so many subjects that had no application to our careers or to life as we know it? The answer is that we were being taught to focus our minds.

No matter how much we might be opposed to the modern world, if we're going to exist rightly in society, and not feel a failure or get depressed, we have to be able to focus our attention for a certain length of time on a particular subject or activity. This was not necessary two or three thousand years ago but today society demands it. We can kick against the world's mental structures to a degree but we can't rebel against them without causing a reaction inside ourselves which will eventually lead to feelings of inadequacy.

Some education methods are very free and liberal and encourage creativity. Others apply academic disciplines from an early age. When a child is moved from one school to another, it is likely to cause some confusion. The way to handle it, of course, is to sit down and talk about the situation together. Explain that this is a phase of change, and why the new stage in the child's life has happened.

Support your daughter and the new school system, as much as you can, so that she doesn't become negative about the school or react against the system. That doesn't mean you endorse it as 'good'. It means seeing the principle behind what's going on so that you can explain to her what lies behind it. And always tell or remind her that nothing is forever; everything changes.

*

Father: Children are taught things at school which are so opposed to some of the things you recommend that it can become quite confusing for both them and us.

As I say, you have to keep informing the children of the difference between what happens in the world and what you are endeavouring to do with your life. You have to explain what's happening and give them a balanced understanding of why life at school is different.

'Going to school is necessary, like money is necessary. Going to school is part of your self-development and self, like money, is necessary to the world. But back here at home it is our job to correct the worldly influences that you are being exposed to. We have to show you that there is both a necessary outer world and a vital inner life.

'So I want to remind you that we are living two lives at once. In one life we endeavour to live the truth and have love and harmony in our home. In the other we go to school and learn the ways of the world. We accept the way the world is and what school teaches us about it. But there are many things that you will not be taught at school. Like the things we practise in this family. Our two lives are led in parallel. At home we are leading you into the inner life of love and truth, while at school you are led into the world. You have to have both . . .'

Father: The main difference I notice is that at school the kids are encouraged to be emotional, to miss people for example. Whereas at home we put a stop to anything sentimental as quickly as possible. Any advice on how to handle that?

Yes. As soon as the children come home from school, be sure to open up a dialogue. If you show them that you have a true and lively interest in what's happened in their day, they will open up to you. Then you might hear something that needs addressing; such as the sentiment you mention, about missing people.

'I want to tell you what happens when you feel that you miss someone. It makes you feel sad. In society, which is the world where your school is, people like to miss their friends when they go away. For them the sad feeling is true; and they really feel it. The more they think about the missing person the sadder they get. Then, when the friend comes back again they get excited. If they hadn't missed each other to start with they wouldn't be able to get so excited. In other words, people in the world like to miss people and be sad because they like to get excited. That's the way the world works and you're going to encounter it all the time.

'Now, because we are endeavouring to live a different way, to be true to life as it is, I want you to know the truth. So we have to ask an intelligent question: If you love me, how can you miss me?

'Look at me now, or look at Mummy, and you feel the love in you, don't you? Every day I have to leave you to go to work. Sometimes I am gone for a week or two. And from time to time Mummy may have to go away. Everybody has to go somewhere at sometime. But even while we're gone you can still feel the love in you. Our bodies come and go but the love stays. That means you don't have to miss our bodies when they are gone. What you have to do is get used to feeling your love of us and then you won't miss us and feel sad. If I have to stay away an extra day, or for some reason I don't come home on time, there is no need to miss me. If you love me it is best never to miss me, because it is best not to be unhappy.'

Speaking like that prepares the child for when someone dies or doesn't come back. Then you can use the same approach: 'Everything has to leave us in this world, but the love is always there.'

*

Mother: What do you do with children who don't want to go to school? My little boy has started at nursery school and hates going. He cries bitterly every time I leave him there. It's very painful for me. I pick him up later and they tell me he's been very shy and quiet and hasn't wanted to join in. He says he feels very lonely.

Why does he cry when you leave him? — because his emotion is attempting to gain your sympathy so that you'll take him home. Of course it's very painful for you. You are being manipulated.

He feels lonely because he's cutting himself off from the others. That usually indicates a problem. Watch to see what it is. Keep asking the child to express all that he's feeling — not just that he's lonely — although he will not open up easily to

231

you if the problem is something he's hiding, or trying to keep from uttering.

I suggest you explain to him why he has to go to school and teach him how to give his sweet nature. It's time for him to open up the socialising aspect of his nature as a human being.

'Come over here and sit down while I speak to you. You have to go to school like all the other children, because you have to learn about the world and learn how to be with other people. Now, you don't want to go on feeling lonely when you're there, do you? If you want to be lonely, that's the same as wanting to be unhappy, isn't it? I don't want you to be unhappy, so I'm going to tell you something important. You are lonely because you are not giving the other children your sweet nature. We all have to learn that if we don't give to others in this way, then we don't receive any sweetness back from them. I know you've got a sweet nature, and it would be good if you could show it to the other children.

'So let's learn how to do it. It's quite easy. All you've got to do is start with a smile or go over and say hello. You'll find that usually other people will respond with a smile. Sometimes they won't, because they might be feeling lonely or unhappy themselves. But, you know, you will find that there's always someone in the playground you can play with . . .'

If you see him isolating himself when you are with him, give him a gentle reminder: 'Do you know you're cutting yourself off again? You're making yourself small. This is a big world and we're all here together, so I want you to open up and then we will all enjoy being with you.'

*

Father: We have two young children and from time to time they show signs of anxiety about school. They say they don't want to go, or Monday morning comes and they say they're feeling sick. We have to work out whether there's really something physically wrong, or it's emotional because there's something wrong at school.

Is it something they do because they need more time at home? Or is it really a refusal to face the situation? I suspect it is mainly just avoidance because I remember skipping school myself at their age.

I also recall having anxiety about school. First of all, find out if there's a particular aspect of the situation at school that causes the anxiety. Make time for a regular dialogue with them about the day at school; not encouraging them to talk too much about any unhappiness they felt, but listening for where there might be real problems, meaning those that they are not likely to be exaggerating. It might be a situation of bullying or something of that kind. Listen carefully to what they say. If there is anything valid behind the anxiety you can take the appropriate action.

There will usually be stresses and strains associated with school which may not be overtly problematical, but will nevertheless be there because going to school is an unnatural activity, albeit a necessary one. Although children have to be told that it is necessary for them to go to school to learn what they are taught there, this in itself can create anxiety. They are likely to build up emotion about going to school simply through thinking about it and looking ahead, which is what they are generally taught to do. Monday-itis is an example of this. After being at home for the whole weekend, the prospect of having to go to school again, combined perhaps with a specific anxiety about what might happen on Monday, will come together in the subconscious as 'I don't want to go'.

Thinking about 'having to go when I don't want to' will produce the symptoms of anxiety, frustration and headaches, stomach-ache or some other disorder. Children can feign these things — I can remember doing it myself — but there may be actual physical pain and I would not eliminate that possibility. However, a child who is repeatedly allowed to get off school because of this anxiety, or symptoms associated with it, will start to approach situations with an excuse rather than facing them directly.

It is important to open this up with your children and speak to them about it.

'I want you to understand that going to school is something you have to face. It's a situation in life, and as you grow up you're always going to have to face situations when really you don't want to. But that's what life is. It's necessary for everybody to go to school, so it is best to face the fact. If you can only face it, you won't have this anxiety in you to the same degree. I understand how it can occur but it's no good being anxious. We have to rise above it and go and do whatever we have to do.

'You know, your headache is quite likely to be the anxiety showing up in your face, because the worried part of you doesn't want to have to front up to the maths lesson tomorrow. Sometimes we give our bodies pains like that by worrying about things that haven't even happened yet. And that's silly, isn't it? So it's best not to think about school over the weekend, and just get up on Monday and go, just like Daddy has to get up and go to work whether he likes it or not. We will help you when it gets difficult. Just come and talk to us whenever you get worried.'

PARENTS AS TEACHERS

O ur job as parents and educators is to raise the consciousness of the children and prepare them for life in the adult
world. It begins the moment we hold the baby in our arms and
speak with love. It continues in every conversation as the child
grows, and we impart our wisdom about the ways of the
world; and in every moment that we reveal to the child the
wonders of the earth and the universe.

To raise children in consciousness is to love them and walk
with them and talk about life. Show them the leaves of the trees.
Dig into the earth and show them the worms. Break open the
apple and have a look at the pips. Show them the difference
between an apple and an orange. Show them all these
wonderful things and be involved as much as you can in their
discoveries. Above all, speak with them intelligently about their
observations of life and listen attentively to what they say.

It is essential that from an early age there should be open
communication with children about what interests them. Much

of the wilful, sullen and rebellious behaviour exhibited by youth arises because as young children they were not allowed to report on what they were seeing or experiencing. Their parents were too busy to spend time with them.

Not listening to children creates a ground of emotion and resentment; a feeling of contraction — of not being able to express myself. As everything within must come out, the feeling of repression inevitably finds expression, sometimes in a violent or destructive form.

As in the youth, so in the adult. A man trying to love a woman, unable to express his love, is suddenly vicious and blurts out a stream of cruel words. Afterwards neither he nor she can comprehend it. 'Look, I'm terribly sorry. I didn't mean it. I don't know what came over me.' This is a typical reaction conditioned by a blockage in the communication between parent and child.

Speaking with children is like speaking with anyone else in the truth. When you are asked a question you reply from your own experience. You don't enter into a discussion that leads away from the fact or engage in any argument that requires the taking of positions.

Don't try to change the child's mind, because you're likely to run into opposition, argument and disturbance. Rely on pointing out the fact and checking to see if it has changed.

The guidelines are: Don't go beyond your own experience. Be as honest as you can. And always endeavour to answer the question.

Children come up with some wonderful observations and give you plenty of opportunity to answer straight questions. Let them ask you anything at all. Take them into your confidence. And then when they get to the age of puberty they will be more likely to come and ask you about sex and love. It's very rare for parents to have that wonderful, honest and open communication with a teenager. But it arises from interacting rightly with them from the earliest days, and from being able to respond to the child's everyday enquiries.

Remember that children are not 'just children'. Every child is an intelligence in a body with very little experience. The intelligence is infinitely old; in essence as old as life itself. It is limited only by the experience of the child's body. When we address the child intelligently and speak with as little emotion as possible we open up an energetic contact with a vast knowledge. The response from that place will sometimes be surprisingly intelligent, even in an infant only one or two years old; and all parents will know how remarkable it can be. That is because life on earth did not begin with my birthday; or your child's. It is at least two thousand million years old. The knowledge and energy of that life is within every body; although whether it's accessible at any time is determined by something far more profound than any of us can ever utter or name.

The more we can introduce a child to the wonders of the natural world and existence, the more we open up a channel into the vast memory of life on earth — the essential life of every child. That is why it is so important to continually introduce children to the works of nature. And when they come up with their questions you will be able to go into your experience of life, your earth experience, to answer them and tell them how things probably developed — because everything develops out of the earth.

There is the potential in everybody to reach into the psyche, to see or realise some truth, and everybody has intimations, insights or experiences of the inner life. But people in this society are so conditioned by the scientific mind, with its pretensions to truth, that any direct experience of the psyche is immediately doubted: 'It must be your imagination!' The conditioning is such that everyone supports the doubt. This will have happened to you at different times in your life, and to your mother and father, and it will be happening to your children.

A boy comes up to his father and says: 'Daddy, I've just been talking to someone in the garden. It wasn't a man and it wasn't a woman. I was just talking to it.'

'Oh yes . . .' says Dad, glancing over his newspaper, 'Dreaming again, are you? Don't be silly. There's no one there. Now go and play . . . I'm busy.'

The boy is in touch with the inner psychic world and all the adult does is kill the communication. The father is in the outer world of The Daily Telegraph; the mental world, not the psychic. He's gone mental. The boy stands no chance of being heard. The more we deny the opportunity to describe experiences, realisations and insights into the psychic world or inner life, the more we kill the inner life in ourselves and our children.

When we are in touch with the earth we are in touch with our being, because the earth is a being. The mental world is not; it's an entity, a momentum, always rolling on, like the television news — passing quickly to the next item, forgetting the last as soon as it's seen because the world's already moved on to the latest news. The mental world is an entity possessing us and it captures our brains as we lose touch with the earth. We have got to preserve the earth, or the being, for our children.

'Come on, let's go and pick some flowers. You choose some . . . Now, look at that! What is it? — climbing up the plant? An ant! I wonder what it's doing climbing up to the top of the flower? What do you think it's doing? We don't want the ant to come with us when we take the flower indoors so let's put it down here. Gently . . . . Okay.

'Now, I'll tell you something about flowers. They have a sort of consciousness, you know. It's a different intelligence to ours, more instinctive, but it's still part of the being of the earth. Although the flower doesn't seem to be moving and living like us, it moves in ways that we can't see and it is as much a part of the whole living world as everything else that lives around us.

'We're all connected by a great invisible being. All the flowers are a part of it, just as all the people are. Deep inside ourselves we're all connected to the same Being. This flower is the same Being — being a flower. And I am the same Being — being Barry. And you are being it too.

'So, we have picked this flower, and because we're going to enjoy having it with us in the house, we will thank it for being so beautiful. Talking to the flower is just like talking to our own being: "Flower, we are going to put you into our house to make it more beautiful, because we love the earth and you are like a piece of the earth suddenly come out to us saying 'Here I am!' You're so beautiful. Thank you, flower."

'That's how we give our gratitude to the being behind the flower. And it's important that we do not just say a quick thanks but really say "Thank you" when someone does something for us, like giving us this beauty, because we're really saying thank you to the being of the person, the same being that's behind everything.'

Talk to children like that and they quickly get the idea that there's a being behind every form. Talk to your children about the life of the earth and it balances all the news stories they will hear. Wherever they go they will constantly be informed about the mental world. Who else but you will inform your child of the truth and the life that is not the world?

The great problem of our times is that mentality dominates our being in the body. We have fashioned a world out of all our hopes, ideas and ambitions and now it sits like a suit of concrete clothes on the natural body of the earth. What we call the world is the proliferating superstructure that we impose on the planet.

Our job as parents is to bring our children back to earth. In reality everything happens on earth and nothing real happens in the world. But the magnet of the world is very strong and we are continually persuaded otherwise. The waves of the world are continually lapping around the house.

The most important thing of all in raising your children in consciousness is to inform them right from the beginning: 'There is not only this outer world. There's another place within us. There's a greater reality behind living and it's called life.'

While Simon lived with me I often took the chance to talk to him about the difference between the inner life and the mental world. One day I was working in the garden when he arrived home from school. He came over and we started to talk about his day. He had been doing a geography lesson, not his favourite subject . . .

'And do they teach you the difference between the world and the earth?'

'Aren't they the same?'

'No. People use the words as if they are, but when there are two words it usually means there are two things. And that's how it is with the world and the earth. The world isn't the earth. The earth is the planet on which the forests grow, the seas roll, the rain falls, the farmers plant their crops. The earth is the giver of life. All life lives on the earth and off the earth. That's what the earth is. The world is what man has made — houses, cities, roads, boats, aeroplanes, all that sort of thing. First there's the earth and all the natural life on it and then on top of it man has built the world.

'But that's only half the story. The world's much bigger than that. The other half is not so easy to see. To understand this, we'll have to play a game . . .'

I asked him to show me the ocean. This was impossible. We were twenty miles inland. He looked puzzled: 'We can't see it from the garden. How can I? I can't.'

'No,' I said, 'You can't. Because the ocean is not here. But you can think about the ocean. And when you think about it, it's there in your head, isn't it? Are you imagining it? Are you thinking about it?'

'Yes.'

'Can you see it in your mind?'

'Sort of.'

'Well, that's where the other half of the world is — in thought, in your head. So, let's have another go. I want you to think about your bike. Are you thinking about it?'

'Yes,' he said, with a very serious look on his face.

'Show me your bike.'

Now he was frowning: 'What? You only asked me to think about it. It's in the garage. No, I think it's by the gate. Anyway it's got a puncture.'

'That's right. Now, we are speaking about the difference between the earth and the world. Everything you've been thinking about is the world. All the people on earth have thought about so many things — like you did just then — that they've built a world of thought. And this world of thought makes people unhappy. I'll show you how. Ready?

'If someone came over and told us your bike had been run over by a car coming in the gate, and it was completely crushed, you would be upset, wouldn't you? You'd think that your bike was smashed. You'd be sure of it. But then if you ran over and found the bike still there, just as you left it, what would you think? Instead of being pleased you would be upset again — because you had been told a lie. You would have found out that the world is a very unreliable place.

'You see, you can think things that are very worrying but aren't real; and people can tell you things that will make you worry and get upset, although the things are just not true. That's the world. It's not all bad. It's just very unreliable. Everyone has to learn that what they think is happening in the world isn't necessarily happening on earth.'

There are constant opportunities to inform a child about the earth. Whenever you go for a walk there are so many things to point out. For instance, walking along the beach . . .

'Do you see the waves coming in? Do you see the way they reached up the beach this morning and came up as far as this? See where they left behind these bits of dead jellyfish? Now look where the waves are. Way down there. That's because of the tides. The oceans are always moving. Backwards and forwards. And the bigger the ocean, the more they move. That's why the tides come in and go out.'

And there are many opportunities to teach children how things work in the world.

One morning Simon and I were listening to the record player as I prepared his breakfast. A velvet-voiced woman was singing a plaintive song.

I feel so bad, I've got a worried mind
I'm so lonesome all of the time
Since I left my baby behind
On Blue Bayou. . . .

I said, 'Simon, what's she saying? Did she leave her little baby behind?'

'Don't know,' he said listening conscientiously for a clue. He was probably eight at the time and at that age you don't know about such things. The woman sang on about how great it is to be on Blue Bayou, and lamented her lot at being away from the place for so long.

Looking forward to happier times, on Blue Bayou,
I'm going back some day, come what may, to Blue Bayou.

'Why doesn't she go back at the weekend and be happy, Simon? What's stopping her?' He looked at me blankly. 'She doesn't want to go, Simon. She prefers to sing about it. If she wanted to go she could hop on a bus. But she enjoys the blues, the lamenting, the crying. This is how people live. They prefer to sing and talk about how good life once was, instead of how good it is where they are now. And if ever they do go back, it's never the same as they think it's going to be.'

Then I said, 'What's a bayou? Let's look it up.'

We went to the dictionary and I asked him to read what it says: 'Bayou. A creek, secondary water course or sluggish body of water.' I always encouraged him to look up words in the dictionary with me.

A dictionary, an atlas and an encyclopaedia — indispensable aids when your child starts to enquire into things and three things every parent would be well advised to have at home. Simon and I often went over to the bookshelf together. When he was having difficulty with his studies at school I would always endeavour to help him.

One evening I found him sulking in his bedroom. 'What's making you unhappy, Simon?'

'Geography'. He wasn't making any connection with the subject and studying it was tedious. 'Why have I got to do it, Barry?'

'Because studying anything is part of learning about the world. Geography is discovering facts about the earth and that never made anybody unhappy unless they wanted to be doing something else. So when you're studying geography (or anything) look at what it is you are doing. You'll find it's enjoyable to study anything if you can see how it connects with your life.

'Geography is the study of the earth. So let's get the atlas and I'll show you where we live and all the countries where I've been. We'll look at the geography of the land and I'll tell you about it.

'Now look, here's Australia, where we are, and on the other side of the earth is England. Here's a map of Europe. There's England, and there's London. I shall be going there soon. See? And then all the way over the Atlantic Ocean is America. Here's the State of Arizona . . .'

'Is that where the cowboys are?'

'Yes. And remember in the films you see the deserts, and the giant cactus, and those extraordinary flat-topped mountains?'

'Like a bulldozer took the top off?'

'Yes, as though the top of the mountain was chopped straight off. I think they're called mesas. We should look that up. Go and get the encyclopaedia and look under M. . . . Okay, here we are: "Mesa, rocky formation formed by geological processes, soil erosion, etc. Spanish word for table." Ah ha! Do you see in the photographs how these look like tables?'

'Why Spanish, Barry?'

'Well, it says here that Spanish-speaking people used to lived in that area two hundred years ago . . . If ever we get the chance we'll take you and show you a mesa so you can actually see how beautifully nature has carved them out of the land.'

That's how parents can contribute to the child's study of geography. Not as an empty lesson but as a sort of story related to experience. When you want the facts trundle off to the dictionary, atlas and encyclopaedia, but make the subject engaging and participate with the child in the knowledge of the earth, making it worthwhile for you both.

Endeavour never to be too busy to answer a child's questions. Our aim as parents or teachers should always be to continually widen the child's awareness of life and the most mundane comment can lead to an instructive conversation.

I was walking along the beach the other day, near where I live, and I overheard a typically awkward question from a boy of seven or eight. He was tagging along behind his mother, a plump lady, and another woman who was talking about her weight.

The little boy called out, 'Hey Mum, what's a stone?'

As so often happens, the adults brushed aside the child's simple question with a laugh. But a conscious parent would not let the opportunity slip.

'Well, most people these days weigh themselves in kilograms, and that's the modern way, but some things in some places are still measured in 'stones' and I should think that once upon a time, when people wanted to know how much something weighed, say a bunch of bananas, they probably put it on one end of something like a see-saw, picked up a few stones and put them on the other end. When the see-saw was level, they knew that it weighed about the same as the stones. So a 'stone' came to mean a measure of weight. That's probably how it happened.

'You know how if you sit on one end of the see-saw in the playground and someone sits on the other, the one who is closest to the ground is the heaviest.

'Come on we'll go over to the playground and I'll show you what I mean.'

*

Mother: I try to explain things to my little boy (who's six and a half) because he doesn't have a father now. Though I try to talk about things, and what he's interested in, sometimes for me it's very hard to make sense of the world and there are always things I feel I can't explain. I'm afraid sometimes he gets confused or bored by what I'm saying.

Remember that you don't have to go into great detail or tell him more than he wants to know. And when you're explaining or demonstrating something, the important thing is to connect in some simple way with the child's own life or your lives together.

Whenever we are speaking to children, or teaching them, we must of course do it in a way appropriate to their age, without giving more information than they need and acknowledging the limits of their attention span. A child of six or seven, for instance, doesn't want to know more than the answer to the question he has asked; which is why children at that age often find school learning difficult or tedious. They can't easily process the details so they need only the broad picture; the filling-in follows on in time. So I suggest you just listen carefully to what he's asking and answer him honestly from your own experience of life. Then the communication will follow on naturally.

Can you give me an example of something you found difficult to explain to him?

Mother: Sometimes he picks up some idea at school or from his friends . . . It might mean something to them but it's not important to me. There was something recently because it was Christmas. Things go on at Christmas that are confusing to him because we are not Christians.

The Christian context of Christmas creates confusion in very many families. What I suggest is that you balance the Christian story of the Virgin Birth and Nativity by explaining Christmas in terms of the earth and the myth of life.

What a lovely story we can tell the children about how the sun brings warmth and light in one season and cold and darkness at another, and how at one special time of the year all the people celebrate the time when the sun and the season changes direction. Speaking about Christmas as that turning point will help to disabuse them of the wrong religious ideas they acquire in this society.

If Simon had asked me about it, this is what I might have said: 'Let me tell you what Christmas is about. It's a celebration of the change of the season, when the sun reaches its lowest point in the sky in the middle of winter in the Northern Hemisphere, which happens round about Christmas-time. So all the people have a party and celebrate because they know the sun has started to climb higher in the sky. With each day that passes the dark nights will grow shorter. And I can tell you that in Europe, in winter, that's really something to celebrate! They've been celebrating this from very ancient times, long before the birth of Jesus. But the Christians say that December 25th was Jesus' birthday, so they celebrate that at the same time.

'All the traditions of Christmas come from the northern half of the earth, where it is cold in winter and there's snow, ice and dark days. But you know, I live in Australia, on the other side of the earth, which is called the Southern Hemisphere. This is where the sun comes to when it's winter in the North. Here Christmas is a celebration of the warmest and sunniest days.

'I'll go and get the photograph album . . . Look, you can see me here, when I was in Europe in the winter. I'm all wrapped up and feeling the cold. There's ice on the trees and snow on the ground. There's not a blade of grass to be seen anywhere. But when the sun starts to warm up the earth, the ice melts, the blades of grass show through and the birds start to sing again.

'Now let's get the atlas out and I'll show you what I mean by the Northern and the Southern Hemispheres . . .'

Do you see what I am endeavouring to do? The aim is to engage the boy's attention and stimulate his knowledge of the earth, in order to balance the information he receives from the world. And the aim is to make every demonstration an invitation to participate in life.

*

Father: What can be done to encourage a child to participate more? My boy (he's four and a half) won't join in the dance class at nursery school. When they did a little play he turned his back to the audience and wouldn't sing. I try to encourage him but it seems counter-productive.

This is characteristic behaviour at his age. He's passing through that stage. Some subconscious emotion is asserting itself. You are probably right not to push him into anything that will hit the emotion. But what does he enjoy doing? How about encouraging him in that? It's your job to find out whatever it is, by observing what he's drawn to, and then to get him involved in it. That would be the positive way of approaching his negativity.

When you find him doing something that you can encourage you could say: 'How would you like to go and learn how to do that? Would you like to do something about it? We could do it together, perhaps. Let's go down to the shop and see if we can get what we need. I'll do it with you.'

He might start by opposing what he thinks you feel he ought to be doing, but sooner or later he'll probably come round and find that he enjoys doing it after all. One day he might even enjoy dancing or singing in a school concert, but at this stage he needs to do more of what he would like to do. Whatever it is, just watch to see that it is constructive and then encourage him in a right way.

*

We should always be watching to see what our children are interested in so that we can encourage the interest. To really love as parents we have to be there for them, to share their love. Don't just leave them to their own devices. Show that you are interested. Give up some of your time to really find out about whatever it is. Go off to the library together and get some books on the subject. And don't just hand them over to the child; read some of them too. The child has to see that you're willing to put your own love and time into the subject because you are truly interested in the same things.

If you're not interested in what your children are doing, in what's important to them, why should they be interested in relating to what you think is important? Communication between you will break down. Would you want to communicate with someone who doesn't have the time to be interested in what you are interested in?

Say your daughter has a love of ballet. You might have no interest in it at all. But you can arrange for her to go to classes. You can take her to the theatre. And then you will have something to talk with her about.

'Tell me, what are the basic movements in ballet? What do they teach you first? Why do they teach you to do that?'

You can be like a child with her. In telling you about it she realises what she knows and she opens up the flower of her love of dance. And you will be showing her that you have sufficient love or interest in what she's doing to learn something about it too.

Does your child show a particular flair or inclination towards anything? Let's say it's drawing and art. It's very important to encourage any interest or skill like that, consulting with the child all the time and bringing books on art into the house. Look at pictures together and get the child to talk about them.

'What do you see in this picture that interests you? Where would you say the beauty is in it? What's the difference between this painting and that one?'

The child's interests might change. Children swing from one thing to another, so you have to be vigilant and watch for developments. It might suddenly be an interest in music and you will have to find someone to give piano lessons. But always discuss the possibility with the child first and get an agreement that this would be a good thing to do. Then be available to hear how the lessons went. Whatever the child's gift or talent, it should be encouraged in love.

Mother: It seems possible to encourage a high degree of

skill, in for example music, if lessons are started very young. There is a method of teaching children the violin — the Suzuki Method. They start children as young as two. It struck me recently how very useful it would be for my daughter throughout her life if she could do something really well.

This question has to be examined very closely. To introduce a child to the violin at two years of age is all well and good, provided she likes it, has an aptitude for it and shows an interest in doing the study and playing the instrument. But if it becomes a burden to the child, that would suggest that you are asking her to serve your needs rather than her own, which would be counter-productive to your intention, of course.

When a child shows any particular propensity towards any form of art or skill, it is important to encourage it as early as possible. But you've got to make sure the child enjoys it. I must have been six when my mother, with the best intentions, sent me to piano lessons. She thought it would be lovely for me and I went on for years and years learning the piano. But my heart wasn't really in it. And although it didn't do me any harm, it faded from me.

Mother: With an obviously gifted child, naturally one wants to give a lot of attention to her development, but perhaps this is at the expense of some other qualities. Do you see any ill effects in encouraging talent?

Yes. There obviously has to be a balanced approach. And while it's important to encourage any emerging gift or aptitude as early as possible, you've got to make sure that it is an expression of the child's love; and that you encourage it in love and not for example, ambition or pride.

The predispositions we are born with are like a field of

potentials waiting for something to activate them. The analogy is with an electromagnetic field between positive and negative poles. At the negative pole is right love (essentially love is an absence of force) and that draws out the positive expression of our predispositions. But if a child's emerging gifts are ignored or they meet with emotional reactions (force) then that positive charge will activate emotionally negative effects.

Encouragement of the child must always come from love, not our own selfish interests.

✳

Mother: I feel it's important to teach kids the basic skills of living — how to manage at the table and feed themselves without making a mess; how to make their own beds and spread butter on their bread. I like to pay attention to how well they manage that sort of thing, because it seems they can be quite skilled in some things and be surprisingly incompetent in others. They might have learned to ride a bike and still not be able to tie their own shoelaces. Do you agree with me about this?

Yes, but it's also important that you don't expect them to acquire these skills easily or quickly. There is usually a natural progression in these things. They can't learn to feed themselves properly all at once. Children learn by making mistakes and some are slower than others in acquiring manual skills, especially in co-ordinating the movement of hand to mouth. But, given that parents can assess their child's level of ability in that respect, it is important to keep the pressure on a child who is getting slovenly. As well as loving and attentive care there has to be an authoritative approach by the parents so that over time the child gets the message about what is right and what has to be done.

Parents have to be very aware and present in these matters. If we look at how children learn to spread butter on bread, we'll see that the skill evolves. They make a mess to start with, and drop the knife, but the way to encourage them is to make a game of it when you are all having your breakfast toast. Make it as much fun as you can, but be stern when you have to.

Be consistent and firm, but make a game of it if you can. So, for instance, when they're learning how to brush their teeth, encourage them by making it fun and let them experiment with different ways of doing it. Then leave them to do it on their own for a week or so. As they get practice they will get better at it and then you can go back into the bathroom with them and give them a bit more help and encouragement. So it is with everything. The parent has to be watching the situation and aware of when the child needs more help.

As always in right parenting, you have to give children your time and allow them to see that they can learn from your greater experience of life. That is their encouragement.

'You watch me juggling . . . Well, it took a long time to learn how to do it and when I was your age I couldn't even catch one ball if it was thrown to me. But one day I just got the hang of it. Juggling two tennis balls in the air is easy. It's when you have three that it starts getting difficult. And then you can add another ball . . . Like this . . .'

The boy sees how easily Dad can use his hands and gets the message that he's practised it for years and years and there's a natural progression to it.

'You'll get the hang of it in time. Just don't get frustrated if you can't do it properly now. One time you couldn't clean your own teeth or butter your own toast, but now you can. We're here to tell you how to do these things and help you, because we all have to learn how to do things in the world — it's called growing up. One day you'll want to ride a bike, and then you'll want to drive a car, but first you have to learn how to do the simple things.'

*

Father: How far should we go in allowing kids to express themselves? I mean in the way they talk — you know, swearing, slang and so on. Lately our boy's got sloppy in his speech. He's nine now, and well under the influence of TV and friends and such-like.

As soon as children start to pick up slang, the mind starts to slide into sloppiness. It's mostly a learned behaviour; acquired by copying adults and, as you say, exposure to the momentum of the world where the quick 'Yeah, thanks' is a fast forward to the next item.

Instructing children to speak clearly is a very important part of teaching them to be more conscious. But first we have to eliminate casual speech and sloppy mannerisms of our own, such as peppering speech with ums, ahs and y'knows. Then you have to encourage the boy to keep his language as precise and right as much as possible. This is the way to keep his mind precise.

'In this house we are all going to start to be more conscious of the way we speak. We will have no more yeps and yups, and no uh-uhs. I want to hear a good, straight yes or no. Is that clear? . . . Okay. But no nodding. Say "Yes" to me, out loud . . . Good.

'You can say "Yes" and then nod, or nod your head while you're saying it, that's all right, but I don't want to see you substituting nods and shakes for right verbal communication.

'We must learn to communicate rightly, not make sign

language. We have the gift of voice and the way to use it is to speak rightly. We all slip up, from time to time, of course, but we should all do our best to be precise.'

Father: Okay, we'll try that. Another thing is, I guess he watches too much TV. I'd like to get him out doing more sport . . .

When he's watching television he's in the mind — even if he's watching sport, it's mental entertainment. A movie may be full of action, car-chases and fist-fights, but it is still only mental entertainment, feeding the appetite for excitement. That is the way the world is in the electronic age.

Participation in physical games and sports, or just kicking a ball, will get your child into using his body, but you'll notice how he and his friends will quickly turn sport into a mental activity. You'll find now that people generally would rather be spectators than doers. So most children interested in football will watch it on TV, adopt their heroes and get absorbed in the scores and records of their favourite team rather than actually play the game. The movement in our times is always towards reading about something and thinking about it instead of doing it ourselves; let the other guy do it.

To balance this trend of course it is essential to encourage children in physical activity. Remember that the most important thing of all is to help them stay in their bodies.

∗

Many of the people I speak to practise meditation. I am sometimes asked if meditation is good for children as a way of helping them to stay in their bodies. Right meditation is always a return to the body and the stillness of being. The point of it is to reach that still place. The stillness can then reduce the restlessness in the mind and eventually overwhelm and dispel any discontent or emotion. Of course a child raised rightly would be staying in the body anyway and not be accumulating emotion . . .

Father: My daughter is only three and a half but she's started to come into the room when I'm meditating. It's interruptive, of course, but I don't want to just cut off from her. Should I try and show or tell her what I'm doing?

Of course it is always good to include your child in what you are doing with your life. If you meditate, then it is certainly good for your child to participate with you, as much as she's able to.

At that age she is only beginning to develop the memory and self-reflection that disturbs us when we are older. So there cannot be the same purpose in it for her as there is for you. But if she is able to join you in your meditation, just for a short while, and is familiar with it, it may help her later on.

In my teaching the idea is to keep unhappiness out by being constantly aware of the being or the good inside the body. That is meditation as a total way of life. The way to introduce this to your daughter is to show her how to be with the sensation of the good as the love or warmth in her body.

How can you do this? At her age verbal communication is limited and the attention span is brief. You can't expect her to just sit still and be quiet. So it's best to do it as a game and give her something positive to do.

If you see that she's old enough and ready for this, begin by sitting down with her and telling her what you're going to be doing together. Choose a time when she's already relaxed and receptive.

'We're going to play a new game. It's called meditation. Do you want to?'

'Yes.' (It helps if the child agrees and says 'Yes' out loud because this creates a sense of willing co-operation between mind and body. A reluctant or churlish mind will disturb the body.)

'Sit down there on the carpet. And I'll sit here, opposite you. Comfortable?'

Again, encourage her to actually say, 'Yes.' And remembering it's a game, smile in response to her. Stay light and easy in yourself.

'We're going to find something together. Something good. And it's inside your body. Ready? Okay. Close your eyes and keep them closed. But not too tight. Now first of all I want you to tell me whereabouts you feel that you love me or Mummy . . . Can you show me? Keep your eyes closed, and point to the feeling . . .'

She will probably point straight to her tummy. She is unlikely to point to her head (although older and more wily children may do so); but if she does you will see that this comes from trying to give you the right answer.

'You can feel your love in your tummy, can you? I can feel my love of you there, too. A good sensation, isn't it? Got it? Yes, it's good isn't it?'

Leave a little pause and then ask her what it feels like. Her spontaneous response is what you are are looking for, not a consideration of the question or a habitual reply giving what she thinks is the right answer. The point is to encourage her to stay conscious of the sensation inside.

'Now, how does it feel? Can you tell me?'

Listen for the word she uses (good, nice, lovely, warm). Once you have her term for it, you can use that word next time you play 'meditation' together.

'Now, I'm going to do my meditation. Do you want to come and be with me for a little while? Good. Then sit down opposite me and shut your eyes like I showed you. Now, can you feel that nice feeling inside your tummy? I can feel it in me. Nice and warm isn't it? Good. I shall just be still and stay here feeling it for a while. When you want to, get up and go and quietly play with your toys but you can come back and be with me any time that you want to sit and feel the good with me.'

The point is not to make the child sit still when she doesn't want to, but to encourage her to discover the good as sensation and make the connection with it on a regular basis. Unless that sensation is discovered, made substantive and continually confirmed with practice, meditation remains an intellectual notion.

*

We are sensuous physical creatures of the earth. Children who lose touch with their bodies find later on in life that they're not able to make love. A man who can't love a woman with his body, or a woman who can't love a man with hers, is going to be unhappy. There will be no harmony between them. That's the fact.

The truth of life is being in harmony and at peace. And that is inside the body. Yet there is the constant endeavour in everyone to have that harmony outside of us, to find peace in existence; or to put things right in the world, which can never be done. It is absolutely impossible to get harmony outside the body for long. Someone close to you will die. Something will be lost. Nothing lasts.

Our children will go on getting mixed up about where the truth is because they will go on being misled by our society, and particularly by science and scientists. People increasingly believe in scientific facts and fictions and think scientists are concerned with truth when they do not practise the truth at all. There is only one truth and that is inside of us. The scientific mind can never arrive at the truth because it only considers objects and energies in the material world.

Father: My eldest son has a strong interest in science, which I encourage, but at the same time I try to give him some sort of spiritual context. He has a natural scientific bent but I'm afraid he's already developed a cynicism about spiritual truth, or things that can't be proved. We tend to have long discussions, for instance about what 'truth' is.

If he is to become a scientist he must enter the scientific mind. So while you are talking with him about his scientific interests, I suggest you stick to facts. It is best not to get into discussion about truth. Truth, of course, is demonstrated in life. If you live the truth, and he is able to see that you do, he can come to you when science fails him. Then you will be able to answer his questions about love or death. What wisdom has science got to impart about death? What can the scientist say to his son when the girlfriend goes off with someone else? Or his own wife leaves him? Can he resort to scientific knowledge then?

There's no truth in science but there are facts that we can agree about. It's four o'clock. That's a fact. But it's not the truth. Truth only relates to life now. Facts relate to objects. Relationships to objects can be either facts or not facts in which case they are theory, speculation or assumption. But fact or theory, relationships come and go. Life is always within us and, as truth, looks out into the world and sees the rightness behind the fact.

As there is no truth in science, there is no love in it. For there is no love outside of us, only relationship. But once you work from that knowledge of truth and love then every relationship in your life seems to fall into place.

Continue to encourage your son in his studies, without getting into a debate. Don't argue or philosophise with him. His scientific studies can then fall into their right context as part of his experience of the world, against the background of your wisdom and intelligent conversation.

You might look and see if you yourself have a need to discuss things. If you are imposing your own interests on him, that may be causing his cynical reaction to you. As always, the way to get better communication is to listen more carefully.

*

We've all learned at some time to ask big questions about the universe we see outside of us. How was everything created? Scientists come up with many answers, but no solution. Meanwhile they discover more and more universe to ask questions about. And this, of course, becomes part of our children's education.

Simon was nine when his class at school discussed the Big Bang theory. Most people have heard of this. It says the whole universe, including space, at zero point in time exploded into existence out of nothing. But no scientist has ever been able to explain the state of nothing before zero time.

After the class Simon wrote to me. (He'd gone to live with his mother after I separated from her, and occasionally he would write to me.) His letter contained the most intelligent scientific question of our times.

'Barry, if you wanted to explain the Big Bang to somebody, how would you explain the nothing part?'

Here's what I wrote in my reply to him.

'The Big Bang didn't really happen, Simon. That's why nobody can answer the question. Things only happen when there's somebody there to see them. As nobody was there it didn't happen.

'I certainly wouldn't want to explain to somebody something that hadn't happened. I'd be trying to explain nothing, wouldn't I? How would I explain the nothing part? — I couldn't. So that's why science can't explain it either and never will — because it didn't happen.

'What's happening in your spare room at this moment? If there's nobody to see it, nothing's happening. You can theorise or imagine that all sorts of things are happening but you'll never know. And for anyone to ever know what has happened in that room in the past, or even before it was built, there has to have been somebody there to see it.

'Nothing can ever be known unless somebody was there to report it. If there's nobody there to report it, then it's only a thought or a theory, something that somebody's thought up. Is that the truth?'

'The scientists know they are on the wrong track, but they can't believe it because all the signs are telling them they are on the right track. But a wise man doesn't believe in signs; he goes by what he knows. What's happening in the spare room? You don't know. That's the nothing in the Big Bang theory. It consists of nothing but signs; it's a theory about signs, not reality.

'Nobody knows or will ever know what the scientists are talking about. That's why you asked the question, Simon. You don't know what they are talking about. I don't know what they are talking about. And neither do they.'

Simon's letter contained a second question, which he had added as an afterthought. It was also a good question: Why do we exist?

'I don't know why we exist. I only know why I exist. I exist to enjoy my life by always being free of unhappiness in myself. Why do you exist?'

When Simon got my letter he quickly wrote back again: 'If the Big Bang didn't happen, how was everything created?'

This question doesn't make sense so I wrote and told him why.

'Your question doesn't really make sense, Simon. Everything is created now. You can't show me anything that was created.

You can't show me anything that was. You can only show me what is now. That is sense, or making sense.

'Non-sense means not making sense. So your question, like the Big Bang theory for the beginning of everything, is nonsense (non-sense).'

When we stop making sense, we start making problems.

Of course I knew what Simon was driving at, but I always endeavoured to help him look at things realistically. That usually means perceiving them in a different way to most people. The difference is between a realistic question and a reasonable one. Most people would say Simon's question was reasonable; and 'reasonable' it may be. But it is not realistic. It's like asking: How does Santa Claus get down the chimney? That's also a reasonable question. But the realistic question is: Does Santa Claus exist? No matter how many reasonable questions are asked about the old gentleman, none will be realistic.

In his first letter Simon had enclosed a picture of himself in a karate outfit, a white suit with a vivid yellow belt, showing that he was a beginner in training. He looked very smart. 'I'm doing karate,' he wrote proudly, 'and I'm a yellow belt.'

'Since you're now a yellow belt,' I wrote, 'I might borrow you sometime to wear with my beige trousers.' He was old enough now to get the joke. At nine, a child has learned not to take everything literally but to see double meanings. Young children can't do this. They are too innocent. They take things and see things as they are.

At nine Simon was losing his innocence. Necessarily, he was becoming educated, sophisticated, civilised, cultured. All these words mean a certain breaking down of the original purity and simplicity of the being. 'To sophisticate' says the dictionary, means 'to alter deceptively, to make worldly-wise, to adulterate' — adult-erate.

Anything cultured is cultivated or produced under artificial conditions. So Simon was becoming one of us. Despite my efforts as his parent and teacher he would soon learn to make a virtue of sophistication and, like everyone else, assume the right to be unhappy.

3

BALANCE IN THE WORLD

Bringing innocence to experience

The Body of Experience
The Influence of the World – The Shadow of Death
Emerging Sexuality – The Knowledge of God

J onathan and I were both in the bathroom at the same time. I noticed that he was playing with my toothbrush.

'Jonathan, don't play with it like that. Be careful, or you'll drop it down the toilet.'

'No I won't.'

Only a second or two later, splash — down it went.

'Barry, how did you know it would drop?'

'It didn't drop.'

'Yes it did.' He was very insistent. 'You saw!'

'No. It didn't drop. I'll tell you what happened. You dropped it. Didn't you?'

'Oh. Umm . . . Yes.'

'Do you see how you tried to get out of it? You tried to blame the toothbrush — instead of yourself. We all do that, but it's not right, is it?'

'No. But Barry, how did you know I was going to drop it?'

'Because I'm experienced. By doing things I've learned what's likely to happen; and I've learned that things don't always turn out as I think. That's what growing up is about. Long ago I dropped things down the toilet when I didn't want to. Now I'm careful about that because I've learned better — just like you. And you have learned now, haven't you?'

THE BODY OF EXPERIENCE

C hildren need experience of the world to protect them from it. Through going to school and exposure to the wider world they grow a body of experience which forms like a protective shield around their physical organism. Through being with other children, playing games, competing with each other, watching television, absorbing many influences, getting into scrapes, encountering unkindness and rough treatment, a body of ignorance is formed.

An analogy is the 'chemical body' that I say everybody in the western world has now acquired. Chemicals produced by modern science in our food, water and atmosphere might make us a bit sick to begin with, but as we gradually absorb them they become our protection against other pollutants. As the pollution of the world increases, our chemical body becomes like a filter, absorbing and discharging the chemicals. In this process modern medicines and drugs have their part to play, a fact which proponents of alternative therapies should not disregard in the treatment of sickness and ill-health.

So a body of experience (or ignorance) is needed for the protection of the organism in a hostile world. Gaining experience is painful, of course, especially if you and your children are sensitive to potential conflict between the inner life and the demands of the outer world. However as a true parent you must be true to the situation and not your feelings.

Be true to the situation. This most important aspect of my teaching can be applied in every part of your life and especially with your children. The situation is that as parent you are there to look after them and give them a home, to do your best for them and then, as they go out to get their experience, to inform them about the wider world and give them the guidance of your wisdom. You have to direct their intelligence to face the world, getting a right balance between the inner life and living in society. If you live what I teach and are true to the situation, you will be able to deal practically with every circumstance and face the difficulties; and you will be able to talk about them, parent to child and child to parent in a straight and open way.

*

Father: I feel quite a strong need to protect my son, and I don't want him to have to go through what I went through.

Indeed you will endeavour to protect him, according to your own experience of life, but you can only do your best to guide him. You can't be responsible for anyone else's life. When you've done everything you can and you are unable to do any more, you have to leave it to God. Then you must detach yourself from what the boy is doing, while remaining available — for the very next moment the opportunity to help him may come again.

We don't want to see our children hurt, and yet their karma requires them to have hurtful experiences, as we have all had.

We offer them guidelines for living, gained from our own experience of the world, but at the same time we must not become attached to what we see as right or desirable for them. We must not live our lives through theirs. That disidentification is love. Often love can penetrate the karmic burden and some of the karmic effects that show up in the child's life may be moderated by the parents' love.

Father: I look back on my own life and see that I had lots of experiences that I could well have done without. I can see that some things did have a purpose, but others had none whatsoever. It bothers me that there's this perversity; that the lessons of my life aren't learnt or can't be handed on.

You can't really say that. Every action serves a purpose. That's fundamental. Your experience has shown you what life's about.

Father: I know of a young man from 'a good family'. They did everything they could to make him responsible and caring and he certainly seemed a sensible chap. Then in the playground he's introduced to drugs, sniffing glue, and overnight he turns into a slob. What purpose could that possibly serve?

These things are inscrutable, but sooner or later the boy will get the chance to come to his senses, even if he gets completely hooked and spends his life trying to give up addictions. Every experience has a purpose.

✳

Mother: I want to look after my son, of course, but not be over-protective. The main difficulty for me is how to give him the attention he needs but also have time for myself. Living with him makes it difficult to maintain my stillness, or have as much balance as I'd like between my inner and outer life.

This is the dilemma of every parent, but particularly of mothers. Woman is essentially concerned with entering her own body, her own psychic system, and going deeper into that profundity. Naturally she wants the same sort of good for her child as she wants for her own psychonomy. But the child is an independent extension in form of herself — not herself. And that is the source of the dilemma.

The solution, as always, is to put first thing first. The more you get rid of your emotion and face the truth inside yourself the more you enter the profundity of your own psyche, and the more you will be able to deal with the difficulties and interruptions which are absolutely necessary and must come in the presence of children. Put your own profundity first and it naturally follows that you will address your child in love, rightness and honesty. Then right instruction follows naturally.

*

Every child is going to encounter the knocks and shocks of existence, some more acutely than others. A child who has been given a little warning, at the appropriate time, will be better prepared. One of the first things to explain is that the values the child will find in society are not the same as those in your family. When your children go out into the world, they will soon encounter the very different values of neighbours, relatives, schoolfriends and other parents, who are going to give them a very different kind of instruction. So it's important to communicate that they are going to experience the difference.

'You have to know that not everybody lives the way that we do. Not everybody tries to keep unhappiness out. In fact

270

almost nobody you are likely to meet would understand if you said "Piggy out and God in" because they don't live like we do. But I also want to tell you that we should not try to change anyone else. Our way of living is for us and what other people do is up to them. We don't condemn them or judge them. We don't react or say we know better than they do. So you mustn't do that. You mustn't try to force your way of life onto another person. It's very important not to do that.'

Discourage a child from taking any kind of position about anything, or there will soon be a tendency to start defending it. Don't let your children become like religious fanatics, saying there is only one way to be and everybody else is wrong, bad or mad.

'We are only concerned with living rightly as we see it. If you try to change others, or judge them, it will cause a problem between you and other people. So it is best not to judge others. And it is best to contain any desire you might have to tell people things that they haven't asked you about.

'Now here's the next thing you need to know as you go into the world. You're likely to run up against unkind people and other children might treat you badly. They do that because they have pain in them and that's their way of expressing it. People do not usually know how to face the unhappiness in themselves. Often they don't even know they have Piggy inside them, so they think it's all right to be moody or angry. Because they are unhappy, they lose touch with the feeling of love and then sometimes they do things that are unkind. They can't help it, because it is the unhappiness wanting to express itself.

'You will find that whenever unhappiness expresses itself it makes other people unhappy as well. The best thing we can do is endeavour to get rid of the unhappiness inside ourselves, so that we do not put it into the rest of the world; but that will not stop other people from being unkind. When people are angry they can lash out at you. This results in a lot of cruelty.

'I'm telling you this to inform you about the way the world is. It's often a violent place but part of growing up is to go out into the world and find out how it works; and I am here to help and guide you.'

*

Mother: Ben's been very ill. I've been quite concerned about it.

Does he have an infection? A temperature?

Mother: He has a headache and his temperature has been very high for two days and two nights. At some stage he actually had some delirium and saw things in the room. He was very anxious and would say things like 'Let's go down, we have to get away from this.' His eyes were wide open and very clear. He could see me but he didn't seem to recognise the house as such.

Children do go through these things, don't they? States of high temperature bring about psychic change. The things he spoke about would have been real inside of him. When he asks to be removed from the bedroom, or wherever he is, it is best to take him out.

Mother: I did that, took him downstairs and asked him questions, like 'What is it you see?' And he explained some of the things to me. I know that at some point he will come back to normal.

Over the last few weeks he's gone through a great change in his life. He's suddenly become separated from me. A family with three children moved into the neighbourhood. It's school holidays and they started knocking on our door. In the beginning Ben didn't want to play with them. I kept sending them away. But then he started going out with them. Suddenly he went from being at home quietly with me, and just going to school for a few hours, to being out all day long, playing in the road with the other children.

And is it disturbing to you that he's playing with them?

Mother: Yes. It is a bit. I was uncertain about it, because they are more rough than he is.

Ben is about six and a half now, isn't he? Between the ages of six and seven children go through this change when they have to take on more experience. From having a mainly physical experience of life, they start to develop a mental relationship to it. Ben is going to want to go out into the world and relate more to other children. They all have to go through this change. It's like having their milk teeth fall out, so that they can grow stronger ones.

Mother: Yes, that's been happening . . . I try to keep my eye on the situation. I encourage them to play in the house and give them toys, so I can be with them, but really Ben wants to go off first thing after breakfast and be with them all the time. Should I insist on him coming back at a certain time?

You are watching the situation. Act from your own integrity. If you say there should be a break in his day when he comes back to be with you, or that he must be back at a certain time for his lunch, then make that a rule. Like any parent, you must be vigilant at all times to see if what the child is doing sits rightly inside of you and if it does not then you must take action, speak to him about it or change the situation. But remember he has to be allowed into the world.

Mother: My fear is that the other children are a bit wild and they might do things to him, hit him. I wondered if his sickness was a way for him to handle his fear.

The little bird has to get out of the nest and take some chances. You are endeavouring to protect your boy and keep him safe but the world is going to pull him out and away from you. He has to be able to mix with others in this world. He has to have the company of other boys and they won't all be like himself or raised as he is. You have to let him go while at the same time you are informing him about life and guiding him as much as possible towards an understanding of what the world is about, so that he does not become too identified with it.

When the other children are rough with him, talk to him about how unhappiness makes the world a cruel and unkind place: 'People are rough and they push other people over for no reason. That's life. We can't change it or avoid it.'

Mother: He has already had to deal with the unkindness of other children. During the last school term some of them were taunting and teasing him. He told me, when I asked him why he was upset, that they were calling him 'a silly girl' and whispering behind his back. So I went to the school and spoke to the other children about it and asked them to stop. But it's as if they are compelled to do it. I suppose it's because Ben is a bit different from them. He's a quiet child, and looks quite angelic with long blonde hair, so he's an easy target.

It happens to many children and I can understand it because it happened to me. Two or three boys get together and strengthen each other. They keep mocking and teasing in concert, and as they look at each other they get a feeling of power out of it. The poor victim doesn't know what to do. And there's very little you can do, in my experience. Endeavouring to talk back or hit back doesn't do any good; the mob approach is overpowering.

I would examine where the problem starts. I would listen very carefully to the words that are uttered. In this case, why were they calling him a girl? Obviously, from your description, his hair and appearance mark him out. He's a young boy mixing with his peers and it's difficult for any child to appear odd or look different from the other children in their group. They will seize on the individual who stands out.

Does Ben appear unconventional? Do his hair and clothes single him out, as the boys single him out? Are you going to compromise and encourage him to join his peers or are you going to have him pilloried for being unconventional? What does the boy say about how he wants his hair and clothes?

Mother: Well, I will have to talk to him about that. The situation is not likely to go away. It may get worse. There is some bullying at the school by the older boys who pick on younger ones and hit them. I spoke to one of the teachers about it and asked her to tell me if Ben gets involved. She said there's not much the teachers can do about it because it happens when their backs are turned. Is there any way I could help Ben deal with the bullies?

It appears he has not come to their attention yet and it may not happen. Some boys can be in a fight and not be too troubled by it. Others get away unscathed. But if you see that Ben is vulnerable you could help him develop his physical confidence by encouraging him to do some activity like swimming or perhaps (at the appropriate time) joining a judo or self-defence class.

Is he in any way separating himself from the other children at school? The bullies pick on the loners. It's important for children to participate in school society. Ben's teacher will be able to tell you if he is getting too withdrawn.

It may be his karma to attract some bullying and in that event all you can do is trust that you have prepared him well enough to be able to handle it. He should have been informed that in this existence everybody has pain inside of them. It comes from a time in the past when they were ill-treated or misunderstood. When the hurt rises up from deep inside it makes people want to hurt others . . .

'What we're endeavouring to do is get rid of the hurt inside of us and one way you can do that is by knowing that you are loved. I love you. Daddy loves you. Your life is good. You have nothing to be hurt about, because we are honest with you. When you have a problem, like this bully at school, you can come up and tell us about it and we'll do as much as we can to attend to it or help you through it. We can't necessarily change the situation, and you can't have everything you want in this world, but there's no need for you to hold on to the hurt.

'Most people don't practise this way of being honest with each other, so the children often feel hurt inside. When they hurt very badly they do hurtful things. You will find that usually they really don't want to have done them; because really it's the hurt that hit out, not them.

'You have to find out how the world is. It's sometimes a cruel and violent place and the bully is teaching you that. But don't hold anything against him. Don't go over what he did to you or think about how hurtful it was. I know it's very difficult not to hold anything against someone who hurt you, but it is our love to endeavour to do that.

'There's something else I have to say to you. It's not a good idea to go and tell people at school where they are going wrong. Don't try to tell anyone at school what we're talking about. They don't teach these sort of things at school. Don't try to change anyone. Just listen to the truth of life, as I tell it to you, and then you will know what is behind the unkindness in people. The important thing is that you know it; and therefore you don't have to get so upset about what people do.'

Mother: Suppose it is not another child that attacks him but an adult. I've never spoken to him about child abuse. Because he is playing out in the street more now he is more vulnerable. How would I teach him about the dangers without frightening him? Should I openly tell him what some people will do to children?

No, not at his age. But you might say something like this: 'There are many good people, but there are some who are not so good and there are even some bad people in this world. So therefore you must avoid anyone who comes up to you and tries to persuade you to go and visit their home, or wants to take you to be alone with them, because they might be a bad person. Even if they offer you sweets or a present or reward, don't go with them, because what they should do is come and see Mummy or Daddy and ask our permission. You just come home if anyone approaches you in this way, and tell me. Don't go off with anyone, because they might not want to help you as they say they do.'

Don't assume that a child will necessarily ask 'What will the bad people do to me?' He might ask that, but don't anticipate the question. Say what you have to say, make it simple and leave it at that. You do not need to introduce a child to sexual matters that are not happening in his life yet and so do not concern him. If you do, you'll make him wonder or be curious. It is generally best to let children ask their own questions in their own time. Then you'll find that just giving simple answers will be sufficient. However with this subject you have to take the initiative, so when the time is right, I suggest you introduce it into the conversation. Just let it come out easily and the boy will receive it.

*

Father: I was at the supermarket last week with Peter — my son, he's eight — when a fight broke out. We heard raised voices between a man and a woman and then, right in front of us, she screamed and threw something and he hit her. We quickly turned away and someone else intervened. But it was disturbing, because the violence seemed to come out of nowhere. Peter was unusually quiet in the car on the way home and so I tried to talk to him about the incident. I think it must have been the first time he's seen random violence between adults, except on the TV of course . . .

It's obviously a shock for any of us to see such a thing in actuality. Or to chance on some horrific sight, such as a car accident. I was a newspaper journalist for many years, for a while a crime reporter, and in those days I saw many results of violence, with people killed. It's awful and harrowing to see such things. But it is so easy to watch them on the telly.

Although our children are continually being exposed to violence and killing on television, it is just a mental experience for them — excitement and entertainment. It does not prepare them for the shock of actual violence. So we have to do what we can to help them handle it. It is best done over time by continually demonstrating the truth and justice of life to our children.

When some incident occurs and they ask their questions, or they are traumatised in any way, speak to them rightly about man's violence and what makes us hurt and kill each other.

'Why did he do it? It was because of his pain. There is so much pain in him that it came up from inside, lashed out and struck whatever happened to be in its way. It's the same pain in every one of us. You know when you're unhappy and we ask you why and you won't answer and you clench your fist and scream and scream . . . that's the same pain that makes men and women want to hurt one another or be cruel and violent.'

And sooner or later the child asks: 'Why can't we have peace in the world? Why won't they stop hurting and killing each other?'

'We cannot do anything to change the way the world is. But when we have had enough pain we can change the way we are. We've got to endeavour to get rid of the pain by loving one another and giving to each other as much as possible. That gets rid of the pain inside of us. And you know, one day somebody may come along and say: "Hey, you seem to be a happy sort of person." And you can say: "Well, I am endeavouring not to have any pain in me." And then they might learn to get rid of the pain in themselves. That's how you can help to stop the violence and killing in this world. It's only a small contribution but it counts, just like drops of rain filling up a bucket. A little drop of water, one at a time, but in time it will be full.'

*

Man: My brother was the victim of a violent attack and had very nasty wounds to the arm and face. His wife took their young son, six years old, to see him in hospital. The boy came away disturbed by the sight of his father, which of course added to the mother's distress. How should the incident be explained to the boy? Would it have been better not to have taken him to the hospital under those circumstances?

In matters like this, children do not have to be shown or told more than they need to know. There are areas of adult experience that do not immediately concern them. In this case, the child needs to know that his Dad had been hurt and is likely to ask how he was injured. How much he should then be told depends on his question, the character of the child and his relationship with his parents.

Remember you don't have to tell a child the whole story. Don't anticipate the dreaded question, the one you think you couldn't answer or wouldn't know how to answer. Children don't follow the rational sequence of questioning that adults often expect of them. If they do, it's because they have been influenced. The fear of an awkward question being asked can actually draw it out of the child. Answer the child's question simply and in one sentence if possible; that will usually suffice.

The sight of cruelty or raw hurt to the body makes a very deep impression on children because they are so open to life, looking around to see what life is, and their psyche is so absorbent. Of course life may involve a child in a situation where he or she has to face the raw cruelty of the world, but I would not recommend exposing a child to such sights unnecessarily. So in this case I would take the boy to the hospital when his Dad's condition is improved.

*

Exposure to the shocks and knocks of existence is, as I have said, a karmic effect. The child's karma cannot be avoided and the parent cannot always control or contain its effects. All you can do as the parent is give the child your love and guidance in the face of a hostile existence.

The world is a cruel, stressful and violent place at times and man is ambitious and competitive. Your child needs to know this and should be instructed in how to be in the competitive world without taking on any avoidable stress or holding on to tension.

Competitiveness is an engendered condition and a form of emotional subjectivity that winds itself up into a tension with no real connection to what actually has to be done. Because it is so subjective we must endeavour to eliminate it in our children. But that does not mean we cannot encourage them to do their best. On the contrary, we should help them with whatever challenge they undertake, as long as they participate without unhappiness, of course.

The appropriate time for a talk about this will arise, perhaps when some incident in the family or at school brings it up.

'There's something you need to know about the world. It's a very competitive place. Everybody competes with each other out there. Competition creates tension and all sorts of emotions — jealousy, envy, pride, guilt, failure, despair. So I tell you that you do not have to compete with other people. What you have to do is join in with them and just do your best. If you always do your best you don't have to compete. Perhaps you could do better next time, but for now you've done your best. That way you take the stress and strain out of whatever you are doing, and you don't get as tense and unhappy as most of the people you see in the world.'

*

Father: There was an incident the other day. Ben was getting disturbed about trying to get a school project finished. All the kids in the school had to enter a drawing competition and their pictures had to be handed in the next day. There were going to be prizes and he wanted to do his best. He was fretting about it, so his mother told him not to make himself unhappy and said he was to stop trying to finish the picture in time. I saw that he didn't want to give up so I took his side and encouraged him to continue. He did as much as he could to finish it and went to bed.

Generally we have discouraged him from being competitive, but now I see that he doesn't handle these situations very well and perhaps we ought to face the fact that his school promotes competition in all sorts of ways and he's got to take part along with the other kids.

Have you talked with Ben about the situation? It would be good for you all to look at it together. What does 'competition' mean? What happens when we compete? What are the ramifications for us and others?

'Let's look at this . . . To compete I must set myself against another. And the result of competing will be that I'll feel some tension inside me. Now you have to do this drawing for school tomorrow. It seems to be causing you some disturbance. Have you got any tension in you? Can you tell me where it is? In your tummy . . . Okay.

'The next question is: Has the tension actually got anything to do with the project you're engaged in? — such as this drawing. And the answer is "No", because we both know you enjoy drawing. You do, don't you? So the tension does not come from what you're actually doing, which you enjoy.

'You have to do your level best to produce the drawing. But if you get tense about it, you won't do your best; you'll be anxious and the anxiety will go through your fingers into your pencil. When we are tense and anxious we can't focus easily on what we're doing, so then we have to concentrate harder and harder, which brings even more tension into what we're trying to do. Then we project the anxiety into the future, and build up a momentum, which is an excitement in the mind that always goes in circles, never straight ahead. So we start thinking and worrying in circles, and we build up more and more thoughts to think about and get more and more anxious. Soon we can't stop thinking and we can't sleep. But none of this has anything to do with what we are actually doing or have to do. So we don't want that momentum to happen to us, do we?

'Your drawing is going to be judged on what the people looking at it think is best. So all you can do is do your best. Take your time over it and when you think you've done your best, when you say it's good enough, take it and put it with all the other drawings. Then you just wait and see what the judges think of it. That's what you have to do in life — wait and see. Nobody knows a result until it happens.

'Nobody knows how things will turn out in life. For instance, I might be going to work, setting out, thinking I'm going to spend the whole day in the office. "I'm going to be very busy today because I have lots of important things to do." I get in the car and head off but when I arrive, I find I have to go somewhere else and before I know it, it's four in the afternoon — time to come home and I never got to my desk at all, because I got deflected. Do you see how life determines what happens, not us?

'People will say they know what's going to happen but they only think they do; nobody knows with certainty. If we start to think we know what's going to happen, or we worry because we don't know how it will turn out, we put ourselves in competition with life. That's why we get tense.

'We don't want the tension in us, so we endeavour to pull back from thinking we know what's going to happen or wondering how it will turn out. So that's my advice to you. Do your best every moment — without competing with life.'

*

Father: Competitiveness is essential in any kind of sport. You can't be involved in sport and not want to win, can you? Our boy is keen on football and has a favourite team. He likes to wear the team shirts and collects bits of football paraphernalia. It's a common obsession at his school, and of course it is so much in the culture that it is hard to stop the identification with 'our team' and whether they are winning or losing. Is this doing him any harm?

Of course it is difficult to break the need for identification that you observe in him. To get his experience of excitement and pain he has to identify with winning and losing. Up when they win. Down when they lose. That's what this life is: the

283

inexorable action of pleasure and pain, like the piston of an old steam engine.

'Pleasure and pain, pleasure and pain . . . That will be your lot, my son — until you are man enough to disidentify with it.'

The more we teach children to choose between one thing and another, the more they become identified with winning and losing.

'I choose this team. They're my side. The other's your side. If mine wins, it'll be great and I hope your lot lose!'

Adult fans who identify with their teams are ignorant. Unlike children they already have the experience of choosing, winning and losing. Now they are just hanging on to it — repeating the experience. Lives of repeated experience are utter boredom at home and at work, relieved only by looking for ups and downs.

'Our side's lost the last three games. They'd better win on Saturday. Or you'll have to buy the drinks.'

There has to be the win and the booze to make up for the downer.

'Oh no . . . We lost! God knows what we're going to do now' — as if he was actually playing.

We are not doers any more. We have developed as a race of spectators, always looking for heroes to worship because we ourselves are such mundane creatures, ignorant, bored and lazy.

Father: So I shouldn't watch football on TV or take my son to the match?

Why not go to the match without getting the emotions involved? You can watch the action of the players, admire their skill and enjoy it without getting identified. Then you will start to glimpse a different world.

In the spiritual life, when we don't need any more experience, we endeavour to reverse the need for it. Withdraw from emotional identification with existence and you'll enjoy it more. It's simple; there's nothing to get excited about, no more ups and downs.

But a child's need of experience cannot be avoided. If you hear the truth of this, you may be able to guide your son through his experience. Encourage him to participate in the physical life and stay in his senses; and by your example and guidance teach him not to indulge the chooser in him, the winner and the loser.

*

Father: My son is eleven and loves any sort of sport. The one he really wants to do is football. His mother is concerned about him getting physically hurt. I played as a child and really enjoyed it so I like to encourage him. My question is whether playing football achieves anything positive?

If he is a sporting boy, as you describe, you have to let him follow what he's drawn to. His mother is fearful of him being injured and that's a right fear. There is no doubt football is an injurious sport. (We're talking about Australian Rules football here; but we may as well be talking about American football or Rugby League.) It's a violent sport as anybody knows who played it in their youth, as I did. It's quite likely to lead to physical injury, especially to the knees, and aches and pains will show up in later life.

What does it achieve? The way I played, it achieved nothing and if I'd been injured it would not have achieved anything either. I could have played some other game which would have used my energies better — and I did. I took up swimming, swam for my school and later for the Air Force.

So I would direct the boy towards some other sport, but if he won't be deterred then all you can do is talk to him about the game. It would be your love to spend time with him following his interests. Find out something about the sport that's more than just the ordinary knowledge of it. I would get him to understand the science of the game.

'Let's have a look at this . . . What's the science of football? What's its object? Every game must have a science to it that's not the rough and tumble. Football is not about getting hurt. It's about getting the ball down the pitch to the goal with the minimum of physical contact. So the science of it is to ask how you can best achieve that.

'The best way to do it is not to get angry — not to compete. Play the game by following the science of it, which is to get down the pitch as far and as fast as you can. Now, according to the science of football, the other team has to try and stop you and we know from our observing the fact of the situation that they are likely to tackle you badly or try to hurt you. You have to know that the people you are playing against will have unhappiness in them, which will make some of them express their pain and competitiveness through the game. You can't protect yourself from the stupidity of the other players and you might get hurt. But if you play just to enjoy the sport and follow the science of it, you will be doing what you can to take the violence out of it. That will make you a good footballer and you will become a scientist in the game because all the time you will know what you are doing and why.'

*

Whenever it becomes necessary to counter the effects of the world on your children remember to return to the earth. Encourage any interest they show in nature so that they get exposure to the cycle of life and death of the natural world; so that they can observe the life of the animals where survival and competition are instinctual — not contaminated by human

286

emotions, anxiety or sentiment. Let them see that on this earth one species of animal must eat another to survive. That is the law. And let them witness the essential innocence of animals in the wild, untainted as they are by human experience.

Father: Our daughter has a great love of animals. She's always loved anything furry. She's nine now and very keen for us to have a whole menagerie of pets . . . This attraction to animals is very strong in so many children it must have some significance?

Yes. We give children animals, as toys and as pets, because they reflect the instinctive nature out of which we come. Children can look at an animal and see a reflection of their love, their own tenderness and vulnerability, their own instinctive sweetness. Your daughter loves animals because they are close to the nature of her mother's womb.

Everyone is looking for a reflection of reality in this existence and children look for it in Mum and Dad. But parents usually have a certain knowingness, a troubledness in them which is also a mirror to the child. There is no unhappiness in the mirror of animals. Children instinctively know that animals are not burdened with the unhappiness of humans. If they are encouraged to think otherwise, or imagine an animal is unhappy, their alarm or concern is acute.

The animals are a reflection of innocence. The parents are a reflection of experience, and reflect unhappiness to the extent that they have it in them. As a child I need the mirror of my parents and their love and experience of the world because in that reflection is the very nature of my developing humanhood. From my very first moment I'm aware of a terrible aloneness and need the reassurance of my mother and father's experience: they know what to do. They reach over to touch me, hold my hand and hug me tight — everything's all right. I feel secure and grow in the expectation that they will look after me. But as I grow in humanhood, I leave my innocence behind. Although I am growing more and more distant from the natural beauty of the earth, the world of the animals is still there for me. I reach out to stroke their fur; to get the feel of their instinctive beauty. This restores me to a place of security. I want an animal to hold and to play with. I want a pet.

We like to give children pet animals to look after.

'I'll look after it, Mummy. Please let me have it. I'll look after it and feed it. Yes, I'll clean out the cage every week. I'll do it. I will!'

And Dad, in the background, knows who will end up doing it. Because experience knows that children cannot remain with their innocence. In their humanhood they will attend to their pets when it suits them and turn away and forget them when it suits them. They may even mistreat animals for their own amusement.

As we grow we make experience our god — until experience, and our attachment to it, drives us into a life of more and more aridity, pain and unhappiness. Finally, by the way of things, we say 'God, I've had enough of this . . .' — meaning, 'Please God, I want to get back to my innocence.'

In the return to innocence, which is the spiritual life, everything we have to pass through is made of human experience and consists of our emotional self. So back we go — through the self and the selfishness that we made in ignorance as we went out into the world.

THE INFLUENCE OF THE WORLD

We would all like to save our children from what might be considered 'a bad influence' but the fact is we can't be idealistic. They are going to be exposed to people, forms of behaviour and habits that in our own experience we know to be harmful.

The three kinds of harmful influence that most concern the parents I speak to are: in young children, irresponsible behaviour copied from other children; in older ones, the impact of television, computers and electronic games; and in teenagers, cigarettes, drink and drugs. This chapter deals with each of those in turn.

*

Mother: Our little girl is starting to copy the behaviour of an older boy who has been staying with us. This is disturbing because he can be wild and foolish sometimes. Last night as I was putting her to bed she was making some noises with her mouth; she had heard him doing the same thing around the house earlier in the day. I told her a number of times: 'No noises!' But she continued and even after a firm smack through the bed-clothes she went on doing it. After a second smack she stopped, but burst into tears. I soothed her down and she fell asleep, but I am afraid of her learning bad behaviour, not only for what that will do to her but also because I'll have to deal with it.

It is inevitable that your little girl, who is looking around for things to imitate, will copy the older boy. But still you have to keep talking to her, especially when she is receptive, telling her that it is not good to copy other people, particularly when they are being nasty or unhappy.

'You mustn't copy that, because it will spoil your joy and your happiness. For instance, you'll often see people frowning. Don't copy them. You don't want to go around frowning, because that will make you and other people unhappy. Just be your own joyous being and don't copy anybody.'

*

Father: When our son first went to school his behaviour changed and I realised that he was copying what the other kids were doing. It used to worry me that he was so easily influenced.

Since all children copy what's around them, it's very important that as parents we are worth copying. We just have to accept that they will also copy other boys and girls and what they see on television. The world of experience is so appealing that they have to project themselves into it. But you can still give them the balance of your own life experience and wisdom.

'Come here and be with me because I've got something to say to you. I've noticed over the last couple of weeks that whenever I ask you a question, you blink at me. Your eyelids flicker. Do you know you do that?' (The child has to be made aware of what has probably become an unconscious or habitual behaviour. You might have to point it out when he's actually doing it.)

'There! See? . . . You just did it again. Do you know why you did it? No? Well, let me give you a clue. Your friend Robin does it, doesn't he?'

'Oh . . . Yes.'

Let's say Robin is the smart boy in the school, an older child and hero model. Our child is trying to copy him, and might even be speaking like him.

'You're copying Robin. If you go on like that you won't be able to stop doing it. It's best not to acquire any habit, let alone one that belongs to someone else. You've probably seen boys in the playground copying each other. If you see one boy hitting another, and you copy that and go over and hit him too, he's likely to hit you back. It's not very intelligent is it?

'While there might be some good things that are worth copying in other people, it's best to be what you are, because you are unique you know. Don't just do things because other people do them. Do things because you know they are right for you.'

*

Father: We try to share the kids' interests and as a family we make a conscious effort to spend time together. But as they get older it's getting more difficult. For example they insist on watching certain TV programmes which I can't stand. Too many evenings are getting used up in front of the screen.

As we all know, children today generally like to watch a lot of television. Watching some programmes may be entertaining or instructional, but generally television excites and stimulates mental activity. The constantly changing images and the beat of the music in videos and computer games speeds up the reception of information, and increases expectation and the need for choice. Children of this electronic age are going to become more easily agitated, less patient and more and more tense because of all this electromagnetic ingestion.

According to your knowledge of what's right for your child you can limit the viewing. When you allow them to watch television on their own, you can say why it is that you don't want to join them.

'I can't watch those programmes. They're entertainment, and that's fair enough, but I find they produce too much momentum in me. Then I want to go on watching — one programme after another — because I need more and more entertainment. And then my mind won't stop. So that's why I don't watch too much of it.

'Have you ever had that trouble? — you go to bed and your mind won't stop; you can't sleep because you're thinking about something all the time? That can come from watching too much TV or having the radio on too long. I don't know if it's true for you, but you might have a look at it.'

*

Father: We have not had a television in the house since our son Julian was born. In our view he has enough to learn from real-life experience, without the virtual reality of television. Nonetheless, helpful relatives seem to be under the impression that we're depriving him of something important, and now he is at school he's subject to peer-group pressure — to such an extent that rather than admit that he doesn't actually have a TV he will make some excuse for having missed a programme. The playground games are often based in TV culture but that doesn't seem to stop him from joining in.

The way you've been addressing this matter is right, if your perception is that television has no place in raising your child. But I have this observation: there must be a tension in him that drives him to lie rather than admit he doesn't have a TV. You will have to look at that. Do you want to have that tension in him?

Father: So far he seems amazingly happy to amuse himself without television.

You have to be careful in making a statement like that. Since he doesn't have a television he has no alternative. We don't know that he wouldn't be amazingly happy watching it.

Father: I do sometimes think he might be missing some of the more interesting films about wildlife and nature, the quality educational programmes, but he has a good supply of books and he involves himself to a great extent in what we do. We are watching the situation and waiting as long as possible before giving in, but we recognise that television has become part of everyone's life and there is always pressure to conform. When the time is right, we'll get a TV but supervise his viewing.

Yes, I'm sure that time is coming and I agree, supervised viewing and selection of programmes is a must.

Father: I'd like to mention a recent incident, which showed us how subtle and corrupting messages continually seep out through the media. Although we have resisted television, we listen to the radio. One evening, as we were sitting down to supper, we found ourselves listening to that long-standing soap opera, The Archers, 'an everyday story of country folk'. After a while I got up and turned it off. Julian said simply 'Why are they always arguing?'

A good question! And it shows that his home must be a place of harmony and not argument.

Well, young Julian, the answer is this: They are arguing to make sure that you learn how to be unhappy. Soap operas reflect our society's idea of how people live, and it is a life of conflict and argument. Soaps provide mass entertainment and this society relies on conflict to provide entertaining drama. Because conflict is presented as entertainment in the media, our children are taught to argue and therefore be unhappy.

*

Mother: My little boy wants to play with electronic toys and video games. I see these things as harmful to his being. Should I just say no, he can't have them?

Well, can you just say no? Can you be as absolute as that in a society which is becoming more and more mental and electronic? To keep a child isolated from television and electronic toys is going to provoke a psychological reaction in him. It is best to give him a balanced approach. Allow a certain amount but not a surfeit. Restrict it as much as you can, but at the same time allow the experience. How much you allow is a matter for your judgment and depends on the child's temperament and development. But I don't see how you can isolate children for very long from what other children are exposed to. They are all going to be playing together.

You say your son wants to play these games and it is true that with the progress of the electronic age our children are going to want more and more. But as the boy's mother it is for you to practise the truth of life as you know it and therefore you cannot satisfy the wanting in him. You might let your son have a certain number of games, but not every game he wants. And of course it must be explained why he can't have yet another one.

The escalation in the use of electronics is a sign that the human race is rapidly leaving the earth; this will be much more obvious in years to come. As creatures we are becoming less physical and more mental. So I would talk to the boy about that.

'The human race is gradually losing touch with the earth. A hundred years ago you might have gone out to the backyard and milked a cow to get your milk. Now if you ask "Where does the milk come from?" most children are likely to say it comes from the refrigerator (according to a newspaper report I read). The nearest most small children come to a cow is through a TV screen and that's likely to be a cartoon animal that talks.

'You see, we're actually involving ourselves more and more in a mental picture of the world instead of getting out into the fresh air, being with the earth. When I was young there were almost no televisions and no computers and now the world is full of them. A hundred years ago there were lots more trees; most of the trees have been cut down. Two hundred years ago most people lived in the countryside because there were very few cities. And two thousand years ago most men were hunters or farmers and lived very close to nature.

'So gradually we have been leaving the earth but recently the process has speeded up. Not so long ago men first went to the moon and now, as you know, astronauts are often up in space-stations circling the earth. The movement of progress is out into space, further and further away from the earth, the trees and the cows.

'The more that you and your generation play with electronic

toys, video games and things made by man, the less time you have for the natural things of the earth. Okay, there's a place in this world for electronics and all man-made things. We can't change progress. But in our times we still have the chance to discover the difference between man-made things and the nature of the earth. Do you ever notice the difference?

'I say we're all here to enjoy our life on earth. Your computer games give you a mental satisfaction, but nature gives you a chance to enjoy a physical experience. So how about giving it a go?'

I would talk like that to the boy and then I'd drive him out into the country. I'd take him into the fields and get him to smell the earth. We would find a dairy farm somewhere and someone who'd show the boy how cows are milked. He'd see the udder, smell the warm milk, get his fingers around the teats, and put his head against the living hide of the cow.

*

Father: My son wants me to buy him a computer. I'm a bit reluctant. He's only ten. How do you suggest I deal with that?

If he has a reason for having it, and if everything he is doing suggests to you that it is right for him, then get him the best computer you can.

Father: But I don't want him to get caught up in computers. We're always trying to unhook him from the TV. . .

You cannot suppress the world in him. I suggest that if you buy the computer, you have a regular talk with him about what he's doing on it; and don't let him spend too long in front of it.

If you deny him the computer, look to see that he does not get unhappy about it. Instead of sitting in front of the screen, is there some other activity that you can do together? Can you find more time to be with him and talk to him?

The same goes for denying him an opportunity to watch television. Is he unhappy about it? If so, what are you going to do about it?

Parents generally have less and less time for their children. You will find that young children mostly want to watch television because their parents haven't got the time to play with them.

That's human progress.

*

We can endeavour to restrict the electromagnetic influence on our children and keep the world out of them as much as possible. But we have to be careful that we don't isolate them so much that when they are old enough to make their own choices, they do so out of reaction. We have to be very wise about how much to allow; what to give and what not to give. 'How much' is up to the individual parent.

The important thing is to retain a balanced approach in these matters and not to lose your connection with the inner life. You have to be able to see through the world, or the media, to the truth behind it.

There's often some point in a TV programme or movie that you can use to help you live the truth. It's like anything else (including listening to a spiritual master or reading one of his books), you're watching out for the one truth that you can take away with you today: 'Ah! That's it. I'm going to live that one.'

For instance I saw a movie called 'Accidental Hero', starring Dustin Hoffman. The hero is a terrible sleaze-bag and con-man. There's a plane crash and being first on the scene he even steals from the dead. That's the sort of man he is. Later on he's pressed to give his son some fatherly wisdom . . .

'Son, you remember how I said I was going to explain

about life? Well, the thing about life is: it get's weird. People always talking to you about truth like it was toilet paper or something and they got a supply in the closet. But what you learn as you get older is there ain't no truth. All there is, is bullshit. Layers of it. One layer of bullshit on top of another. And what you do in life, like when you're older, is you pick the layer of bullshit you prefer and that is your bullshit — so to speak. You got that? No? Well it's complicated . . . Maybe when you get to college . . .'

That struck me as very good worldly advice from a father to his son. There ain't no truth in the world. It's all bullshit. So know what the world is. And then go and make use of it.

*

It took my intelligence a long time to inform my silly mind that my body did not need to smoke tobacco or drink alcohol in any form. As a young man I smoked and drank. Why? Because when my body was open to all the wonders of life it was instructed by the example of society, my parents and my peers that it was good to have a drink and a cigarette.

What would make children smoke, except the influence of others? You know how awful it is when you start — all the coughing and spluttering. It doesn't come naturally. You've really got to learn how to do it.

When I started to look at this many years ago I couldn't understand why I ever started. Then I saw that we smoke because it's about the only thing we can do that's not against the law but is against almost everyone's wishes. Nobody wants you to smoke when you're twelve. But we want to be adult and do whatever we want and in this we are encouraged by those around us.

'Go on, have one. It's good.'

If you've smoked and tried to give it up, you know who the

devil is. It's the smoker who says: 'Go on, have one.' He wants you to be as degraded as he is, which means he wants your consciousness slowed down to his level. Cigarette smoking and drinking alcohol slow down your consciousness by speeding up your mental activity. The momentum dissipates your stillness. You will notice that smokers and drinkers can't be still for very long.

As living is a progress of experience my body had to go through drinking and smoking. But I only had to go through it because nobody had the power or authority to tell this little boy what was right. My parents endeavoured to tell me, but they didn't have the power and authority because they themselves were doing what they advised me not to do. You don't have authority when you have double standards. You have to live what you say. Then you have power.

*

Father: I have a severe problem with my son. He's 26 now but when he was two, my wife left me and took him away. The boy was brought up without a father. Now he has a severe drug problem, with heroin and cocaine. He has no moral standards. He is a drifter and a criminal. Sometimes he gets depressed and mutilates himself. He steals to get money for drugs. He was caught in a stolen car and put in prison for a while, but as soon as he got out he got even worse.

I stay in touch with him as much as I can, and I've tried everything I can think of to help him. I have been on the spiritual path for many years and it is an absolute hell for me to have this problem. I am always being tempted to think about what I could have done if I had looked after him, instead of letting him go. So I must ask for advice. I went to a famous psychiatrist. She said 'Take him to the police and have him put away.' I went to my guru in India. He said I should let him be and let life look after him. Please, what can you say to me?

'Let life look after him': that is the truth. Life looks after everything. In the East, the real East where the spiritual master sits, we can leave everything to life. But here in our western world it is different; we have a worrying mind. So what can you do? What is most practical?

I understand your love of him and that you want to do something to help him. If you love him, you must do whatever you have to do. But you must not go on torturing yourself. Put him into the care of therapists or a rehabilitation centre. Do whatever you are moved to do. But give up your attachment to him, or you will continue to suffer.

I understand that you want to do something to try to make him change. It may be that you have to give your whole life to him which will require enormous love. Such love can bring about a change. But he might die anyway or revert to his old ways, and if he did, you wouldn't suffer because in your enormous love you would have given to him in the knowledge that everything that happens is done to serve life's purpose.

Nobody changes without being willing. If your son loves his life the way it is and does not want to change, he does not want your help; he will not listen to you and wants nothing from you except, possibly, a handout from time to time.

Does he want to change? If he were in front of me I would ask him straight: 'Do you want to change?'

'What do you mean?'

'What are you prepared to give up? Name it.'

'I'm not prepared to give anything up. I like my life the way it is.'

'Okay. Then have your life. Now go. I don't want to see you again. Go and live your life. When you want to change, I'm always here for you and I will do everything I can for you.

Even if you're dying and you still want to change, I'll be here. But as you don't want to change, you must go on your way. Go and live the life you love.'

He would have to give something up, and go on giving up, to get the necessary energy to make a change, but when the influence of the world is so extreme it requires enormous love and one-pointedness.

When there's nothing more we can do, we must let go and leave it to life.

*

Father: I've had to recognise that there's a limit to the lessons I can pass on to my boys. I can no longer influence their choices. The eldest is now seventeen. For him it's okay to get drunk or stay up talking all night. And of course, like me at his age, he knows much better than his elders.

I recognise that youth can't respect the values of older generations. And in a way that's quite healthy. A sort of God-given protection from our failures. I used to look up to my parents, and teachers at school, but when I saw that they didn't have all the answers, I started questioning life and carved out my own individuality. I was influenced by many things at that age — except for whatever my father or teachers put in front of me.

Isn't that how it has to be? For better or worse?

Yes. To small children, age represents wisdom, competence and something to look up to, but as they grow and become worldly-wise they are more discriminating. They start to see through the shortcomings and posturings of their elders. In adolescence they tend to regard their parents as failures and hypocrites — rightly and wrongly. They see Mum and Dad as fallible; and they themselves as infallible.

It happens because every adolescent carries within him a perception of guru, the wise one. He sees his unlived years as offering the certainty of that achievement. But what he does not see, and cannot see, is what living does to youth's untried ideals, how it reduces all (except the exceptional few) to the mediocrity of compromise, worry and the old-age pension.

In adolescence the youthful vision has not yet been smeared by fear of death. Death, the end of all achievement, is still well over the horizon, and interesting only as a subject for late night discussions. But as the years of experience pile up, its shadowy presence creeps over the horizon and clouds the vision. This hazy perception of approaching death makes man world-weary. He realises unconsciously that there is no hope. He starts to give up. And as though he were death itself he rounds on youth and decries the vision splendid. Thus all generations follow each other into mediocrity.

Man's only immortality is to imagine he lives on through future generations — instead of realising guru, the immortal being in himself.

Guru, the wise one in every youth, is not an ideal. Guru is he or she who retains the vision of youth undeterred by the fog or fear of death. Guru sees through to the horizon, to the vision splendid. There is no death. The fog was simply fear.

THE SHADOW OF DEATH

C an you speak to your children about death as you speak
to them of love or life? Or are you living under the shadow
of death, afraid to speak of it and afraid of dying?

It's very important, right from the start, to tell the children
about death and how people die. Although at first it might
seem difficult, the more you open yourself to truth and reality
the more you will communicate with your children about life,
love, God — and death.

The more you speak the language of truth, the easier it will
be. Your own genius for the truth will speak through you and
you'll be amazed at what comes out of your mouth. Once we
are able to get through the fear and rationality put into every
one of us as our self, we discover that under the emotion is
the wisdom that has no fear of death, and the knowledge that
all forms of life come and go; but I, love, am forever. That is
the reality — to be lived if we will only give up the fear,
excitement, pain and hurt that we've accumulated and which
is generally passed on to the children as our ignorance.

Talking to your child about death it is best to come from your own self-knowledge and keep all explanations simple. Of course as the child is a reflection to you of relative innocence, you will be able to observe your own hesitancy and fears about death. And you will have to face up to those fears in yourself.

You have to know that the fear of death is only imagination. The fear is neither the fact nor the truth. When a dead body is in front of you it is absolutely self-evident that the life has gone out of it. But in our society there is almost no opportunity to see this. Dead bodies are quickly spirited away and hidden from view; with the result that everyone is terrified of death — and forced to use their imagination instead of being able to see the simple fact and truth of it.

Everyone is afraid of death. In some the fear is more overt than in others and in many it will not rise to the surface sufficiently to be evident at all. But death, or the fear of it, is always with us. How on earth can we stand to live with it? How do we survive? — by forgetting about it. Everyone plans to go on living. 'Time I took out life insurance for when I'm seventy-five. Payable on death? Well, that isn't going to happen, I trust. I hope and pray that I will be spared.'

Every body dies. But everyone likes to forget that every body dies. People are afraid of dying only because they are not exposed to its reality. Death is ignored; and that is our greatest ignorance. But when you face the fact that you're going to die, do you die?

Facing the fact of death makes you intelligent. You no longer think that you are going to live forever so you don't get so worried about immediate problems. If you're going to die anyway how much do the problems matter? People who fret and get angry believe they're going to go on living. When you realise you are going to die, you start to give up your anger and worry.

Because of the usual avoidance of death, most adults do not approach the truth until they suddenly have to face either the imminence of their own death or the loss of someone they love; and then the pain and shock is truly fearful. But parents endeavouring to live the truth are able to introduce death to their children, raising them with awareness of what it is and diminishing the fear and the pain.

From an early age children should be helped to see that the death of bodies is a natural process. This can be done using the example of plants, insects and animals. When it comes to the death of people children need to be shown that what they love is the invisible life in the body, the spirit; in other words, that people are not their bodies but the love we have for them and they had for us. Unlike our bodies, this love — this spirit, this life we are — can never die.

'Do you see that magpie? What is it doing on the lawn? Can you see what it's doing? It's eating worms. Do you see how it turns its head to the side and actually seems to be listening, to hear where the worm might be wriggling under the ground? Then in goes its beak, out comes the worm and the magpie eats it.

'Do you know that everything on this earth has to die to keep something else alive? Isn't that amazing? That's the law of life. The berries on the trees have to die to feed the blackbird. One day the bird will die and its body will rot and go back into the earth where the plants grow that bear the berries that the birds eat. That's life and death; that's how it is.'

Whenever you mention death to a child, always demonstrate love. That is most important. Always mention love in connection with death.

'You know how when the sky is blue and the sun is shining and there's a nice breeze blowing through the trees we say "Oh what a lovely day!" That means we recognise the love-ly in the day.

'We can feel our love of the day now, inside us. That love

is always there. Even when our bodies die, the love has no end. Because you love it, it cannot go.

'We see and enjoy the loveliness in the trees and the birds, the grass and the flowers, because our bodies have senses, like sight and touch-feeling. When the body dies, the senses disappear. But the love of the day is still there. Love is forever.

'Plants die. Animals die. It doesn't matter what it is, it's going to pass away. Everything that we see around us is going to die, including all the people. Mummy and Daddy and Auntie and Uncle and Granny and Grandpa . . . One day we will all be gone. But you needn't worry about it because the love you feel for us doesn't die. The love is the truth; that's what's real. So when you feel your love of Daddy, you are feeling the real part of me. And the love for you that I have inside of me is the real thing. My body, or your body, which we can see and touch, is nothing like as real as the love. It's just a body that is going to die, like all the other bodies that always die.

'In the world, people get very upset by talk of death and when somebody dies they weep and mourn. They don't know that when the body goes, the love is still there. "Oh my God" they cry, "My love is dead" — because they think the love and the body are the same thing. From the moment of birth every body is bound to die, yet all those people weeping for their loved ones are mourning the inevitable death of the body. You're not going to do that when somebody dies, because we will keep reminding you that love can never die.'

'But Daddy, you're not going to die and leave us, are you?'

'Life will decide when I die, and no one ever knows when that will be. (Even if they think otherwise, nothing in life is certain.) But whenever it is that my body dies, I can tell you that if you look inside for your love of me, you will feel the same love in you that you feel now.

'Every body in time must go, be buried, burnt or destroyed, but though my body will have gone, you will have the knowledge that I am truly with you; I am not dead.'

*

Every love comes from a place deep down in the human psyche where all love is the love of God. That essence of love is in every body. When a body dies the love in it goes back into the psyche towards that place — to the love of God, which in the living individual had become the love of some other living body. It goes to where it is loved. If I am love, then when the body dies I must go into the one who truly loves me.

This is beyond the rational, doubting mind: 'If your love goes into everybody who loves you, then it will have to be distributed in so many little bits that there will be very little left for me.' The scientific mind is so ignorant. The love of God is ever-present and totally fulfilling.

Whether the love is of mother, father, child, lover, or whoever, the love is one love, yet it bears a distinct and unique 'fingerprint', a knowledge: 'Yes, this love is the love of my mother (or whoever).' It is all love, yet the miracle is that each facet of love has that print of individual love upon it.

Only doubt, fear and rationality stop us from feeling the energy that goes into us when someone we love dies; an energy that informs us 'I am loved'. That is why, when somebody you love dies, it is so important to open yourself to the mystery of the love that does not die. Be still, poised, alert and sensitive; and preferably be in nature. The important thing is to stay with the love.

When my body dies, if you love me, keep being true to me inside of you, in stillness as much as you can; and get on with your life, doing the best you can. You will find a smile on your face at the oddest times; and in that smile there will be the knowledge: 'What he said is true.' There will be no visions, no knowing; just knowledge.

In the western world we are so far from reality that the truth of love and death is buried in notions and ceremonies. The complication of existence is that we are so far away in time from our beginning that it's very difficult to be still enough to be the love that has no form except as knowledge. Seeing through death is the way back.

*

At the end of the movie 'Shadowlands' the Christian philosopher C S Lewis sits with his adopted son as they sob their hearts out in grief. The woman Lewis loved, the boy's mother, has died after a long illness.

Sobbing on those occasions is a release of the force invested in facing what had to be faced. Man and boy sob together and the film ends — without a word of wisdom about death, although it is at just such a time that the truth can be most clearly heard. In the same circumstances I would do my best to speak intelligently to the boy.

'Son, at times like this, will you notice, please, that the sobbing does not continue. It is the release of the force of a great pain inside of us. For a few seconds it works to open us up to the pain and then it stops. Notice, when it suddenly stops, that you feel a release inside of you, a kind of joy — not that we are joyful because your mother is dead, but because there's been a release from the terrible pain that supported the unhappiness while we watched her die.

'Do not be afraid to be joyous in these moments of release. The sobbing may occur again, in a few minutes, or tomorrow, or tonight; but it won't last. Don't hold on to it. Don't try to perpetuate it. People won't know what to say to you and because of their sentimentality they will sympathise with you.

308

You may want to continue sobbing to show them you hear what they say, but don't do that. Don't be sentimental.

'Know, my son, that inasmuch as you love your mother there is no death. Wherever love is, the essence of her is there. Your mother has no body of her own any more, so she has died into your body, into your love. If you love her inside, she is there. But if you try to think about her, miss her or are sentimental about her, you will miss the living truth of her love, which is still there inside you.

'When anybody you love dies, that's where the love goes. But it doesn't die there. Love lives there. Doesn't it?

'If you can feel your love now you will know that it is the love of everyone you ever loved, with no reference to any particular person. Can you feel the absence, the emptiedness? That is the love of nothing. All love lives there in the living being that you are. All love — the one undifferentiated love called the love of God.'

*

Christopher: Just before the end of last term a boy at school was drowned.

You knew him?

Christopher: Yes, at school.

What was the reaction inside of you? What did it mean to you when you heard he had drowned?

Christopher: I was sad.

Everyone in the world feels sad when a friend dies, but do you know why you were sad?

Christopher: Because I used to see him every day and now I don't.

When we do the same things every day a certain momentum occurs in us, an expectation that things will continue as they are. But life is not like that. We can't expect things to go on as they are. Because you saw your friend every day, you expected to go on seeing him every day. Then he disappeared. People are disappearing around you all the time, but you don't get sad about it. The people you had breakfast with this morning have all disappeared, haven't they? (They aren't here.) You wouldn't say they are dead, because you think you're going to see them again. When someone dies that expectation is broken. You realise you are never going to see your friend again. That is what makes you sad. But can you see that your sadness is not because he has died, but because you expected him to live?

Now the truth of death for everybody is this: You are going to enter death tonight. At around ten o'clock or eleven o'clock tonight you are going to withdraw from your senses, from your sight and your hearing, and your body is going to disappear. That's your experience, isn't it? Every night you go to sleep and disappear — just like your friend, who from his point of view, simply withdrew from his body, just like you're going to do tonight when you go to sleep. To you, he drowned and died. But for him, it was just like falling asleep.

When you are asleep tonight, where is your body?

Christopher: In the bed?

No, that's not the truth. To say it is in the bed you would have to be awake looking at it. I'm talking about when you've gone to sleep. Where's your body then? There's no body, is there? So it was for your friend when he drowned. From his point of view, death is just like being asleep with no body. We who are awake, looking at his body, see that he is dead. We see that he is certainly not just asleep, because he's withdrawn from his senses forever. He has disappeared. Soon his body will no longer exist. But so what? What is there to be afraid of? We withdraw every night from our senses, and we're not frightened of going to sleep.

I am not frightened of 'not existing'. Are you?

No — because when you're in deep, dreamless sleep and you're not even dreaming, you don't exist. Where's your mother? Where's your father? Where's school? Where's all the worry about your homework? All gone.

When any of us die we go into a place that we already know is most desirable, because every night without fail we love to go to sleep; and every morning, without making any decision about it, we wake up and find ourselves back in our bodies. What would it matter if we didn't wake up? Your friend didn't wake up, but it didn't matter to him. It only matters to his family and friends who wish he was still alive. It only matters because they can't face the fact of his death. The time had come for him to leave his body for good, but they imagined and expected that he would go on living.

Christopher: But we miss him.

You will only miss him if you think about him. Most people put all their faith in the appearance of things, so they tend to miss the presence, or love and sweetness that is within everyone. If you enjoyed being with him, what you loved was his presence. He was really a mirror of your enjoyment as you looked and saw that you were in harmony with him. He reflected your own presence of love and that has not died.

How can presence be in the past? It is always now. And you will be able to feel it as a good sensation inside yourself, if you are still enough. So don't think back about him or think about the times you had together; and then you will not miss him.

*

Father: It won't be long before I am arranging my Dad's funeral. He's dying of cancer. In the back of my mind I wonder . . . When the time comes, and he is dead, will I take the children to see the body?

As anyone who has ever seen a dead body knows, it is very obvious that there's nothing there, that what was loved has departed. What was sweet, gentle, wonderful and full of life is now an empty shell. The reality we recognise as a living being has withdrawn and nothing remains. There is nothing to fear in death for there is no one 'there'. Most children in our society are denied this experience.

We get fearful about death because we are not shown the fact of it. So there is a value in showing your children a dead body, although beforehand you should make it clear what the point of the exercise is — to demonstrate that when a body is dead there's nothing there. Of course it requires your own wisdom and judgment to determine whether the children are old enough or ready for this. They have to have been rightly instructed about death, so that they don't get at all fearful about what they will see or start to imagine what it will be like; or refer to what they've seen in horror films. If they have been prepared by right instruction, then there won't be a problem. Indeed, it will be a very intelligent moment for them.

'Yes, I see. There's nothing there. Look, you can see. It's actually dead. Grandad is not there any more.'

'No. That's right. What we loved was the life in his body,

312

and that has now departed into another place inside of us, where the love still is and the being never dies.'

*

Mother: My little boy, who's four, said to me, quite out of the blue, 'I wish I didn't have to die. I wish people could live forever.'

He doesn't know he's going to die. He's been told he's going to die; he wouldn't know otherwise. We are the product of the suggestions put into us. We are conditioned to believe in death. When he mentions something like that again, and provided he's receptive, you could prepare him for the truth of dying . . .

'You go to sleep every night, don't you? And you know it's very nice to go to sleep. We do enjoy going to sleep when we are tired, don't we? But if we didn't wake up the next day, how would we know? We wouldn't — would we?'

A child who has not yet been too conditioned by thought and emotion may get the point quicker than an adult. But it's a question everyone should ask themselves: If I don't wake up tomorrow morning, who's to know?

Continuing to speak to the child: 'You see, death is like going to sleep. While we're asleep we don't have any worries and we don't know anything about dying. So if you didn't wake up one morning you wouldn't be worried about it.'

'But why do people have to die. Why can't they live forever?'

'Well, just imagine what the world would be like if everything lived forever. If the ants lived forever, the whole place would be crawling with them. If nothing died there'd be vines growing over all the buildings. Every vine that ever lived would go on growing over the whole place. We wouldn't be able to hold them back. We wouldn't be able to get down the road. We wouldn't be able to walk on the footpaths or drive our cars. There'd be vines and trees and grass intertwined and growing everywhere and the roads and the houses would soon be covered over. If nothing died and people lived forever there would be so many people the streets would be filled up and you wouldn't be able to go out. You wouldn't be able to have your dinner because nobody could cook enough meals for all the people. My goodness, don't you see? It is good the way things are; that everybody has to disappear. Then we are not crowded out. So death is good because it allows those of us who are alive now the room to exist!'

*

Man: I'm not clear what you are saying about sleep and dying. There is a difference. When I die I won't be waking up in the morning!

First of all, how do you know you're going to die?
Let's look at life as it is. Tonight you will go to sleep. That's just like when you die. There's no difference between being dead and being in deep dreamless sleep.

Man: But Barry, when I go to sleep I know I'm going to wake up again.

Did you know that while you were asleep?

Man: No. Maybe I dream, that's all. Otherwise I'm asleep till I wake up again.

How do you know that's not the same as death?

Man: Because I wake up next morning.

How do you know you don't wake up when you die? You can't wake up here when you die, because you're dead. But how do you know you don't wake up?

Man: Wake up where?'

Well, why don't you wait and see. Death's a wonderful adventure. I always wake up. You can't tell me there was a day when you didn't wake up, can you?'

Man: No, I can't . . . So, Barry, are you saying we die and go to heaven or somewhere?

Wherever did you get that crazy notion? I said there's no difference between being dead and being in deep dreamless sleep. What do you know about heaven when you're fast asleep?

Man: Nothing.

That's right. Get rid of everything you think you know. Die to every thought, belief, and every bit of conditioning. And then you know nothing.

∗

Mother: When we are frightened, is it basically the fear of death? I have a five year-old who gets very frightened about all sorts of things. For instance she heard about an earthquake in Japan and now she's scared it's going to happen here. What can I say to her?

Yes, that's the fear of death. But as she grows older she will gradually acquire the heavy burden of living — more information about the world and more unhappiness — and she'll get so concerned with her problems that she won't have time to be worried about death. It won't cross her mind. She will assume that she's not going to die.

It would be good if you could speak to her about life and love and death. Find a time when she's in a good place within herself and speak to her reassuringly, taking account of her sensitivity.

'Now, listen to me, there's nothing to worry about. It's true there has been an earthquake in Japan and there were a lot of people killed. But do you know that a few years ago in Mexico the same thing happened? And I remember when it happened in Greece. Japan and Mexico and Greece are different countries in quite different parts of the world . . . Let's get the atlas. Here it is. See there . . . That's Greece. See? There were people killed in the earthquake there too, a few years ago.

'But you know, people are dying every day. Every body has to die, but there's nothing to worry about. The wonderful thing is that though every body dies, what you are doesn't die. You are not your body. You are the love that you have for me and that can never die. I want you to know that as long as ever you feel your love of me, I am there. Even if my body is not. Isn't that amazing? That's life and that's love. So don't you ever worry about people dying.

'Next time we go for a walk, we're going to look around and see if it's true that every living thing dies. The leaves fall off the trees and die. The flowers die. The little birds and the flies and the mice die. You can point out anything to me that has died and I'll point anything dead that I see. And yet, although living things are always dying, they are always being born. Some body dies: another body is born. Life keeps coming back in different forms.

'That's life and death — a continual amazing process of appearing and disappearing. You may as well say there is no death! So there's nothing to be afraid of, is there? No, don't be afraid.'

*

Father: On two or three occasions in one week, without anything prompting it, my six year-old boy said, 'I don't want my body to be buried when I die. I want to be left where I am.' He was concerned about being buried in the ground.

There is a confusion in his mind between two states. One is: 'I see that if I am buried I will be cut off from the air, the light and from natural living as I know it.' The other is: 'I want to be where I am when I die.'

The truth is: It matters not what is done to my body when it's dead because then I do not have a body. I am where I am when I die, just as I am where I am in deep dreamless sleep. Only when my consciousness comes into my brain (as my awareness) is my body created.

So if I was to demonstrate this to your boy, I would do it like this: 'Let's play at making shadows on the wall. I'll get the candle and put the handkerchief over my hand and you watch as the shadows make a rabbit . . . Now, if Mummy puts her hand out, look, there's a tree! Suddenly we take our hands away, or I blow out the candle, and the wall is just blank again. Well, that's what it is like to live and to die. In reality nothing's happened, but the shadows on the wall have come and gone.'

Father: I hear the truth of that, but it doesn't seem to be the whole story. I'm more than a shadow. I'm not just being manipulated by some other intelligence . . . To a large extent I'm responsible for what happens.

That's right. Our bodies are shadows on the wall and yet we

317

have to be responsible for them. We have to engage entirely in the shadow game. We have to come right into our shadow bodies. Then this game of life seems so real it is no longer a game. If we really participate in it and are fully engaged, somehow we automatically connect up with the light, or where it's all coming from. But we have to engage in it. We can't try to get back to the light by saying "Oh I don't like this game. I don't want to be in this world." If you do that you keep yourself away from the light and then you know tension and fear.

Father: I suppose we all feel at odds with the world, parents and children, to some extent.

Even when you feel at odds you must do your best not to withdraw from life in existence, although the natural impulse is to fight against it, to try to get away from it because it is such a divided condition to be living in this world. I must be able to be in this existence, to be what is, for obviously it is created by some intelligence and has some source or cause. And if I can't divine the cause, or have the knowledge of it, then I have to say, 'What is, is best' — for what else can I say?

Can I change it? I can change it around, I can move something from here to there, but can I change it as a whole? No, I cannot.

Finally, when I realise I cannot change anything in life, I surrender to what is. And that is peace. I bow to an intelligence which I do not understand, and do not need to understand, and in so doing I align myself with that intelligence, where I come from, and then somehow I am that. There are no more shadows.

EMERGING SEXUALITY

T he time comes when your child asks a question about sex.
Don't project forward to that moment before it happens;
and in the moment, don't allow yourself to think, 'Oh, this is
going to be tough!' Answer the question as truthfully as you
can, according to the experience of the child, and remember
that it is important not to anticipate the next question. Children
don't put things together like adults so they don't follow up
with a stream of enquiry. They ask their questions at the right
time, and when they get an answer sufficient to their need they
go on their way.

Sex arises from secrets. If men and women in this world were
as innocent of sex as little children, nothing would be hidden
in their sexual experience. There would be no secret fantasies,
private guilts and unspoken desires, and no parent would be
afraid of speaking openly about sex to the children, or
uncertain about how to help them face their emerging sexuality.

For man, woman's vagina will always be a mystery; but the
mystery should not be a secret. In every action of love a man

should be able to see through what he's looking at, into the beauty behind it. The most glorious beauty is inside the female vagina — the shrine for man. Sex only arises when man thinks about what he can't see, and then makes a secret of it.

How can we best prepare the boy for this mystery when we live in a sexually corrupt world? Is it for instance a good idea for a mother to let her son see her naked body? Sooner or later, even in all innocence he will ask you the question: 'What's that under the pubic hair?' Should both parents walk around the house naked so that their young sons and daughters can see their genitals? I cannot make any categorical statements about this; it is for you to look and see what is right. As parents you have to determine if and when it is right for your child to see you naked and that will depend on your own openness in these matters and the age and innocence of the child. You will be guided by your own lights. But whatever way you deal with this, you have to watch for the sexuality that will enter the child's mind under the influence of the world.

By seven years old a boy is likely to be sexually curious. No matter how much he's been with the naked bodies of his parents as an infant, by now the sexuality of the world will be entering him through the conversations he hears, what he sees on television and observes around him. As children become more sexually aware, more sexual curiosity and excitement is put into them. Sexual talk amongst themselves fuels their curiosity. They learn to associate excitement with sex. Soon sex and excitement amount to the same thing.

The parents have to be the judge of what is suitable for their children to see at any time. I am sometimes asked if it is a good idea for children to see their parents making love. I say that I do not recommend it because the way things are there's too much sex in boys and girls, and too much sex in the environment. Their minds will get to work on what they are seeing because of something they've heard from one of their friends or something they saw on television which excited them. So as parents you have to ask each other, 'Is our child still innocent enough to be with us when we're making love?'

Why as adults would we want to watch a couple making love, even on a movie screen? — because we want to indulge the sexual excitement of watching something normally hidden from us. Anything hidden can be emotionalised and the sexual emotion in everybody is always waiting for the chance to get excited. Some people say they are offended by the sight of making love; but emotionally that's the same as being sexually excited by it. Sex hides in both secrecy and shame.

The truth of making love is that it should have no effect whatever on an observer. You should be able to watch without any excitation, with eyes that just see the action. You should be able to watch with no identification whatsoever.

The truth is that when a man and woman make love there is really nothing happening. The man is inside the woman. He's going through the actions and doing what he's doing. She's responding in her way. There are two bodies interacting — that's all. That's the truth of the matter. But we have invented a subconscious world of fantasies, sexual secrets, hiding, shame and excitement; a place where we identify with what's happening and distort reality.

The identification is in the watcher; and in the performer when he or she is watching and thinking. If the couple were punching each other instead of making love we might say, 'Look at them fighting. They're so angry.' But we don't really know that they are angry. They are just two bodies punching each other.

We assume so much from the actions we observe, yet really our entire emotional life is inside us; it's not in the physical world at all. The physical is just the performance. In reality it's all happening inside of us. We are repelled by anger because that's what happens inside of us. We are excited by the sight of a couple making love because of the sexual emotion inside of us. If just the intelligence is watching, it's only an act. But if our emotions can be excited they can watch through our eyes.

There is no secret in two people making love. There are just two bodies in interaction. If everyone could face this truth, it would soon clear the hidden fantasies and sexual secrets out of the subconscious world. If everyone, including the children, could see couples making love at any time and anybody could make love at any time without sexual excitement, the world would be purified of sex. But of course that is a very long way away from where we live today.

Father: We have been quite open with our two young children [a boy and a girl]. We don't hide our bodies from them, but we don't walk around displaying them either. We've been able to preserve the innocence, I think, so they can look through us.

Mother: The girl once asked why she doesn't have a penis.

Yes, the question will come. Why shouldn't she ask a question like that? If her father was walking naked from the bathroom to the bedroom, why wouldn't he stop and talk to her? And that might be just the moment for her to ask the question. What did you answer?

Mother: Men have a penis and women have a vagina instead.

And did she ask about the relation between them? No? — because that was sufficient for her in the first instance. You left it at that. Good. Always take it one step at a time.

322

Father: How would you answer the next question, though? Say it was 'What is a penis for?'

You have to answer as honestly as possible and with the fact: 'What is my penis for? Well, first of all it is for passing water. We've all got to go to the toilet. Boys do it that way and girls do it the way you do it.'

Then one day the question will be 'Mummy, where do babies come from?' But you can't tell them that until they are ready and the question is asked.

Father: Our boy knows that babies come from a woman.

Does he know how they get there?

Father: No, he hasn't asked that one.

At some stage he will and that's when you have to take him out into the garden and tell him about the birds and the bees.

'Come on, the best way I can tell you about this is to show you what the bee does with the flowers. So there's one, over there. You watch and see what he's doing. The penis is like the bee. The bee is carrying pollen which has got to get into the flower to make more flowers. See how he has to go deep into the flower? That's like the vagina. The flower has a place inside, like a woman has a place inside her. And the bee goes in there and puts some pollen down inside.'

Draw natural parallels, wherever you can, to instil the knowledge that procreation is a natural function. Then, when they are ready, you can introduce the idea that in the intercourse of man and woman there has to be love.

'Because the flower is pleased to have what the bee brings, she gives him some of her pollen, which is her fragrance. And that's like the love between men and women.'

Be watchful when you are talking to children like this that you do not have any excitement in you. Always keep the excitement (the sex) out of anything to do with love. You can explain this to your children as they approach puberty.

'Excitement gets mixed up with love. People like love so much that they make the mistake of thinking about it when it's not happening. This gets them stimulated and excited and that gets mixed up with love. Really love is not exciting at all, but it is very pleasurable. It is a great feeling of sweetness and rightness. Love is very good. So you see, when adults make love with their bodies it is not just about making babies. Love is about making life good. Men and women have to have love between them to make their life good.

'You know that when life is good it's not exciting, don't you? Remember what we said about your birthday party? It's best not to look forward to it and you can enjoy it much more if you don't get excited. It's very important that you remember this: love is best if you don't get excited about it.'

Always do your best to keep the excitement out of children. It's that excitement that fuels their sexuality in later life and causes most adult sexual problems.

*

Mother: My eleven year-old daughter is beginning to be attracted to boys. We had a meeting with the teacher at school who said she's apparently very bright and was doing well in lessons but because she's attractive her head is being turned by boys. It's distracting her from her work.

How does she feel about boys? Have you talked to her about it? No? Then choose the right moment, for example when she mentions something to do with a boy she's met. Open up a conversation so that she can say what she feels.

Mother: Her general attitude is that she has friends who are boys and friends who are girls. But then all of a sudden I hear there's been a falling out and a friend has become almost an enemy.

Girls of that age do tend to favour someone then go off them, don't they? 'Oh I hate him.' This is part of their development around the age of puberty and it is important to say to her, 'Ah, well, yes . . . I understand. You've gone off him' — so that you prepare for a more serious dialogue with her when the time comes.

It's true of course that she will be distracted from her studies but I don't know that you can do anything about it except talk with her as much as possible. Encourage her to confide in you. She needs to know that you will listen to what she says without wanting to correct her behaviour (until the time comes to do that). It should not be a mother-daughter dialogue, where you have all the authority, but the conversation of 'two girls together'.

'I'll tell you about something that happened when I was your age. Gosh, I did take a shine to this boy! Can't remember his name now, but he was a bit older than me and lived down the road . . .'

Mother: Does she have to go through what I went through? — the embarrassing sexual experiences, the heartbreaks and depressions? I suppose it's an unavoidable part of adolescence, but can I do anything to help her?

She has to get her experience, but you can certainly help her to get through it by being open with her and addressing her questions about love and sex. It is very important for a young girl to have an open relationship with her Mum — important for both of you and very reassuring for her. Speak to her about the reality of love so that when she's talking with

325

her girlfriends about the facts of life she knows she can always come to you or her father to get the facts straight. She must know she can confide in you and that you are able to instruct her from your own experience of love.

Take the opportunity when it presents itself. For instance, when her breasts become prominent enough she may refer to them. Or she might not mention anything but her behaviour will show somehow that she is becoming selfconscious about her breasts. So take the opportunity to inform her about the maturing process in a general way. Tell her that the sexual energy has started to come into her and although it isn't fully developed yet, this energy is the power to make babies and of course the breasts are needed by babies when they feed from the nipple.

It is important to talk to her about menstruation before her first period. Inform her of what it means to have a period and why it happens. You will probably already have explained the fact that children are born out of the womb and how they get there; but make sure she hears it rightly, and hears it from you and not just from her schoolfriends. Tell her the biological facts about menstruation: the period is the shedding of the lining in the womb when it is not needed; but when a woman is pregnant the period stops because the womb has to develop a placenta to nourish the baby. Tell her the facts of the body scientifically, but always relate them to the living of life, speaking perhaps about your experience of your own body as a girl and as a mature woman.

Now that she has an interest in boys, talk to her about the attraction between man and woman and how there is a drive in man for him to enter woman's body with his private part.

'The sexual drive is in all the species. That's how the earth is populated and it's quite natural. In animals the sexual drive is an instinct, and in us it is instinctive too. Our sexual drive to reproduce ourselves is blind and in a man it just endeavours to get into a woman's body to mate and produce children.

'But then man and woman are not like the other animals, just driven to populate the earth. We are animals, but we do not just act with animal instinct. We have the power of self-reflection and self-consciousness; and there are many other considerations in us being together, apart from just populating the planet.

'As man and woman together we have discovered that we have the power of love. The sexual drive on its own doesn't make love. It takes the added quality of knowing or being love. So man and woman bring the power of love to sexual instinct, which means we don't make love just with the sexual drive, or just to make babies.

'Of course the drive to procreate is very strong in us and there is the possibility when we make love of becoming pregnant or conceiving a baby. But there's such a thing as contraception, which in most cases protects us from pregnancy. It certainly doesn't protect us from sex, though; in fact it makes us open to mistake sex for love. So it's important that you start to learn about these things. When you are a fully grown woman it will be very important to you that you don't mistake sex for love, but find real love instead.'

In this way you can start to instruct your daughter in the difference between love and sex. Invite her to ask you what the difference is, any time that she's confused. Go on to discuss the girl's experience of herself. If you apply what you say to your own life and to hers it will be easy to show her where the love is and where the sex is, and how as man and woman we have the power and the consciousness to bring love into the sexual drive. Always put personal experience against the background of what life and love are about.

'You see how careful we have to be not to confuse love with the sexual drive? Sex is a drive to come together. It is urgency

and excitement and, as you know, anything that introduces
excitement into you later brings unhappiness. In love there is
no urgent need to do anything; there is just passion and the
sweetness of the senses. So it is best not to allow a man's
private part to go into you unless there is love.'

*

Mother: I am raising two boys on my own. The older one
seems to be having wet dreams and I have wondered how to
deal with the subject of masturbation with them. Is it a
necessary thing for boys to go through?

Not many boys will avoid masturbation. Once they discover
it there is a natural move in them to re-experience the beautiful
feeling it engenders. And when they reach puberty there is a
natural urge to sow their seed.

This is a lusting society and all boys are psychically
impregnated by all its sexual influences. They will be driven
to masturbate and it cannot be stopped. When they are men
with some experience of real woman, they may learn to love
her direct. Then, if they can give up sexual fantasising, the
habit of masturbation will fall away. But you can't talk about
that to a young boy. In fact the reason boys masturbate is
because they have not yet had the experience of actually
loving woman.

Wet dreams can introduce a boy to the idea of real
woman. It may depend on the individual but I recall in my
own experience that the form of a woman would appear to
me in wet dreams. I know now that even though I was very
young, it was the same woman I speak to today; the woman
in every woman, the female principle that draws us into
existence through sex; that draws us back into death — the
death of self. That's how it is for men: woman draws us into

existence through sex; then she turns into God and pulls us back inside.

The best way for you as a mother to deal with this area is to be honest with your boys and if it happens that one of them is having wet dreams, or a question about it arises, sit down with him at a suitable moment and talk about it. You would have to ask him what his experience is, because I don't know that every boy has a woman in a wet dream. You must gain his confidence so that he can talk about it freely and not be ashamed by what is just a natural process. Then, at the right time in his life, you may be able to talk to him about real woman.

'There is a divine female principle, the most beautiful thing to man on this earth. It is divine because it comes from God, which means it is not in existence. But it can come into existence in an abstract way, through your dreaming, and make this extraordinary thing happen to you — a wet dream. It is this principle of woman that man really loves. When she comes into his life she gives him the extraordinary pleasure of what is called making love. You will engage in that when you are old enough and you are a responsible man. Until then I advise you not to try to make love to a woman. It is best to wait.

'Generally a man starts to become responsible when he can pay his own way. If before then you need to love woman, then you must be very careful, because when people are not responsible sexual experience makes them very unhappy.

'Also, I want to say something to you about masturbation. Most boys do it. Often they keep it a secret and feel bad about it. But it is nothing to feel guilty about. There's nothing wrong with masturbation. But all the same, don't do it too often, don't go to extremes . . .'

Whether a parent can really help to restrain a young man from sexual fantasising is very doubtful. Life's just got to take its course. But as the mother of your sons you will be watching to see what is right for them and will do your best to guide them.

*

Father: I went into my son's room and he was embarrassed because he'd obviously been playing with his penis. I'd like to be open with him about masturbation but it is a difficult subject for me to talk about. I can't really say it's natural and okay when it's taken me so long to realise that it's not. I have said he can speak to me about it if he wants. My own parents never mentioned it so I felt secretive about it and used to wonder if they knew. I guess I still feel uneasy about the subject.

Yes, I hear the difficulty. You should certainly dispel any secretiveness about it. Speak to him from your own experience, bearing in mind his age and exposure to the sexual world. Remember also that you do not have to say anything to him that he has not actually asked about.

Sexuality is programmed into the brain and manifests at a very early age for both boys and girls. In a very young girl it is often clear to the men around her, especially her father. All children are likely to experiment and play with their genitals, because it's the human condition to be fascinated by them. The reason is that the genitals contain the means of being in both heaven and hell on earth; and man and woman are fascinated by heaven and hell.

All animals go where the pleasure is. As food is pleasure, pet animals will always come to us for their food. We human creatures want to enjoy life and find the pleasure in it. The penis is a source of pleasure and the easiest pleasure to find when we're alone, apparently, is to play with our genitals — even when we are very young. At a very early age boys start to play with the penis to enjoy its particular pleasure.

Unlike the pleasure of food, which is integrated with the body's internal sensation, penis-pleasure is genetically associated with a separate consciousness. The programming in the brain makes the penis separate from the body and when boys start to play with their genitals that confirms the sense of the penis as a separate entity. To the self-consciousness of the body this separate existence of the penis is mysterious. The ignorance of our society and the human condition in which we are entrapped turns the wonder and mystery into something hidden and secret.

For man to be fully responsible in making love with woman he must stop giving his penis this separate identity. Then it is not just an appendage of the body but a sensation integrated with the rest of his sensation — it is one with his being. He must become the power of the penis.

The two most powerful organs in existence are the penis and the vagina for they generate all the life in existence — all the beauty and pleasure of it. No one ever saw the beauty of a sunrise who did not come from the penis being in the vagina. They also generate all the problems; no one has ever felt the pain of heartbreak who did not come from the penis in the vagina. They have the power to bring heaven and hell to earth, but this society is so far down the track of time that man and woman are deep in ignorance of it. And yet, behind all the intellectual and scientific speculation about life on earth, what is the power of existence if not the penis in the vagina?

Unless I am that power, I cannot be free of existence. To be that power through the whole of my body is true enlightenment. I am that power. Therefore there is no penis separate from my body. In man's unenlightenment, however, because of the divisive consciousness of the genetic programming and the sexual conditioning of the society, we are persuaded to go for the passing pleasure. So as boys grow into men they go for the orgasm; they masturbate and go for sexual excitement because they can't help it; it is inevitable.

I have no solutions to save your son. I can only address you, the man who can hear the truth of love in this existence.

Father: I know that when I find my own power, I can speak about these things clearly and with much less selfconsciousness. When the time comes I see that it will not be so difficult to speak of these things to my son.

Yes. Speak in the moment. If when he comes forward with his problem you address your own state and condition in that moment you will speak from your own truth. The right words will come out and the solution will be your action in the moment.

*

Father: I have some anxiety about my young son being exposed to some sort of negative sexual experience. Sexual abuse seems to be so common. I recognise that the anxiety comes from my own boyhood when I was interfered with on a couple of occasions, by different men. Nothing has actually happened to the boy, as far as I know (he's eight now) but I feel there is always the possibility and I'd like to know what you have to say on this subject.

There are sexual secrets in everybody's life and only we know what was done to us — if we can remember. Nobody knows what the treacherous sexual mind in all of us is up to. Everywhere in the world there is more and more sex, more sexual sophistication, more sex-shops, sexual advertising and selling of sex. Yet when some secret sexual act is revealed, such as the abuse of a child, everybody is so shocked.

332

More and more the people are being taught not to make love but to imagine it. If the penis is in the vagina and as a man you have the woman's body around you, if you are really there as the body, can you have any more pleasure? Can you get any more out of it, really, if she is in a black leather outfit or you are wearing a peculiar kind of condom? Or is the thrill all in the stupid sexual mind? That's where it is, and that is what's running the world — the sexual mind.

That mind is in all men and women, to some extent, and when the natural sexual energy starts to rise in a boy he is vulnerable. He doesn't yet have enough experience. His natural sexual desire can go in any direction. It might go towards other little boys and he will go and play sexual games with them. Or he might find a little girl and play doctors and nurses.

His desire may not go towards woman. Some mature man may get hold of him and point him in the direction of homosexuality. He may be encouraged that way by other boys, or some other influence. If he is given that slant he may one day be telling everyone he's a natural-born homosexual. But that would not be true. There is always an experience which directs the natural sexual energy of boys or girls one way or the other, according to the influence that is put upon the child.

As a man, and as father of your boy, you have to go against the stream of sexuality in the world. You have to endeavour to reverse in yourself the irresistible momentum of the sexual mind that runs this existence and drives the DJ's, the television presenters, the pop video makers and all the other contributors to the frenetic escalation of sexual restlessness in this world. Everything in this world has to be kept moving because if it were to stop, the people would get bored and depressed. Then they would have to face their self, and that would be too painful; so there is more television, more music, more games, more excitement, more sex — anything to keep the people on the move.

But the time comes for the individual when life says: 'No

more. Stop.' Fortunately, for most of us this is done rather gently and slowly, except at those critical moments when the extreme of experience imposes a halt. The spiritual life is the conscious endeavour to slow down, stop and reverse the way of the world in us. So the question for anyone endeavouring to be more true is: Can you stop? Or are you attached to the momentum? Can you desist?

By going against the stream in yourself, you set your son a good example. If you are open and honest with him, and you've been raising him in justice and truth, he will know that he can come and talk to you about anything that occurs and then you will know in the moment what to say to him, or what action to take.

And if, despite all your care and attention, he has some bad sexual experience, if he is subject to some negative sexual influence or is physically abused, you will have to accept the fact. That is one of the most difficult things to accept for a parent; knowing that the child is going to get into trouble, loving him, not wanting him to suffer, and being unable to do anything about it. But that's how life is. There is no escape for anyone.

*

Mother: My teenage son likes the pop singer Madonna . . . Her shows are full of sex and aggressive personality and I had to question what it was in her that he liked. He said it was because she wasn't afraid to be who she was and had the guts to do what she does. Then he turned to me and said: 'The trouble with you, Mum, is that you're too soft and feminine and spiritual.' In other words, why aren't I more like Madonna?

He's under a lot of peer group pressure at school at the moment and I think he feels that because I live the truth as best

I can that I'm not a normal mother. This incident disturbed me more than I realised at the time.

This is a good example of the ingestion of the world by the young and the pressure exerted on them to be like other people. All children want their parents to be like other parents and if their own mother and father seem to have some individuality they get selfconscious about it. There's one way to counteract this. You'll have to stand against the stream of the world in him.

Have you told him what you are doing with your life? Does he know what he's saying when he says you're too soft and feminine and spiritual? Perhaps it's time to speak to him as woman.

'Well, from what I have seen, you're right about Madonna. She does have the guts to stand up and say what she stands for. But now I'm going to tell you something: I also have the guts to stand up and say what I stand for. The difference is that you don't like what I stand for, do you?

'Silly boy! Why should women be the same? Don't you see how different I am? You admire Madonna for being what she is, but I have the guts to stand up for the truth I live, don't I? When you are living your truth and have the guts to stand up and be as honest as Madonna or as honest as me, then you'll be worth listening to.'

Have you spoken to him about your life as woman of love? Have you spoken to him about woman?

'I am endeavouring to live my truth. I go inside my body every day and absorb the stillness of being, without looking for any entertainment. That gives me a strength; an ability to speak straight to you about things like this. This stillness and love appears to you as soft, feminine and spiritual. One day, when you've been out into the world and had your experience of girlfriends and women partners you might come back and tell me that all you ever want to find on this earth is a soft, feminine, spiritual or truthful woman.

'You're responsible for your life and you will have to pay the price for everything you are worthy of receiving. Although you haven't learnt that yet, that's the way it is. But I love you and of course I am always here when you want to come and speak to me about woman.'

*

The adolescent is a product of our times. Boys and girls used to pass almost directly into men and women. At puberty they were initiated into adult ways and able to come together to make love, raise a family and take their part as responsible members of their society. But in our times, in the eight to ten years between childhood and adult responsibility, the lure of the world has been getting stronger and stronger while the opportunities to love and exercise real responsibility get fewer and fewer.

The world's substitute for love and individual responsibility is sex. All of living now reflects the momentum of a society gone mad with sex. To get through the adolescent years the youth has to have momentum. He has to have loud music with a heavy beat, constant background noise, discos with flashing lights, videos with frenzied images. All these things reflect the pent-up sexual energy in youth because sex is based on restlessness and the constant need for change.

Continually instilled with sexual imagery, young people are increasingly hyped-up to take their place in the sexual aberration that is our society — where more and more electronic gadgets convey information faster and faster; where men with mobile phones do business walking through the park and all the men and women sitting on the grass are busy thinking and dreaming of the past instead of being conscious in the presence of nature. Life on earth is being destroyed. The pure and the beautiful is progressively contaminated with sexuality — the inability to love or be still.

Sex, like adolescence, can't wait. It can't wait to come up with the next thing in our society — the 'New'. That's the word in the newspapers, on the washing powders or anything else in the shops; because we are always looking for the new thrill, the next bit of satisfaction. Sex always goes for the satisfying thrill of the orgasm. Passion, on the other hand, is never in a hurry. Passion makes love for the beauty of it, every moment; and is measured in the rightness of every moment.

Teenagers should be taught what passion is. They should be shown how to make love. But how can this be done in a society like ours? When parents can hardly communicate with youth about anything of importance, how can they even talk to them about love and sex? When everyone is caught in the sexual aberration and almost everyone has forgotten how to actually make love, what chance have the young people got? What they are told about love only excites the sexuality in them and fills them with wrong notions. This lack of right communication about love and sex is the cause of most of the confusion, turmoil and unhappiness of the adolescent condition.

If I, man, cannot love woman, then I cannot love my children rightly. I will give them the wrong idea of love. If in my own life I cannot break the grip of the sex in me I will never know my passion or even begin to discover the reality of love. But if my partner and I put love first, and we learn to always make love, not sex, then there is a chance that we can communicate something of that knowledge and love to our children.

I endeavour to get man and woman to realise what love is and to make love rightly. An aspect of this is communicating the importance of what I call 'the psychic sense' of love. This is something that you can endeavour to communicate to young people at the appropriate time. It is especially important for young men, although they are usually too busy with the rising of sexual energy in their bodies to fully realise what it is. But if you can give your sons some hint of it, even when they are quite young, then later on the psychic sense of love may blossom.

For me the sense of love begins with the smell of woman. She has a psychic perfume, more subtle than the physical smell. It is the smell of her flesh, not her skin. This is only perceived with the psychic sense, an inner state within the outer senses of smell, sight, taste, touch and hearing. The psychic sense is one state of sense from which each of the differentiated physical senses sprout.

To get back to the truth of love, the passion, a man has to realise this inner state of sense, but it can only be realised through the physical senses and in the absence of sexual momentum. The man has to be able to just smell the flesh of the woman, smell her hair, take the time to touch her and kiss her, just for the sheer love of woman.

Youth is usually so quick to go for the sexual experience that he misses this subtle psychic contact. So he doesn't really know anything for instance about kissing a woman. Who is there in this world who can show him? — unless he can find a real woman to take away his sexual force.

Can we find a way to instil in our sons and daughters an awareness of this psychic sense? Of course it helps them to connect with it if from an early age they are encouraged to really enter their senses. For the same psychic sense is behind the sweet smell of the flowers and the grass, and you can teach them how to smell the grass; to get down on their knees and put their noses into it and really smell the earth. If you always encourage them to really see the beauty in the trees and the leaves, the sense of the beauty of nature arises in them. Then that will be there later on, when as adolescents they struggle through their sexuality to discover the real sensation of love.

The opportunity may come for a talk to a young man about lusting and what it leads to.

'I'd like to talk to you about a discovery that I made in my life, but I have to tell you, it's not an easy lesson to learn. So I'd just ask you to hear me out and in your own time and your own experience you will be able to see what it means for you. The discovery I've made is this: Lusting after woman drives her away.

'You know what lusting is. It's when we look at a woman with a sexual feeling in us. It means that we will soon be tempted to imagine being in bed with her. It gets us thinking about sex. We get excited and then emotional and perhaps end up masturbating.

'What I have to say to you is this: If you can see woman without lusting after her it will help you to get closer to the psychic sense of love, and that's what you need to develop if you are going to really be with woman.

'So what you have to do is just see her beauty, whoever she is, young or old. Observe the way she dresses, even the older lady, and notice the trouble she's gone to in order to look attractive. Just appreciate woman without lusting after her. See her skin, her breasts, just the beauty in her smile, without having any thought at all. That will bring you psychically closer to her and then, when you are physically with her, stay with your sense of her; and that will bring you closer to real passion.'

Most young people are so confident of their own perceptions of the world that they cannot listen to the wisdom of experience. They are the new generation looking for new experience and they haven't got the time. In their hurry to be grown-up, they are always trying to be something they are not.

So adolescence is characterised by a certain disrespect and casualness, aggravated by the physical awkwardness of accommodating strange new sensations as sexual energy flows into an immature body.

I would endeavour to instruct any teenager willing to listen to me not to be in such a hurry to grow up; to stay in the body and practise grace in the world.

'When you walk, don't just stomp along. Don't just shuffle along with your shoulders down and your arms swinging, like a robot. Why not practise consciously placing your feet? Don't make an effort of it, but just be aware of your feet.

'Why not put your head up? Look straight ahead instead of down at the pavement.

'Can you have a go at walking gracefully? That doesn't mean trying to create an effect. It just means that you notice when you slump, or are slopping along; and that you are conscious of your body walking along with more ease and grace.

'When you eat, don't have your knife and fork poised like a couple of swords over the plate. Don't just shovel it in. Have a bit of grace when you're eating.

'Don't use slang and don't swear any more than you have to. Don't run your words together; you don't have to try to get it all out at once. When you talk, be open and as often as you can speak gracefully or sweetly.'

As we all observe, teenagers make a pretence at asserting their individuality but are quick to follow fashion and the habits of the herd. I would tell any young person who would listen to me: Don't try to be something you are not. Don't be robotic. And I would endeavour to communicate this especially to young girls.

'I know it's difficult when you are in that transition between being a girl and a woman, but I am here to stop you suffering if I can and this is what I have to say to you: Don't try to be grown-up. It's best to wait and just be graceful. Grace is not casualness. A casual way of speaking, leaning up against things, talking out of the corner of your mouth, smoking a cigarette — that's not graceful.

'Please don't think that when you smoke, you're being cool or that anybody thinks you're grown-up. Smoking makes you pretend you're something that you're not and then you lose touch with your beauty. It also attracts wrong company. Sexual man is looking for you, just waiting to see if you are available for sex. When you smoke you advertise that you're looking for experience, and man is waiting to give it to you.

'Being casual is about taking a shortcut, getting by the easy way, and if you do that in your life you will get shortcuts in your love. That means sex without love, which always leads to unhappiness. If you give yourself to sex, man is waiting to devour you and then leave you. He will always leave you, and then you will suffer.

'It's not smart to be casual. It leads to familiarity. You might meet a man and want to love him, but the casualness will come between you and you'll grow apart without even noticing it, until one day you find you've been taken for granted, and he's gone. Practise being graceful and you will find that a loving man will come to you — not some awkward boy, not a youth who just wants to experiment with you for his own experience, nor some guy who thinks he knows what it's all about and hasn't got a clue what love is; but a man will come to you who has the grace to love you.'

＊

Mother: I have a son going to college. He has a steady girl-friend now and in the vacation I think he would like to have her come and live with us at our house. I feel uncomfortable about this and I am not quite sure why . . . Maybe because I

341

will have to go out and buy them a double bed. Nothing's been said about it yet, but somehow it's in the air.

If you don't give him the opportunity to be with her and make love, he's going to love her elsewhere, isn't he? If he's reached the age where he is mature enough to handle it (and you in your wisdom know whether he is or he isn't) then you have to face the fact — the time has come. You might want him to hold off a while longer, but if you have been open with him about man and woman, and you want to see him love woman, at least you will be there to help him. So for instance, if you see him being unloving to the girl you'll be able to say: 'Hey, I thought you said you wanted to live with her here because you love her!'

It's so much against the old ideas of things, isn't it? — for you to help him learn to love woman. But if you have some uncertainty in you, open up the subject and discuss it with him. Get it out; it will be helpful to your psyche to do that.

However, it is really his responsibility to ask you whether it would be all right for her to come. Can you wait until he raises the subject? Then you will know what the situation is and be able to respond in the moment. All the practical things will follow. The moment will come and he'll say 'Well, Mum, how about a double bed?' Don't worry. You'll say the right thing at the right time.

No matter what happens, don't think you've done the wrong thing. Remember that you're in charge of your life and if any domestic arrangement is not right then you can immediately speak to them and address the situation. Do what is right for love, and for your enjoyment of your life, and that will be right for the situation.

Mother: I'm glad he feels open enough to bring her to stay with us, but I see that he's not the little boy any more that I cared for. Now he's a man. I'm probably quite attached to being his mother, but under that, there's enough love, I hope, to let him go.

Yes, real parental love is the love that lets go when it's time. It is not just the embrace or the service of caring and providing for a child for all those years. It is a love that will go on taking the world out of him as long as you can, helping him to take responsibility and opening him up to love. But finally you have to let him go and get on with his life. And he knows that you are always there if he needs you.

Mother: Yes, I'm sure he knows that. If you were speaking to him, would you have any advice for him and his girlfriend, as a young couple just starting out together?

Yes, and this is what I would say to them, or to anyone, young or old: Sex will crucify you.

Every bit of unhappiness on this earth is due to sex. Whereas love never hurt anyone. Love never broke anyone's heart and never will. It is sex that breaks your heart. Sex means you get attached to each other and then when he or she leaves you, as one day must happen (because everybody dies), you are heartbroken. As soon as you get attached to anybody, you prescribe your own heartbreak.

If you ever fall in love you are doomed. Falling in love is like falling asleep, and you're not supposed to be asleep in love. Love is present, active, alert. Love is filled with vibrancy and the vitality of life. Fall into it and you fall into a dream that the storybooks have prepared for you to go to sleep in . . . Suddenly you will be jarred out of it by a broken heart: 'What's happened? My love is gone!' But of course the love has not gone; it's inside of you, not in another body. If you put your love onto that other body and then the body leaves you, you will suffer.

So love wisely. Give yourself to love but never give yourself to sex.

KNOWLEDGE OF GOD

Never teach a child to believe in God. Believing in anything is folly. Whatever you believe in you'll be able to find someone else who doesn't believe in it. And then you've got someone to argue with, or something to fight for. One of us believes in Islam and the other believes in Christianity. The two beliefs collide and soon you've got war. I do not believe in Islam. But I say that I know the essence of Islam which is the love and worship of God, as preached by Mohammed. I do not believe in Jesus Christ. But the essence of Christianity is 'to love the Lord thy God with all thy heart, with all thy body and with all thy mind'; and indeed I do love the Lord my God with all my heart, with all my body and with all my mind. The essence of the religions is the worship of God, the whole of life. As for the beliefs that they adhere to, with their partial knowledge of life, it's best to just inform yourself about them, if you have to, but don't start believing any of it — for God's sake. I don't believe in anything. If I know God, why would I believe in God?

Every religion depends on belief. When you believe in something you can be manipulated and made to imagine that life is as it is not. That's what belief is. The world is full of it. For instance, everyone believes (or wants to believe) that they are going somewhere. Scientists believe in progress. Most Christians believe they are going to heaven or hell. But the truth is that everyone is going to die and we are all going nowhere.

The trick the religions use on the children is to make them believe in something. What I teach you to do is to give the child the fact as it is, in this life now, and that removes the belief.

You know the intelligence you are. Speak to that same intelligence in your child. When the truth is shown to you, you can see it clearly and accept it — provided you can know it for yourself, without having to believe in anything or anyone else. As it is for you, so it is for your children.

If you have heard the truth in this book, and I have demonstrated it to you through the fact of life, you will not need to believe in anything I have said. When you hear the truth and live it, it is beyond belief. You know then that it is not Barry Long's truth but your own. And if you are living the truth, according to your lights, then you are informing the children from your own truth and experience; you are instructing them in a right and practical way about the divine life and about living in the world, and your own demonstration to them in ordinary family life is their teaching. Meanwhile, of course, they are receiving the instruction of the world and through Christianity, or some other religion, are being informed about spiritual life as if it were extraordinary. Their young minds are being stuffed by emotional teachers and priests with confusing, imaginative, irrelevant and impractical doctrines.

The religions do not address in practical terms the most important things in people's ordinary lives, such as how to deal with a demanding child and how to make love rightly so that we don't make problems and trouble for each other. We are all ordinary people. Jesus and Buddha were ordinary men. I live in our world, where men and women make love, raise children and are unhappy. That's where I work, because I'm an ordinary man.

*

Mother: My daughter is a spiritual and sensitive child, but she says she thinks about all the bad things going on in the world and it stops her sleeping at night. I don't know what to say to help her.

Our children are the product of a society which has taught them to think. We are all responsible. They must suffer because of our ignorance. What can you do? I suggest it is very important for your daughter to have a knowledge of the good. Our society teaches the children that there is an opposite to good, for that's the Christian way; there is God and the Devil. But I say we must teach the children the good that has no opposite.

I would sit by the child at night and speak to her: 'We've got a new game. We're going to see what we have that is good. You go first. And I will go next. What do you have that is good?'

'Well', she might say, 'I've got my bike.'

'Is that good?'

'Yes.'

'That is good. And it is good because it doesn't have any opposite does it? Even if you didn't have your bike, if someone stole it, you would have something else instead and that would be good too. No matter what you lose, it's always all right.

'So, now it's my turn. What have I got that's good? Well, I've got you. I love you. And I love to be in the house while you're sleeping. My love is always with you while you're sleeping. Even if I am away from you, I am always here in my love of you. So that also is the good that doesn't have any opposite.'

Talking to children like that might seem ineffectual to begin with but you have to start somewhere. You have to endeavour to give them a sense of the good and teach them, as much as possible, not to think.

'You don't have to think about the good. The good is always here. I am here. You have air to breathe. If you want a glass of water, you're able to go and get it. You have all your senses. It is good to be alive. So with all the things you've got that are good, you can go to sleep in peace.'

If you can teach children to acknowledge the good like that, they may start to embrace a new consciousness.

The consciousness of opposites is the world of cause and effect. Hot and cold. Up and down. Love and then hatred, despair or heartbreak. We deal in opposites because we have a mind that lives on opposites: 'I love Mary. I don't love Jane. I love John. I don't love Jack. This is my friend. That is my enemy.' Where I come from (and I come from the same place as you do — from me, the being) there are no opposites; just the One, which is good, or right.

The good is not a feeling. It is not even necessarily a good sensation in the body. You might just have a knowledge of rightness in you. When you are dying, for instance, it may not feel good, or you may be in pain, but there is the knowledge that it is right and good that you die and you cannot die until the very moment that you do.

Always acknowledge the good that has no opposite, for it is just God with another 'o' in it.

*

Woman: If we can encourage young people to turn within, that must shorten their journey to the truth, mustn't it?

If they are encouraged to be still with nature, to see life as it is and not as we like to imagine it, or as it is in the movies, then of course that's encouraging them to reflect on the state within — their being. And then, as they get older, they will be able to get back to the state more quickly. I trust that's what is happening for all the parents who live this teaching. I trust they are reflecting more and more on the reality of life and their own being and are demonstrating that to their children. Indeed I trust that is going to change the world — just the little bit of the world that individually we alone can change.

*

Father: I've got two children but I don't live with them. They are with their mother who's a strict Roman Catholic and they go to church every Sunday. I'd like to bring them along to see you, Barry, but I don't want to cause them any conflict. What should I do?

I don't see that you can bring them to me if the mother would resent it. As you quite rightly say, the children would be confused, receiving two values at the same time. How old are they? Do you see them often?

Father: Eight and nine. I get to see them four or five times a year.

Well, whenever you see them, it's important for you to take them for a walk and talk to them. Don't deprecate the Catholic religion in front of them. You mustn't criticise a religion that is being inculcated in the children because that will only confuse them. And you must be very careful not to criticise what their mother does. But it is very important for you to communicate to them as their Dad — 'man to man'. You have to give them a wider spectrum of life, not denying what they have got but opening their eyes to other ways of looking at life. You can

349

communicate something of what happens at these meetings, from your own experience, so long as it doesn't cause division.

'So, you and your Mummy go to Church. Would you like to hear where I go? I go to meetings where all we do is endeavour to be still and be with God. Now, you know about God, don't you? God is within us. That means inside my body and inside your body. We don't pray or anything like that, because if we were praying we would be speaking inside ourselves wouldn't we? — and we want to be very still and silent so that we can align ourselves with God. By being still we can connect with a place inside our bodies. It's a very beautiful place, of course, because it's God. Of course it's the same God as your Mum talks about.'

Whatever you say, you've got to put something across that broadens their outlook without condemning what they are doing. And then, in time, they might come to you (as so many people come to me) to be rid of what I find is the terrible indoctrination of guilt and fear so often imposed on the people by the Catholic religion.

＊

Father: We practise the things you teach about man and woman and family life and we've recently begun to value the company of other parents and children who live the same way. We find that supports us in communicating the truth to our son, who is five.

Yes, the company of others who are committed to this teaching is important sometimes, for both children and parents, when it can be arranged.

Father: Unfortunately most of the people we know tend to have material values and are unquestioningly orthodox.

Inevitably there's always someone who's suspicious of our commitment to your teaching. We're also frequently in contact with practising Christians and unfortunately some of these people sometimes indicate their disapproval to the boy.

The child is not old enough to make a balanced or convincing response. Facing the authority and certitude of an adult, he is likely to be overwhelmed by the bias and prejudice of these orthodox people and Christians who are so sure that they are right. If they were honest they would not use the boy to express their disapproval of your life; they would speak to you, the adult, and say where the teaching is not true.

The only way we can develop equilibrium and balance in a child, or ourselves, is by developing the ability to see the truth of the situation. That means: first of all, not being biased in any particular direction (not adhering to any belief or opinion acquired in the past); and secondly it means using our own experience of life to reach a conviction of what is right and true, but only for the moment.

Father: When a child has so little experience of life, I find it's difficult to convey matters of self-knowledge. I might say something in the truth, but to my son it's a concept and just another part of his burgeoning mental structure.

Yes. That is why we have to be so careful about what we feed into the young. I'm reminded of something that was once reported to me about the Roman Catholic priesthood. Apparently the Jesuit schoolmasters have a saying: 'Give me a boy until the age of seven and he's mine forever.' In other words he'll never forget what he's been indoctrinated with — until God or life, the great truth within the boy, brings him to his senses, or he comes to someone like me, the master consciousness. That will disabuse him of indoctrination, but it will be a very painful and disorientating experience.

You have to give the child room to form his own response to life. It's not enough just to talk about your own self-knowledge, because that will indeed be beyond his experience or understanding and may just get picked up, like notions implanted by a priest. Talk to the child about what life is so that you continually reaffirm his own experience of it. You have to get the balance between the knowledge or information you impart and the child's own observation. In this way the child acquires the equilibrium with which to assess a situation for himself, to see what is true and what is false.

Equilibrium is the ability to go straight ahead, or respond to left or right, whichever wind is blowing, without being blown off-course. Indoctrination destroys that equilibrium and will predispose anyone towards judgment or prejudice so that they become biased, always turning to one side.

So demonstrate truth and self-knowledge to the child in practical ways and never allow or encourage him to depend on belief.

Father: We can't just ignore the fact that living in England it's still a Christian society, nominally at least. There's a background pressure to conform. My parents wanted to see our son 'christened'. At school there are hymns every morning and religious and moral instruction is biased towards the Christian Church. Someone at a playgroup told our boy he'd go to hell if he was naughty! That sort of continual reinforcement of Christian values in the culture is quite insidious and confusing, I think, to our son.

'Christ died for our sins' they say, so every Christian becomes a sinner. I say there are no sinners on this earth.

Living is not easy, but everybody is doing their best. Wouldn't you say that's true? Or do you think your own Mum and Dad were not doing their best, according to their lights? Everyone is doing their best, even when it might seem that they've made a hell of a mess of their lives. Look at what you've done with your life. It's hardly been a perfect jewel, has it? — any more than mine has. But I did my best, as everybody does.

Isn't that the truth? Isn't that a relief? I suggest you look at that. Either the Christian religion of guilt and redemption is true or I am true.

Father: Are there not some Christian values that children can usefully learn and apply? Such as the virtues of love, as taught in the Gospels — loving thy neighbour as thyself and turning the other cheek . . . 'Love your enemies, bless them that curse you, do good to them that hate you, etc.'

Does that make any sense to your child? Is it any wonder the children are confused? What kind of love does it take to love your enemies? Certainly not 'love' as it's generally understood. Quoting bits of Bible like that only confuses the children — because they can't love their enemies, any more than you can. But you can endeavour to give up your anger towards them and not hold on to your unhappiness.

Two thousand years ago the man Jesus of Nazareth, a Jew who was a master, taught his people not to hold on to any hurt or resentment, but the Christian priests made a god of him and in their ignorance quoted his teaching without being able to live it.

Christianity is not the truth. Here is a parable for you. I was living with my first wife in Australia when I started waking up to the reality of life (this was in the 1950's). I started talking about truth all the time and eventually I had to separate from my wife and leave the children. Later my daughter embraced Christianity. It was an understandable reaction. She married, had a child of her own and raised her as a Christian. My mother loved this little girl and she loved her great-grandmother very much, so when at the age of ninety my mother lay dying, my daughter took the little girl to see her in the hospice. And she said: 'I hope you're a Christian, Granny, because if you're not, I'll never see you again.' My own grandchild — indoctrinated with disgraceful notions of God, truth, life and death. But that's what Christianity does to children.

There should be nothing between me and my God, my love. The true master says to the people: 'Nothing must come between you and the reality you love in the stillness within you. It is that reality you love, not I who am speaking to you. I will not call myself God for that would fool you. I am here only to help you realise the God or life or love within you.'

The priest is not the master. Priests come between my children and the God or life or love within them. The Christian religion gets hold of young children and condemns them to suffer later in life from the dreadful agony of guilt put into them by the notion of sin and the fear of hell. I hear it over and over again from the people who speak to me about their love and their pain — so many lives utterly ruined by the Christian religion. It is a terrible thing to indoctrinate the children with stupid notions about a God up in heaven when the truth is that God does not exist.

You can say if you like that the whole of existence is God's reflection, but that is still not God. The whole of the universe is a tiny mirror image of God, made by our senses. And the world of our senses is very far from being the whole of reality. Yet in the tiny fragment of existence inhabited by the priests and followers of the Christian religion, God is made to exist. 'He' takes on form and substance, and the part is taken for the whole. Every other part of existence then becomes problematic for the Church, and the terrible consequences are written in the history of all the peoples who ever came into conflict with its doctrines.

Does God exist when your child is dying of cancer? Painful, horrible and tragic as that is, can you take that as the act of a God that exists? Or had you better say 'No, God does not exist.'

Can there be anything that happens on this earth — the killing of a child, the torture and murder of man or woman — that is not God's will?

The truth is that it is all God being God. But it is a terrible dilemma for Christianity. So the Devil was invented to overcome the problem. An effective political compromise with the truth that has corrupted the minds of the children down the centuries and is still putting 'the fear of God' into them.

*

Mother: I had a lovely conversation with Ben about God. We had been talking about going on a boat and being seasick. I said it felt like dying. Quick as a flash he replied, 'But you don't know what that's like Mummy, because you haven't died!'

'No, quite right' I said, 'It's what I think dying must be like.'

'You shouldn't think about it, Mummy, or you might really die.'

I had to tell him he was right again, because I'd been teaching him that we get what we acknowledge. 'Anyway,' I said, 'when it comes to dying we are all in God's hands.'

'God's hands?' he queried.

'No, you're right, God doesn't have hands. That's just an expression. He is formless.'

'God is nothing, Mummy.'

'Right. He's nothing and he's everything.'

'Am I God then?' he said, 'I must be, if he is everything.'

I started to answer him and then lapsed into silence, no longer sure what to say.

'Mummy, does twelve and twelve make twenty-two?'

'No, twenty-four. Why?'

'Because I'm counting my teeth.'

I am amazed by conversations like this. He shows me how uncertain I can be.

355

How would you express the truth, Barry, in what Ben was saying: 'Am I God then? I must be, if he is everything.'

Ben embodies both child and guru: 'Yes, Ben, you are God. But your mind hasn't realised that yet.'

To realise something is like putting your hand in water. When you take your hand out and think about what it was like, you know from the experience what having your hand in water is like, but the experience is no longer real now. As Ben said, you can't know what dying is like if you haven't died; you can only think about what it would be like.

If I say to you 'God is everything', and you reply 'Then I must be God', that's thinking about it, isn't it? — working it out with your mind. It's not realising it, because realisation only exists in the actual time of doing or being it.

The realisation of God is apparently one of the rarest states on earth. It is an inner state where there's no body and nothing but intelligence. It is realised in the moment and once realised, as God is nothing, that's the end of it. Any word or thought about it will be a 'something', therefore not God-realisation.

Once the state 'I am God' is realised, it cannot be said that 'I am God', because it is not possible to be God outside the moment of realising it. There is the knowledge of the state of the being of God, but since that is nothing, there is nothing more to say.

AFTERWORD

Parents Respond – Teachers Report
Barry Long and Education
Bibliography – Index

PARENTS RESPOND

*T his book can only open the door for you. It is here to help
you discover your own genius as parents. The points I
make and examples and illustrations I give are like dots in a
children's drawing book. It's for you to join them up, complete
the picture and colour it in.*

• I realise it's not the children that are the problem, but
rather our reactions to the children.

Not 'How can they!' but 'How can I?'

In some ways this is a great relief. The battle is here, not there.
It frees us all of blame and makes me instantly accountable.

• My son is 10 months old now, my first child. He's lovely.
Generally speaking he's very happy and full of energy and
playfulness. It's the hardest work I've ever done, very hard
sometimes. Particularly at the beginning, I didn't know where
I was or what I was doing. I didn't know why people have
children. Why do people have children . . . ?

• He gives us an awful lot of enjoyment and teaches us a lot. I think the thing I get out of him the most is the opportunity to see how much we look for attention, and how we get angry when we don't get what we want. And I find I get an awful lot of opportunity for that, if I can just see it.

• How to deal with 'the demanding child' — this seems to be a key to many things. When my child demands, he is instantly outside himself — not himself. He of course is my reflection, because I see that I do exactly the same thing. It's very useful to see this, because it's a principle that I can apply to all situations.

• There was a period of several weeks where my partner and I were not being honest with each other. For the whole of that time the child was difficult to deal with. He was whiny and obstreperous. He caught a cold and wanted to cling on to me all the time.

One evening, with all three of us at the dinner table, we started to face what we had been avoiding. It was great to be talking honestly to each other again. What was extraordinary was that as the conversation went on the boy became much more still. He was happy to just listen. By the end of it he was looking us straight in the eye again and when he spoke, he spoke calmly. We could feel his love again.

This was an astonishing and instant reflection for us. Yet again I was reminded how responsible I am for the environment I live in and for my emotions.

• Sometimes what you say has been very new to me. Other times you just confirmed what I was already doing. But I needed that, because my main problem is self-doubt. I have this need sometimes to keep hearing that what I am doing is all right. But when I can relax then things go easier. I might do the same things, but the child is affected differently. He responds more easily to me. When I am tense he doesn't really respond and struggles away from me. I realise now that my self-doubt was going into him. It's what I feel that comes over to him, not just the words and actions.

• One of the most important things is realising that I have to let my son go into the world, into experience. I used to have the conviction that I could spare him the world and the suffering if only I could find the right way to do it. I know now that's not possible.

• I must say I don't seem to have any real problems any more. I find we all work in harmony together these days and that's a beautiful thing. There is very little mood in our house.

Living this teaching really has helped me in dealing with the situations that occur. I find it quite easy these days to handle any disturbance with my son. He is mostly joyful and easy to be with and when moods occur he is able to deal with them quickly.

I do see that I mustn't let him get away with anything — everything must be dealt with. I have to deal straightaway with any disturbance that comes up in him or in myself. But everything is well as long as I am clear, free of emotion and present.

• I have been talking to my son about the truth since he was about two years old. We have a quiet time together and we will meditate or just be. He absorbs it avidly and quite seriously. Although he is still only five he makes statements of remarkable insight. For instance I asked him what it is like to simply look into space within, and he said, 'Silence listening to silence.' He had learned the phrase from a storybook in which a boy was calling down a mine shaft, but he immediately translated the image into an inner experience and applied it rightly.

Another time I asked him: 'Are you are good boy? Are you growing up to be a good man?' He looked very serious and replied: 'You tell me.'

361

'I'd say so, yes.' I replied, 'The more you keep the unhappiness out.'

'It's getting harder,' he said very honestly, 'There are so many distractions.'

Thank you, parents, for your contributions to this book. The children are always mirrors for the parents to look into. Our looking into the mirror together I trust has served us all.

TEACHERS REPORT

From a primary school teacher in Australia, a woman who has lived Barry Long's teaching for some years:

The children I teach are between four and six years of age. They are just beginning their independent life. Their vital energy is tumbling out, asserting itself in a most uncontained way. It's both magnificent and ghastly. My response can be of wonder and it can be of despair.

How do I use Barry Long's teaching in my life at school? Firstly and most important has been my own individual transformation, through love of God and the master. I care that the children might not be made as superficial as the world would have them; so I magnify God, life, love, truth and death wherever a chance arises in the day.

I might say, as we sit in a circle ready to do our language and music lesson, 'Listen! What do you hear? The birds are communicating to us.' We are fortunate enough to have a nature strip next to our suburban centre which is graced by two wise

363

gum trees and home to many birds. Or I might say, 'Please be tender with that beetle. It is one of God's creatures, just as you are. If you like me to stroke you softly — like this — then that's how you should touch an animal.'

I am rewarded by such incidents as this: Matthew said to his neighbour, 'I know why that cat has a bell around its neck.' The neighbour asked why and Matthew said: 'So it will protect God's creatures, the birds.' This type of perception is sweet to me. His mother attributed it to me as his teacher, but really it was Matthew's creative perception — coming out of his own potential.

The children are very focused on 'having' and 'not having'. I find this a difficult area to address. When they come in the morning with their plastic possessions, to show me what they have, they immediately set up a dynamic for others who 'have not'. A certain competitive energy is cranked. When there is conflict over an object, if it cannot be sorted out, my bottom line is: 'If this is making you unhappy then I will put it away.' Immediately the response is 'I'm not unhappy.' So I say 'Well, you must show me that you are not unhappy.' Then I see the child reaching down inside himself towards his inner smile. I tell him how good that is. But if the child is stuck in his unhappiness there is very little I can do, except give him a little tickle to break the tension. There are some determined children who can hold a moody beyond my efforts at school.

When a child is possessed by his possession (a toy) he is unable to appreciate the day's offerings. To try to bring him beyond his possession can sometimes set off a wild reaction; he may run around wildly, knocking others and disturbing their activities and constructions. Some children lose their security, God, at a very early age and put their trust in objects outside of themselves. Without the object they are like kites not held. So life in its great compassion helps bring children back to their senses by providing an accident. Interestingly, it is often the most outrageous children who are the most fragile.

They lose their equilibrium and it takes an accident to bring them back into their senses.

It is some children's nature to give to life. They are willing to participate in life as it presents itself. These children evoke an equal response from me. They enrich our work with their spontaneity and expansiveness, joy and harmony. I would love to work with a group composed entirely of such children. The rhythm of the day would have the naturalness of the moon and the tide working together. Circumstances gladly rearrange themselves for the giving and willing. But then there are the 'oppositional' children who demand a greater share of the cake than seems equitable. With them I have to face my own stubbornness and maintain my clarity in the face of emotion. This I could never have done without Barry Long's teaching.

My imbibing of the teaching has given me a more expansive view of a situation and a certain authority. I can (at times) stand unattached, with a 360 degree view, able to communicate unemotionally and impersonally with the children and their parents. This is directly due to the reduction of my person (my emotional self). My trust in 'the situation' is because Barry has declared: 'What is the closest thing to God in existence? — the situation.'

When I have no other way of addressing a conflict, such as one child hitting another, I can speak with authority, and I hear the rightness in my voice: 'There is no need to do that.' In such a moment I know that the master is with me.

In helping children to be more responsible I help them to travel back through conflict so that they might see how they contributed to the conflict that is now making them unhappy. Young children need to know what is required of them. So sometimes I offer them another option, demonstrating how the situation could have been resolved. Another adult observing me do this commented, 'You were so logical.' This was a very real moment, when I knew that Barry's teaching was in me.

There was another instance last week. I was telling the

children a myth from The Dreaming — the mythic world of the Aboriginals. At the end I added something: 'Where is this dreaming? It is in me. It all comes out of me and now it returns to me at the end of the story.' I expressed this with rhythmic gestures indicating its appearance and disappearance. The children were stilled — momentarily!

Before I started to live Barry's teaching I was very self-conscious. Now I find myself spontaneous and able to perform in front of other people. I see how all the four and five year-olds are acquiring personalities and how their masks are a compilation of the behavioural traits of the adults around them. One boy was demonstrating one of his father's mannerisms so plainly that I found myself calling him by his father's name. The children also take up my traits so I am grateful that my persona is a little softer and more fluid than it once was.

Speaking of things picked up from others, I notice how peer-pressure affects my twelve year-old daughter. There was a recent case. She had been to a dance and said it was very noisy and crowded; it was not really to her liking. 'Will you go to the next dance?' I asked her. 'Probably,' she said, 'My friend likes going.' I saw that if a child (soon to be an adult) doesn't honour her own insights and intuitions she will no longer get them. She will become used to the discontent of doing what is not pleasing and that will be what she will unconsciously seek. She will be unhappy and not know why. So I was able to point out to her the importance of heeding her own perceptions.

With my daughter and at school I have introduced many of the things Barry has shown me; for instance, what I am and where I come from — 'There is only one I in the universe. I am in my body and I am always here.' The children love the simplicity of this. When I ask them 'Where am I?' and they reply 'Here!', pointing to their own bodies, I see their eyes light up. They really get it.

I can tell when young children delight in some key to the mystery. They shine. Because I recognise and acknowledge this it grows where it can. Is this not what Barry has done with me?

*

From a secondary school teacher in England, a woman who trains other teachers:

In my early years of teaching in comprehensive secondary schools, I was frequently stressed, exhausted and consumed by the job. Like my colleagues in the staffroom I thought that this was normal and hardened myself to the task, becoming harder and less open to life in the process. Although I fundamentally knew teaching to be the right profession for me, given the emotional and physical demands of the work I did not think I would last too many years. I could see that to be a drained teacher would not enable me to contribute in a vital way to the learning of the young people in my classes, which was, after all, my principle motivation in doing the work. But then I was introduced to Barry Long's teaching. In living the truth that I hear in his words my experience in school has been transformed.

As I began to take responsibility for my life, I began to see how much I taught through my personality. The effort needed to maintain and project this mask was a major source of energy leakage. I had to be prepared to face my classes as naturally as I could. As a drama teacher, dropping the mask was particularly painful as the impulse in me was to entertain, and the children had grown to expect this. I was afraid of becoming boring and thus losing control. But if I had one exciting class the next one would suffer because I was drained or unsettled. Within a short time of readjustment I found that I had not lost the children's interest and I am more consistent throughout the day. Students do not come into a lesson wondering what mood I am in and thus what sort of lesson they will have. I realised I had created trouble for myself by projecting my personality as a defensive shield to protect me unnecessarily from children and classes that I perceived as difficult. Actually the difficulties had arisen either because of the children's reaction as they tried to cope with my inconsistent personality, or because my personality prevented me from properly responding to their needs.

Having acknowledged the problem of my personality to myself, I now quite openly ask pupils to point out where they see me being inconsistent. This keeps me on my toes. I have also made it a priority to observe how certain pupils take on roles within the group (or are made by others to adopt them) such as the joker, the swot, the victim. Having identified these roles, but without focusing on individuals, I explore with the group the reasons why people adopt roles or positions and whether these aspects of their personality are natural and necessary. I find Barry's fable 'The Being behind The Mask' a very useful starting point [see Bibliography]. As this work develops we examine whether their moods are natural to their being or caused by events, people etc. My intention is primarily to open up a dialogue with the pupils so that when they bring anger, frustration or moods into the class we have a shared language to address the situation. I now have a point of communication with pupils who are distressed or threaten the harmony of the class and perhaps some individuals can see that moods are not natural. Of course I have to practice what I teach and make sure I am free of moods. I have to see that I am not carrying the momentum which might have been generated by one lesson into the next.

From my own experience in schools and particularly from my present work with student teachers, I have seen that there is a great tendency in teachers to spend time worrying about a problem class, pupil or situation. Other than doing the necessary planning for a class I now endeavour not to think about a situation until I am faced with it. This was difficult to achieve at first and student teachers say it is the hardest exercise I give them. This is not only another great way to conserve energy but has meant that the problems I would have worried about often do not materialise, because I do not bring expectation with me into the room. I encourage pupils to adopt a similar approach and to endeavour not to worry in between the lessons they don't like or find difficult.

I have taught in a number of schools over the years, some of them very challenging in terms of pupil discipline, but the experience has been invaluable in enabling me to see that I am best able to quieten a situation of conflict through stillness. Any force in me simply adds to the trouble. As I have less momentum, my classroom management improves. I am able to sense a disturbance before it flares and take appropriate action without thought. When there is a problem, the body does indeed move to where it is needed.

As a drama teacher I am fortunate in being able to spend time at the beginning and end of lessons encouraging pupils to become centred in their bodies, to drop the momentum of what has gone before and become focused on what is happening now. The exercises in Barry Long's 'Meditation a Foundation Course' are helpful in introducing stillness in a practical way. [See Bibliography.] Although pupils accept this practice as part of what happens in drama I don't see why this could not be built into other curriculum areas. I know that many colleagues have strategies for quietening classes. However I say it is crucial to inform pupils of exactly why we are doing an exercise and why it is important for them to be stiller. It's not simply so that they can get down to work better. Invariably some pupils are disturbed by the greater stillness they either sense in classmates or in themselves and become more agitated and restless. This I accept and let happen until the point where they want to mention it themselves, or it is right for me to talk about it with them.

One of the major sources of anxiety I had as a student was the fear that I would forget everything I had learned. I constantly felt like a fraud having passed an exam but knowing that soon after I had left the exam hall I promptly forget most of the facts and references that I had crammed into my brain. No one, until Barry Long, had told me that I already have all the knowledge I need and that the information I digest is needed to get on in the world and pass exams but is not necessary for life. It was a blessed relief to realise this and forms the central core in how I now present both the curriculum and my own knowledge.

There is an inevitable imbalance of power in schools between pupil and teacher. One central and frequently abused aspect of this is the relationship between power and knowledge. My intention is always to keep addressing this relationship, and de-mystify my knowledge. I endeavour to strip away my supposed power by telling pupils that any facts or information I give them are to enable them to pass exams. Important though this is in terms of the world, that is all it is. Knowing lots of facts may bring worldly qualifications but the work we do with material that is to do with our own lives, and arises out of our own experience, is different. As Barry says, real knowledge doesn't add any information to us, so nothing of it can be forgotten. If the children give the work their full attention the knowledge they need will be provided when the situation calls for it.

My authority must come not as the bearer of knowledge but through being as present and honest to the situation as I can. I tell the children that my role is to reflect what they already know within them and to encourage them in expressing their individual potential and creativity. That I can do this is simply due to my having more life experience.

Perhaps the most fundamental change in my perception as a teacher is how I communicate with the individual child. I make a commitment to acknowledge their presence, their individuality and give them my full attention for whatever time is available for our dialogue. Through Barry's description of the child possessed by emotion I have seen the emotional baggage that each child carries to a greater or lesser degree. It is a service of love for me to endeavour not to add to it by any lack of presence in my interaction with a child. I also see that the children serve me beautifully. By surrendering any self that is disturbed in me by my interaction with them I am made more pure.

BARRY LONG AND EDUCATION

Study brings more questions.
Self-knowledge brings the end of them.

B arry Long was preoccupied with the question of education
and the raising of children even before he formally started
teaching groups of adults. In 1976 he was living in an English
country cottage, working as a freelance writer. It was then
eleven years since his initial spiritual realisation and the time
was coming when he would offer himself publicly as a teacher.
He determined to move to London and start a school. It would
be called The Children's School for Philosophic Development
and Understanding of Studies.

It took about six months to sell the cottage and move house
but a few weeks after settling into his new home in Highgate,
North London, he placed an advertisement in the local
newspaper: 'If your normally intelligent child, aged nine to
twelve, has a problem in understanding any school subject so
that it causes the child to fret or worry, I might be able to help.
I do not teach subjects. There is no charge.'

It has always been Barry Long's way to teach from his own
life and realisation. What most concerned him in 1976/7 was

what he identified as a blockage to the understanding of life or truth that arises in adults because as children they were given inadequate tuition at school. He was aware of this blockage in himself. His own education in Australian state schools had been basic and terminated at the age of 15. He knew the frustration and confusion of the child who misses out some essential principle of a subject and is forever afterwards unable to catch up.

'No subject matter is complicated,' he wrote at the time, 'No matter how complex it is, the complication and confusion occurs in the mind . . . and starts to arise with the first anxiety of not having understood something. We spend our lives trying to compensate in external terms and in self-justification for the emotion, the guilt, of not having understood something, perhaps many things, so long ago when our busy teachers and parents assumed that we knew what they were talking about — and we were afraid to ask "Why?"

'Most of us had this learning ceiling fall on us as children but we managed to duck and scramble through into adulthood — not cured, but by developed cunning able to cope and conceal the conflict, confusion and anxiety it generated. Mostly this happened because our teachers or parents did not have the time or the will to go back to the beginning, or to where we first failed to understand what the subject was about, its significance to us as learners — at a point where our teachers assumed that we comprehended something when we did not; and we could not admit it in case we seemed foolish, or were made fools of, or, worst of all, discovered that we might in fact actually be less intelligent than the person next to us who did seem to understand.'

In planning his school for children he was not proposing to teach subjects from the normal school curriculum. Instead he proposed to teach children how to learn. By engaging their interest, understanding and enjoyment of a subject he would seek to eliminate the students' fear of dependence on memory, which he identified as probably the chief subconscious cause of a student's anxiety.

'Learning is not an end in itself,' he said, 'except for the curious, and the computer and quiz-master mentalities. Meaningful learning is a means to understanding and from that flows the possibility of true individual creativity and fulfilment.' In other words, he would teach self-knowledge.

Barry Long maintained that all he needed to relieve children of their difficulties or problems with school subjects was his own love of truth and the child's intelligence — defining intelligence as 'the ability to see the fact or the truth'. Since the child with a study-problem has a blockage and cannot see the fact of what it's about, Barry Long would ask questions until the fact is seen — 'and the truth will set the child free'. He would teach the children to ask 'Why?'— and then how to listen to the answer. And he would show them how to assess for themselves whether the answer was the truth. It was always basic to his teaching that to recognise the truth of any answer is simply a matter of being able to listen openly, without emotional blockage; it's not dependent on knowing anything.

As he waited for parents to respond to his advertisement he mused about the school's significance: 'If my feeble effort (for I can only reach a few) ever becomes a movement of many, the children helped will be of more use than any of us. They will be truly creative and produce in the world something of which we cannot even dream.'

He waited, and then the phone rang. The man on the other end wanted to know, 'What are you up to?' and, after receiving a lengthy explanation, he hung up. The phone rang again. This caller asked if he had the right number. He didn't. The same advertisement was placed in another three issues of the paper but no one else made contact.

As the parents weren't interested in helping their children, Barry Long decided to teach the parents. Settled now in

Highgate, he was more accessible to the few men and women who had by now discovered him as their teacher. They were ready to form a small group, meeting on a regular basis. Later, in the 1980's, there were public meetings, mainly in London, attended by more and more people from all walks of life. Much of the teaching at that time focused on meditation and stilling the mind, but there was always an equal emphasis on facing the fact or the truth through question and answer, and the demonstration of the truth in one's own experience.

As his audiences and reputation as a spiritual teacher grew so did the power of his teaching. The endeavour to teach how truth can be discovered in direct experience became a moment-to-moment demonstration of simple being in which his audience shared. The blockage of the human condition was now simply identified as negativity — unhappiness plus thought. And the single question, the only 'Why?' that remained: 'Why are you unhappy?'

As always, the truth of Barry Long's teaching must be lived in individual everyday lives — in the practical detail of partnership, work and family life; and, as this book so clearly demonstrates, in the raising and education of children. So, finally, through many parents' living of this teaching, and their many questions, Barry Long's school has been brought into being — without any classrooms, but now I trust with a kind of textbook.

Clive Tempest

BIBLIOGRAPHY

The following works by Barry Long have been referred to in the text or contain material specifically useful to parents and teachers.

ONLY FEAR DIES
(Barry Long Books)
See particularly the essay titled 'The Child Possessed' and the first chapter of the book, 'The Being Behind The Mask', which contains the fable mentioned on page 368 and which Barry Long recommends reading to young children as a bedtime story. An audio version of this chapter is published as 'How To Live Joyously'.

SEEING THROUGH DEATH
(Barry Long Audio)
Suggests a way of speaking to children about death and dying.

TALKS FROM TAMBORINE MOUNTAIN
(Audio Tape Collection: The Barry Long Foundation)
A series of talks recording day-to-day spiritual observations during the four year period when Barry Long lived on Tamborine Mountain in Queensland. The talks include many references to Barry's conversations with Simon, who was six years old when these recordings began.

TO TELL YOU THE TRUTH
(The Barry Long Foundation)
A cassette tape containing two talks, one specifically 'For Youth'. Here Barry Long helps young people to see through the confusing dishonesty of the world and talks about the

importance of distinguishing between power and force in handling the difficulties of living.

MEDITATION A FOUNDATION COURSE
(Barry Long Books)
A straightforward introduction to meditation, including many useful exercises that can be adapted for children.

START MEDITATING NOW
(Barry Long Audio: two tapes)
How to become still, enter the sensation of the body and begin to stop useless thinking. Contains instruction in the meditative practice mentioned on pages 152-153.

MAKING LOVE
(Barry Long Audio)
The key to Barry Long's teaching on love and sexuality is contained in this set of two audio tapes.

*

Full details of Barry Long's other works and his teaching programme may be obtained from The Barry Long Foundation International via the following addresses:

BCM Box 876, London WC1N 3XX, England

Box 5277, Gold Coast MC, Queensland 4217, Australia

In USA or Canada call 1-800-497-1081

INDEX

Various topics concerning children in the following age-groups